GW01606623

FAMILY HISTORY RESEARCH

Vol.1. The French Connection

FAMILY HISTORY RESEARCH

Vol. I.

"The French Connection"

by

Patrick Delaforce

Regency Press (London & New York) Ltd.
125 High Holborn, London WC1V 6QA

Copyright © by Patrick Delaforce

This book is copyrighted under the Berne convention. No portion may be reproduced by any process without the copyright holder's written permission except for the purposes of reviewing or criticism, as permitted under the Copyright Act of 1956.

ISBN 0 7212 0688 3

Printed and bound in Great Britain by
Buckland Press Ltd., Dover, Kent.

Chapter	Contents	Page

	Introduction	7
1	Genealogical sources in the UK	10
2	The Port Wine Shippers	57
3	The Fishmongers of London	63
4	19th and 20th Century English families	67
5	18th Century English families	76
6	A Short History of Pawn Broking	86
7	The Chevalier, the Card and the Philanthropist	91
8	17th Century families	98
9	The London Guilds — moneymen, tailors and others	105
10	The Silk Weavers of London	111
11	16th century Huguenot families — first arrivals	122
12	The London Churches & the Threadneedle Street Capers	130
13	The Guisne Huguenots in France	137
14	The Secret Agents	143
15	James and the Queens of Scotland & England	149
16	Henry VIII's theological trouble-shooter	156
17	Sir Anthony and Perkin Warbeck, the Pretender	162
18	Sir Bernard — Ambassador for four English Kings	167
19	The Gascon Lord at the Battle of Barnet	177
20	The Australian families and sources	179
21	The American families and sources	186
22	The Canadian families and sources	195
23	Last Wills and Testaments from 1625	199
	Family Trees	201
	Appendix	222

List of Illustrations

Plate		Page
1	John Delaforce, founder of the Port Wine Shipping family	58
2	Three generations of Port Wine Shippers, Henry (centre), sons Victor and John, grandsons Patrick and David	60
3	Douro boat carrying Port Wine	62
4	John Delforce, founder of the London Fishmonger family	64
5	The London Fishmonger scene at Billingsgate mid 1850's	66
6	A London Pawnbroker mid 1850's	88
7	A London silkweaver at work 19th century	113
8	Indenture of Thomas Alfred Delaforce, lighterman 1868	106
9	Freedom of City of London for Joseph Delaforce, 1842	108
10	Certificate of Fellowship of the Huguenot Society of London	140
11	The French Huguenots arrive on the English beaches — 1685	123
12	The original French Huguenot Threadneedle Street Church — 17th century	131
13	London Scene 17th Century	100
14	Last Will & Testament of John Delaforce, alias Delafors 1702-1779 Courtesy of the Public Record Office, London S PROB 11/1057 1C/411	78/9
15	IGI computer printout — courtesy of Church of Jesus Christ of Latter Day Saints, Utah	18
16	William Delaforce, ex-convict Second Fleet, founder of Australian family	179
17	Marriage Certificate of John Fleurriet Delaforce 1842	26

Nos. 5, 6, 11 and 12 courtesy of BBC Hulton Picture Library.

Introduction

Wordsworth 1770-1850
And they are gone; aye, ages long ago
For old unhappy far-off things,
and battles long ago.

This is a true story of Kings and Convicts, Princes and Pawnbrokers, Barons and Silkweavers, Prelates and Tailors, Admirals and Lombardsmen, Goldsmiths and ... Spies.

It concerns a family called Delaforce.

Their earliest ancestors — three generations of them — were hung by Charlemagne after the two battles of Roncesvalles in the 8th century. They were directly related to the old Kings of Navarre in the 9th and 10th centuries. They were Princes of Verdun and Savennes (near modern Montauban) in the 10th and 11th centuries.

Later on they fought at Hastings, married into the Conqueror's family, appeared in the Domesday Book, were personal friends of Richard Coeur de Lion, King John and other Monarchs. One signed for the Barons at Runnymede, others served personally Mary, Queen of Scots, Queen Elizabeth I, Henry VIII and Richard III.

Another sailed in the *Mayflower* as a member of the crew!

Now in the twentieth century they are scattered to the four winds. A few are to be found in London. Others in Portugal, America, Australia and Canada. And the author lives in France not far away from the feudal princes' stamping ground of a thousand years ago.

This book is more than just a history of a small unusual Anglo-French family. It is also a serious work on genealogy and the fascinating art of family history research.

It is possible for most families to trace their ancestry back several centuries. it requires time, patience, some luck, a little money, but it most certainly can be done. The author had time, patience, a lot of luck, a little money, and, venturing into the unknown, came up with over a thousand years of well documented family history. Some of the highlights of the history and most of the sources from 1500 are shown in this book. The author discovered new (but old) families of relations in England, Australia, USA and Canada as a direct result of his research.

The many sources of data, references and historical facts spanning a thousand years or more are spelt out in detail. In chapter 1 for the UK, and in chapters 21 for the USA, 20 for Australia and 22 for Canada.

Many of Britain's population derived from the Normans of the 11th century and Huguenots of the 16th and 17th centuries. Many British have emigrated to the USA, Canada and Australia. It is felt that genealogical sources for those countries will be of interest.

Most families have a legend lurking in the background — perhaps true, perhaps a fantasy!

Some of the Delaforces believed that they descended from the illustrious Dukes De La Force who were marshalls and pairs (peers) in France from the moment when King Henri IV (Paris was worth a Mass) ennobled the Caummont family in 1637. They were Huguenots, so were the Delaforces.

However it is clear that the Caumont la Forces were not blood relations to the Delaforces, a very old French family deriving from Navarre, Gascony and the Gironde, with the original names of Fources, Forces, Forca etc.

The Caumonts acquired the town and chateau of La Force near Bergerac when in 1554 Philippe de Beaupoil de la Force of Perigord, daughter of Francois de Beaupoil, Seigneur de la Force married Francois de Caummont. Neither the Beaupoils nor the Caumonts were related to the Delaforces who at that time were either in England, Paris or on their way north to Guisne near Calais.

The author's family has been, and members still are, Port Wine shippers in Oporto, in northern Portugal. For many generations it was a privately owned firm which meant that records were kept and a family tree preserved as far back as 1781. It could be said that a headstart of two centuries is a great advantage to a family historian.

True — but this family tree concerned an English family living and working mainly in Portugal for that two hundred year period. There was little knowledge available of other Delaforce families living elsewhere.

In a sense this has been written as an adventure story. Always round the next corner was a new hero — or a villain — sometimes simultaneously.

Chapter 1

Edmund Burke 1729-1797
"People will not look forward to posterity, who never look backward to their ancestors"

Genealogical Sources in the UK

This chapter concerns sources available for Family Historians and Genealogists in the UK. Sources for USA, Canada and Australia are shown in the respective chapters dealing with the Delaforce family in that country. This chapter also briefly covers some sources in New Zealand, South Africa, Eire and other countries.

Certain major sources have been covered in more detail and are shown in the following order:

1 Parish Registers.
2 Public Record Offices.
3 Census Data and Records.
4 Wills and Testaments.
5 CFI/IGI — Mormon Church.
6 Aliens and Immigrants.
7 Guilds and Livery Companies.
8 The Society of Genealogists.
9 The British (Museum) Library.
10 The Guildhall Library.
11 The Huguenot Society.

Other sources are then shown in alpabetical order.

Part 1 Parish Registers

Registers of births/baptisms, marriages and deaths are of course the single most valuable source for family history and genealogy. A lot of excellent books have been published on the sources pre 1837. These should be consulted before research is undertaken to reduce the amount of time that may be wasted.

From 1837 the civil registrations of births and marriages are to be found at the General Register Office at St.Catherine's House, Kingsway, London WC2 and the Death Registers across the road at Alexandra House, Kingsway, London WC2. The indexes are arranged alphabetically by surname in quarterly volumes. Put another way, to examine all the records to piece together an unknown family 1740 volumes need to be consulted! Consulting the indexes is free: purchase of certificates costs £4.60 by personal application and £8 by post. The search rooms are open Monday to Friday 8.30a.m. to 4.3 pm.

Birth certificates give (a) the place and date of birth (b) the child's given names (c) the name and occupation of the father (d) the name and maiden name of the mother and (e) the name and address of the informant for the registration.

Marriage certificates give the (a) names and (b) the ages of the two parties to the marriage (c) their respective addresses (d) the names and occupations of both parties fathers (e) and date and (f) the place of the marriage and (g) the names of the witnesses.

Death certificates record (a) name (b) date (c) place (d) age (e) the cause of death (f) the occupation of the deceased and (g) residence if different from the place of death (h) the name and address of the information for registration purpose. Neither place of birth nor parentage are shown on the death certificate.

It can be seen that since 1837 tracing of ancestors by painstaking cross-analysis and a certain expenditure of key certificates is perfectly possible but extremely hard physical work iniitially and hard mental work afterwards! For instance some 500 Delaforce entries over the 145 years would have cost over £2,000 if purchase of all certificates had been warranted.

Pre-1837

Records from 1538 are held (a) either by the Incumbent (b) or the appropriate county record office. Many of them are on microfilm and quite a few are indexed. For instance the Greater London Record

Office, 40 Northampton Road, Clerkenwell EC1 holds the parish registers of well over 300 parishes within the former counties of London and Middlesex (excluding the City of London held at the Guildhall, and Westminster held at the Victoria Library, 160 Buckingham Palace Road, London SW1). Norman H. Grahams first-class "Consolidated Guides to the London area" should be purchased and consulted, and the Guildhall Library 'Parish Registers' handbooks consulted for anybody researching the Greater London area.

The Society of Genealogists in London hold the biggest collection of transcripts of Parish Registers which are invaluable 'shortcuts' for researchers. They have also published a National Index of Parish Registers, not yet completed but equally invaluable. Their Boyds Marriage Index is vital. The Mormon Computer File Index (sourced in this book) is absolutely vital to any researcher of parish records in the period 1550-1837.

Publications worth reading are:

"Public Record Office Leaflet No 1" — *free* and excellent!

"Guide to City of London Parish Registers" at Guildhall Library.

"Genealogists Consolidated Guide to Parish Registers in London 1535-1837" 3 vols. Graham.

"Original parish registers in record offices and libraries" pub LPS, Tawney House, Matlock, Derbyshire.

"A list of Parishes in Boyds Marriage Index" by R W Massey

"British Museum Library pamphlets 6/7/8" — free: BML also have many copies of Parish Registers.

"Society of Genealogists leaflet No 2" also "Parish Registers copies Part 1 & 11".

"LDS Church Parish & Vital records listing" lists CFI Index registers. (LDS stands for Latter Day Saints i.e. the Mormons).

"National Index of parish registers" Ed. D.J. Steele at Soc of Genealogists.

Nearly all records and registers *other* than the Church of England are kept by the Keeper of Public Records, PRO, Chancery Lane, London WC2.

Crockfords Clerical Directory (at your local library) will give you the name and address of the Incumbent (Clergyman) and address of every diocese in Great Britain for direct consultation if post 1837 records. If he does not hold the particular year needed he will tell you where it is (PRO or CRO).

Recommended Reading

"How to find Marriage Indexes" M.J.Walcot and Family History Societies Federation.
"Bishop Transcripts and Marriage Licences, Guide to Locations" J.S.W. Gibson
Pallot's Marriage Index covers 1780-1837, for London, Middlesex, Kent Surrey, Essex and Middlesex: small fee payable to Institute of Heraldic & Geneological Studies, Northgate, Canterbury, Kent.
"Phillimores Marriages" BCM Pinhoras, London WC1V 6XX.

Part 2 Public Record Offices

There are three main buildings in London (1) Chancery Lane WC2 (01-405 0741) (2) Kew at Ruskin Avenue, Richmond, Surrey, TW9 4DV (01-876 3444) and (3) Land Registry building in Portugal Street WC2 (01-405 3488) (which houses the original data on microfilm of national census of 1841, 1851, 1861, 1871 and 1881).

The division of records between the two major national reposition of records deriving from the 11th century has been logically planned. Readers tickets are needed to the Reading Rooms at both Chancery Lane and Kew. They are issued free of charge to applicants who can satisfy the Keeper of the Records of their suitability to be allowed access to the original records.

At Chancery Lane there are two famous Reading Rooms — the Round and the Long rooms. The Probate Reading room (see wills) and the North Room (maps and large documents) are both on the first floor.

At Kew the main Reading room (Langdale) is on the first floor. Kew is highly computerised and most researchers will need to learn how to master the individual TV set machines.

Researchers need to know how the immense amount of records are divided between Chancery Lane and Kew before they visit the PRO. Chancery Lane has Chancery (C), Exchequer (E), State Papers (SP), Prerogative Court of Canterbury (PRCB), amongst 44 categories. Kew has 108 categories including Colonial

Office (CO), Foreign Office (FO), most of the General Register Office (RG), Historical Manuscripts Commission (HMC), Home Office (HO), Inland Revenue (IR), Public Record Office (PRO), Board of Trade (BT) and War Office (WO).

Chancery Lane collections include 'Ancient Correspondence, Ancient Petitions, Court Rolls, the Hundred Rolls, Papal Bulls, non-parochial registers (French, Dutch, etc church registers), Estate Duty registers of the Dept. of Inland Revenue.

PRO issue a leaflet explaining where each category can be found.

Other Record Offices in Great Britain

(a) The Record Office, House of Lords — Westminster (01-219 3000) records of Parliament.
(b) The Office of Population Censuses and Surveys, St Catherines House, 10 Kingsway WC2 (01-242 0262) — registrations of births, marriages and deaths since 1837.
(c) The Scottish Record Office, General Register House, Princes Street, Edinburgh EH1 (031-556 6585).
(d) The General Register Office of Scotland, New Register House, Princes Street, Edinburgh EH1 (031-556 3952) — register of births, marriages and deaths in Scotland.
(e) The Public Record Office of Northern Ireland, 66 Balmoral Avenue, Belfast, Tel. 661621.
(f) The General Register Office, Oxford House, 49-55 Chichester Street, Belfast BT1. Tel. 35211 — register of births, marriages and deaths in N. Ireland.
(g) Principal Probate Registry, Somerset House, Strand, London WC2 (01-405 7641).
(h) General Register Office, Douglas, Isle of Man. Tel. Douglas 3358.
(i) Registrar General, States Office, Royal Square, Jersey.
(j) National Library of Wales, Aberyswyth, Dyfed SY23 3BU. Tel. Aberystwyth 3816/7.
(k) County Record Offices are in Bedford, Reading, Aylesbury, Cambridge, Chester, Truro, Carlisle, Matlock, Exeter, Plymouth,

Dorchester, Durham, Chelmsford, Gloucester, Bristol, Winchester, Portsmouth, Southampton, Hereford, Hertford, Huntingdon, Maidstone, Canterbury, Preston, Manchester, Liverpool, Salford, Wigan, Bolton, Leicester, Lincoln, Grimsby, Norwich, Northampton, Newcastle, Nottingham, Oxford, Shrewsbury, Taunton, Bath, Stafford, Lichfield, Ipswich, St. Edmunds, Kingston upon Thames, Guildford, Lewes, Chichester, Warwick, Coventry, Kendal, Newport Isle of Wight, Trowbridge, Salisbury, Worcester, Northallerton, Wakefield, Sheffield, Bradford, Leeds, Beverley, Kingston upon Hull.

(l) General Register Office (PRO), St Catherine's House, 10 Kingsway, Aldwych, London WC2 (01-242 0262) — all UK births, marriages and deaths since 1837. GRO at St Catherine's House also holds separate indexes for (1) Army returns of births, marriages and deaths from 1761 (2) for RAF from 1920 (3) Consular returns of births, marriages and deaths of British citizens in foreign countries from 1849 (4) births and deaths at sea 1837-74.

(m) Greater London Record Office, County Hall, London SE1 (01-633 8166/7808) but is currently moving to 40 Northampton Road, Clerkenwell, London EC1.

Recommended reading

PRO leaflets (free) 37,1,2,4,6,7,26,32 and 34.
"Guide to the contents of the Public Record Office"
HMSO — 3 volumes.
"Record Offices: how to find them" by T. Gibson and P. Peskett.
"Tracing your Ancestors in the Public Record Office" by J. Cox and T. Padfield.
"Record Repositories in Great Britain" HMSO.

Part 3 Census Data and Records

The first census of population in England and Wales was held in 1801, and have been held ever since, apart from the war year of 1941. From 1841 they are of significant value to family historians provided a reasonably accurate geographical area can be pin-pointed before the search begins, since a complete family with names and ages can be located. For 1841-1881 census data are held at the PRO in Portugal Street in the Land Registry building, London WC2. A day pass can be obtained at the door without charge.

The Guildhall Library has census returns for the City of London for 1841-1881. The County Local Record Offices all hold microfilm data for the 1841-81 census data. Very few indexes have yet been published, but those that have should be consulted in Mr Gibson's books mentioned below.

Essential reading

"Census Returns on Microfilm" 1841/1871 by J.S.W. Gibson
"Census Indexes and Indexing" by J. Gibson and C. Chapman.
Public Record Office leaflet No 2 — Censuses of Population.
Guide to Census Reports, Great Britain 1801-1966 HMSO.

Part 4 Wills and Testaments

To some extent this subject is covered in chapter 23. This is such an important subject that many leaflets and books have been written about the problems of locating wills, since there are 300 locations for pre 1858 wills! Many were rightly called 'peculiars'. After having thoroughly checked the Principal Probate Registry at Somerset House, The Strand WC2 for post 1858 wills, the best advice initially is (a) to visit the PRO Chancery lane to examine the major source there, the Prerogative Court of Canterbury (PCC) in the Wills Room on the first floor (readers ticket necessary). The Death Duty registers (PRO leaflet 34) are on open shelves at the PRO Chancery Lane, Wills Room, for estates since 1796 liable to duty). (b) to read the PRO free leaflet No 4 on Probate Records. (c) visit the Guildhall MSS section which holds the original records of the Commissary Court of London; the Archdeaconry Court of London and also the Royal Peculiar of

St.Katherine by the Tower. Also PCC Indexes 1383-1629, 1653-1660, 1671-1700. (d) Visit and consult the Society of Genealogists which has the best collection of regional wills for England, Wales, Scotland and Ireland. (e) Consult your local Public Records Office. (f) Consult your local Family History Society. (g) British Record Society publications.

Essential reading

"Wills and where to find them" J.S.W. Gibson.
"A simplified Guide to Probate Jurisdictions" by J.S.W. Gibson.
"Records of Prerogative Court of Canterbury" PRO
"Index of London wills before 1700" Marc Fitch for British Record Society.
"Commissary Court of London 1374-1488" by M. Fitch, Index library vol 82/86.
British Record Society's County Indexes for Wills
"Wills and their whereabouts" by A.J. Camp
"Family History — Wills and inventories, chap XVII" by D. Steel
"London Consistory Court Wills 1492-1547" by I. Darlington
"Indexes to the ancient testamentary records of Westminster" by A.M. Burke
"Calend of Wills in the Court of Hustings 1258-1688" by R.R. Sharpe.

Part 5 Computer File Index/IGI

From 1894 the Church of Jesus Christ of Latter Day Saints, in Cottonwool Canyon, Salt Lake City, Utah, (The Mormons) have been engaged in collecting records of baptisms and marriages for their own purposes not necessarily for research. A computer file index (CFI or IGI) has been produced which is updated every few years and produced on microfiche on small cards. There are 2914 fiche for the British Isles, each covering about 16,000 names

COUNTRY: ENGLAND COUNTY: LONDON AS OF AUG 1981 PAGE 35,201

NAME	SEX M MALE F FEMALE H HUSBAND W WIFE — FATHER MOTHER OR SPOUSE	SEX	TYPE	EVENT DATE	TOWN, PARISH	B	E	S	SOURCE BATCH	SOURCE SERIAL SHEET
DELAFORCE, MARY	DANIEL DELAFORCE/ELISABETH	F	C	06JUN1785	SHOREDITCH,SAINT LEONARDS	05MAR1975OG	03APR1975OG	14AUG1975OG	C040801	1813
DELAFORCE, MARY	JACOB DELAFORCE/MARY	F	C	10SEP1786	BETHNAL GREEN,SAINT MATTHEW	20AUG1976PV	11NOV1976PV	03DEC1976PV	C046982	14207
DELAFORCE, MARY	THOMAS DELAFORCE/REBECCA	F	C	18APR1813	SHOREDITCH,SAINT LEONARDS	29JUL1975LG	14NOV1975LG	04DEC1975LG	C040803	4991
DELAFORCE, MARY	AUGUSTUS DELAFORCE/MARY ANN	F	C	07NOV1830	BETHNAL GREEN,SAINT MATTHEW	30JUN1976SG	09NOV1976SG	26NOV1976SG	C046984	2090
DELAFORCE, MARY ANN	EDWARD DELAFORCE/MARY	F	C	16JUL1815	SHOREDITCH,SAINT LEONARDS	30JUL1975LG	21NOV1975LG	11DEC1975LG	C040803	9886
DELAFORCE, MARY JANE	AGUSTUS DELAFORCE/MARY	F	C	08OCT1826	SHOREDITCH,SAINT LEONARDS	20MAY1975PV	08JUL1975PV	26JUL1975PV	C040805	2686
DELAFORCE, REBECCA	JAMES DELAFORCE/SARAH	F	C	22JAN1786	SHOREDITCH,SAINT LEONARDS	06MAR1975OG	03APR1975OG	14AUG1975OG	C040801	2434
DELAFORCE, SAMUEL	SAMUEL DELAFORCE/ELIZABETH	M	C	06MAY1795	SOUTHWARK,SAINT SAVIOUR	01MAY1976IF	11JUN1976IF	11JUN1976IF	C055181	16850
DELAFORCE, SAMUEL	THOMAS DELAFORCE/HANNAH	M	C	10JUL1796	SHOREDITCH,SAINT LEONARDS	22APR1975OG	24MAY1975OG	14AUG1975OG	C040801	16290
DELAFORCE, SAMUEL	SAMUEL DELAFORCE/ELIZABETH	M	C	19OCT1804	SOUTHWARK,ST. GEORGE THE MARTYR	19SEP1970LA	08DEC1970LA	06JUL1972LA	C022441	3095
DELAFORCE, SAMUEL	SAMUEL DELAFORCE/ELIZABETH	M	C	16SEP1829	SOUTHWARK,ST. GEORGE THE MARTYR	22JUL1970SG	29JUL1970SG	27JAN1971SG	C022442	6660
DELAFORCE, SAMUEL ALEXANDER THOMPSON	SAMUEL DELAFORCE/MARY THOMPSON	M	C	14NOV1828	SOUTHWARK,ST. GEORGE THE MARTYR	22JUL1970SG	05DEC1970SG	23JAN1971SG	C022442	5990
DELAFORCE, SARAH	JOHN/ELIZABETH	F	C	12JUL1761	LONDON,ST. BOTOLPH BISHOPSGATE	INFANT	INFANT	13APR1971IF	C001616	3166
DELAFORCE, SARAH	EDWARD DELAFORCE/ELISABETH	F	C	30APR1775	STEPNEY,SPITALFIELDS CHRIST CHURCH	19MAY1978OK	12AUG1978OK	23AUG1978OK	C069692	4415
DELAFORCE, SARAH	JAMES DELAFORCE/SARAH	F	C	19SEP1779	SHOREDITCH,SAINT LEONARDS	08FEB1979OG	30MAR1979OG	08MAY1979OG	C040811	29694
DELAFORCE, SARAH	THOMAS DELAFORCE/REBECCA	F	C	25DEC1810	SHOREDITCH,SAINT LEONARDS	23JUL1975LG	11NOV1975LG	03DEC1975LG	C040803	0463
DELAFORCE, SARAH	JAMES DELAFORCE/SARAH	F	C	14OCT1827	BETHNAL GREEN,SAINT MATTHEW	29JUN1976OG	25AUG1976OG	25SEP1976OG	C046981	7064
DELAFORCE, SARAH JANE	EDWARD DELAFORCE/MARY	F	C	09AUG1807	SHOREDITCH,SAINT LEONARDS	12APR1975OK	22MAY1975OK	01JUL1975OK	C040802	14553
DELAFORCE, SUSANNA	THOMAS DELAFORCE/HANNAH	F	C	27JUL1794	SHOREDITCH,SAINT LEONARDS	12MAR1975OG	10APR1975OG	20AUG1975OG	C040801	13573
DELAFORCE, SUSANNA	THOMAS DELAFORCE/REBECCA	F	C	21SEP1817	SHOREDITCH,SAINT LEONARDS	03SEP1975LG	02DEC1975LG	16DEC1975LG	C040803	14661
DELAFORCE, THOMAS	ISAAC DELAFORCE/ELISABETH	M	C	30JUL1756	STEPNEY,SAINT DUNSTAN	17JUN1976PV	10SEP1976PV	08OCT1976PV	C055761	1422
DELAFORCE, THOMAS	EDWARD DELAFORCE/ELISABETH	M	C	07MAR1780	SHOREDITCH,SAINT LEONARDS	22FEB1979OG	20APR1979OG	10MAY1979OG	C040811	30194
DELAFORCE, THOMAS	THOMAS DELAFORCE/HANNAH	M	C	25DEC1785	SHOREDITCH,SAINT LEONARDS	12APR1975OG	17MAY1975OG	08AUG1975OG	C040801	2358
DELAFORCE, THOMAS	THOMAS DELAFORCE/REBECCA	M	C	08JUN1823	SHOREDITCH,SAINT LEONARDS	19FEB1975OG	22MAR1975OG	30APR1975OG	C040804	9669
DELAFORCE, THOMS	DANL. DELAFORCE/SARAH	M	C	04APR1777	BETHNAL GREEN,SAINT MATTHEW	19AUG1976PV	13NOV1976PV	04DEC1976PV	C046982	10338
DELAFORCE, WILLIAM	EDWARD DELAFORCE/ELISABETH	M	C	08MAY1774	STEPNEY,SPITALFIELDS CHRIST CHURCH	24MAY1978OK	15SEP1978OK	26SEP1978OK	C069692	4074
DE'AFORCE, WILLIAM	DANIEL DELAFORCE/BETTY	M	C	10AUG1787	SHOREDITCH,SAINT LEONARDS	15APR1975OG	21MAY1975OG	09AUG1975OG	C040801	4310
DELAFORCE, WILLIAM	? WILLIAM DELAFORCE/MARY ANN	M	C	15JUN1817	BETHNAL GREEN,SAINT MATTHEW	18SEP1976OG	18NOV1976OG	06JAN1977OG	C046983	16429
DELAFORCE, WILLIAM MATTHEW	THOMAS DELAFORCE/HANNAH	M	C	23AUG1789	SHOREDITCH,SAINT LEONARDS	16APR1975OG	20MAY1975OG	08AUG1975OG	C040801	6911

*DELAFORD , ** SEE DELAFORTE
*DELAFORE , ** SEE DELEFOUR
*DELAFORS , ** SEE DELAFORCE

= EVALUATED ENTRY

A = ADULT CHRISTENING B = BIRTH C = CHRISTENING D = DEATH OR BURIAL F = BIRTH OR CHRISTENING OF FIRST KNOWN CHILD M = MARRIAGE [illegible] = CENSUS W = WILL ALL OTHERS = MISCELLANEOUS

IGI computer printout
Courtesy of Church of Jesus Christ of Latter Day Saints, Utah

equivalent to 360 pages of parish registers! The 1981 version is available at the Society of Genealogists, covering some 30 million ancestors. Also available at the Mormon Library, Exhibition Road, South Kensington, London SW7 (Wednesday afternoons).

There is an index of the surnames covered on each fiche at the lower right hand corner of the fiche. Usually for a small sum a printout of the whole page can be obtained at the press of a button, for study at home. Mormon Chapels with CFI index are in Huddersfield (0484-27099); Loughborough/Leics (0509-214991); Merthyr Tydfil/Glamorgan (0685-2455); Southampton (0703-767476); Sunderland (0783-284561).

Each entry has eleven columns of which the first six only are vital (1) name of the person married or baptised (2) name of the parents or spouse (3) Sex shown by M, F or H, W (4) Type of entry Birth, Christening or marriage (5) Date (6) Parish.

Indexed by each English County, arranged chronologically by surname, given name and date. Sections for Scotland, Ireland, Isle of Man, Channel Islands and two each for Wales and Monmouthshire. Strongest in the London, Cornwall, Devon, Lancashire, Lincolnshire and Yorkshire areas where the majority of original emigrants lived. There are 23 million entries for the British Isles. London/Middlesex has 3 million, Lancashire 2 million but some counties have under 200,000 entries.

Baptisms and marriages are mixed up together on the same microfiche. Surnames are grouped under standard spellings devised by the Genealogical Society.

The Index can be seen at Mormon Chapels; Guildhall; Society of Genealogists but some CROs have local data available: also some Family History Societies.

"Parish & Vital Records Listing" published by the Gen. Dept. of the Church of Jesus Christ of Latter Day Saints available from L.D.S. Chruch, Exhibition Road, London SW7. Many other countries have been covered including Scandinavia and other European countries. The new title is the International Genealogical Index (IGI).

Part 6 Aliens and Immigrants

There are two major sources of information available for research into names of foreigners coming to live in England in the last six hundred years.

(1) The Public Records Offices in London (mainly at Chancery Lane and Kew) hold vital originals
Chancery Miscellanea (C 47)
Exchequer Extents of Alien Priories (E 106)
Exchequer Subsidy Rolls (E 179)
Exchequer Accounts Various (E 101)
Parliamentary Rolls (C 65)
Patent Rolls (C 66, C 67)
Chancery Close Rolls (C 54)
Calender of State Papers, Domestic, vols I-V (SP 14,15,29 and 30)
Aliens Acts (HO 1,2,3 and 5) inc Entry Books
Domestic Entry Book (SP 44/67)
Swearing or Oath Rolls (KB 24)
Oaths of Allegiance (E 169/86)
Chancery Original Denizations (C97)
Original Patents for Denization (HO 4)
Bouillon Papers (HO 69)
Privy Council (PC 1) and (FO 95)
Passenger Lists (BT 26 and 32)
Treasury Records (T 93)
Certificates of Naturalisation 1844-1900 (Home Office)
Registered Papers (HO 45 and 144)
PRO Lists and Indexes

No.XXXV pp 103-7, No.XLII, No.XLVI
PRO Lists & Indexes No.XLVI (1922)
Genealogists Magazine Vol XII 1956 (pp 149-154, 185-188)
Guide to the Contents of the Public Record Office, 3 vols HMSO" see at all major Public Libraries. Treasury (T), Colonial Office (CO), Home Office (HO), Board of Trade (BT) and Foreign Office (FO) documents should be consulted at PRO at Kew.

(2) The Huguenot Society of London have published excellent records of Aliens and Immigrants which can be consulted at the Society (members), or at major libraries such as the Guildhall, and British Museum Library.
Volume VIII Letters of Denization and Acts of Naturalisation for Aliens in England 1509-1603.
Volume X lists of Aliens resident in London, Henry VIII to James I in three parts and index (1523-1623) by R.E. and E.F. Kirk.
Volume XVIII letters of Denization and Acts of Naturalisation for Aliens in England and Ireland 1603-1700.
Volume XXVIII letters of Denization and Acts of Naturalisation for Aliens in England and Ireland 1603-1700.
Volume XXVII letters of Denization and Acts of Naturalisation for Aliens in England and Ireland 1701-1800.
Volume XXXV is a supplement to vols XVIII and XXVII by Dr. W.A. Shaw.

These five volumes are indispensable to any researcher who knows or suspects that his ancestors came into England in the period 1509-1800, not only from France but from the Low Countries and elsewhere. They are very well indexed. Care must be taken to trace *all* spelling permutations of the modern name. For Delaforce this meant over 20 permutations!

(3) Other sources

"Lists of foreign Protestants and Aliens resident in England 1618-1688" by W.D. Cooper.
"Register of Dutch Church Austin Friars 1568-1872" by J.H. Hessels (Camden Society).
"House of Lords Record Office for naturalisations 1801-1947.
"A list of Strangers 1567/8" by A.W.C. Hallen, Genealogical Magazine 1898.
Visitation of London 1568 by S.W. Rawlins (Harleian Society).
Agnews 'French Protestant Exiles' 2 vols.
Jules Berthaut "Les Emigrés Francaises à Londres".
J.S. Burns 'History of French Protestant Reform'.

N.H. Grahams "Nonconformist and Foreign Registers in Inner London".
Lart 'Huguenot Church in Caen, 16th Century'.

(4) All Huguenot and Walloon church parish registers have been documented and well indexed b the Huguenot Society: vols I, IV, V, IX, XI, XII, XIII, XVI, XVII, XX, XXI, XXIII, XXV, XXVI, XXVIII, XXIX, XXX, XXXI, XXXII, XXXVII, XXXIX, XLII, XLV. The registers cover the main London churches such as Threadneedle Street, but also Canterbury, Norwich etc. Anyone with a French name or names in the family should join the Huguenot Society of London c/o Miss Scouloudi, 67 Victoria Road, London W8.

Part 7 Guilds and Livery Companies

This source has proved to be invaluable to the history of the Delaforces particularly the silk weaver guild records. Ironically enough although there were a number of Tailors and Goldsmiths, neither the Merchant Tailors nor the Goldsmiths have any records of Delaforces.

Guilds of traders and craftsmen originated in the early Middle Ages to regulate admission to the trades and crafts by maintaining standards of workmanship and trading. The Statute of Apprentices of 1563 forbade anyone to enter a trade who had not served an apprenticeship. The Guilds centred on London but their power and authority was widespread. For instance the Guildhall in London has local indexes for apprentices from Surrey, Sussex, Warwickshire and Wiltshire. Apprentices usually entered their craft at the age of 14 probably sponsored and initially paid for by their father and served a term usually of 7 years before being made Free. Apprentices and Freemans records are therefore invaluable to genealogists as the age of both can usually be calculated with some precision.

From 1710-1804 a stamp duty was paid on apprenticeships and the records of stamp duty paid in the PRO is a valuable source of information. By 1900 there were 77 livery companies plus two which did not receive their livery. Parish Clerks and Waterman/Lightermen.

The main London Livery Guilds are or were as follows:–

Apothecaries
Armourers/Brasiers
Bakers
Barber-Surgeons
Basketmakers
Blacksmiths
Bladesmiths
Bowyers
Brewers
Butchers
Carmen (Conveyors of goods)
Carpenters/Cabinet Makers
Clockmakers
Cloth Workers (Fullers, Shearers)
Coachmakers
Cooks
Coopers
Cordwainers
Cutlers
Drapers
Dyers
Fanmakers
Farriers
Feltmakers
Fishmongers
Founders
Fruiterers
Glass-Sellers
Glaziers
Glovers
Gold & Silver Wyre Drawers
Goldsmiths
Grocers
Horners
Ironmongers
Joiners & Sawyers
Leather Sellers
Masons
Mercers
Merchant Taylors
Musicians
Master Mariners
Needlemakers
Painter Stainers
Parish Clerks
Pattern Makers
Paviors (of paving stone)
Pewterers
Plaisterers
Pouchmakers
Poulterers
Saddlers
Salters
Scriveners
Shipwrights
Skinners
Soapmakers
Spectaclemakers
Sheathers
Stationers
Tallow Chandlers
Tinplate Workers
Turners
Tylers & Bricklayers

Vintners
Weavers/Silkthrowsters
Wood Mongers

The main sources are (a) to enquire of the Guildhall library both Printed Books and Manuscripts, reference L.37. (b) to read 'London & Middlesex Published Records' pp 21-28 by J.M. Sims which lists specific documents for every Guild and (c) to visit the PRO at Kew Gardens and consult the Apprenticeship Books (IR1) for records 1710-1811, (IR17) for 1710-1762: also at Kew or Chancery Lane, PRO Lists and Indexes LIII and WO 25/2962 for apprentices and the Army; ADM1, 12, 73/421, 106, 448 and CSC10 for Admiralty apprentices. BT 150/1/2 for Seamen Apprentices. Also BT19 for Board of Trade Indexes. (d)) to visit the City of London Records Office in the main Guildhall building, which house the Lord Mayor's Court records. CLRO also has a card index of Freemen 1498-1670 in the Repertoires of the Court of Aldermen. CLRO houses lists of members of the Brokers and Stockbrokers since they started. (e) to visit also in the main Guildhall building, the excellent City of London Freedom Registers which are beautifully bound and presented indexes to the original records which show the apprentices' father's name, occupation and address. See also Freedom Minute or Declaration books: Apprenticeship enrolments/indentures: Freedom enrolment books: the Ward Mote Inquest returns and the Complaints books.

Some Guild records are still held directly by the Guild concerned — the Clothworkers, Drapers, Fanmakers, Goldsmiths, Leathersellers, Merchant Taylors (but microfilm at Guildhall Library), Mercers, Salters, Skinners and Stationers.

Recommended reading

(a) For the earliest period 1275-1497 the London Letter Books A-L are excellent not only as a source of names but other social, trading activities. Edited by R.R. Sharpe they can be read at the B.M. Library, Guildhall or on open shelves at PRO County Hall/Clerkenwell.

(b) PRO leaflet No. 26.
(c) English provincial, Scottish and Irish Guilds — Guildhall Library (GSC 338.6).
(d) "A Guide to the records of CLRO and Guildhall Library Muniment Room" P.E. Jones and R. Smith.
"Gilds: their origin, constitution, objects and later history" by C. Walford.
"City of London Freedom Registers" by M.T. Medlycott.
"The Apprentices of Great Britain" by Society of Genealogists.
"Register of Freemen of the City of London in reigns of Henry VIII, Edward VI" by C. Welch.
"The London Goldsmiths 1200-1800" by Sir Ambrose Heal.
"English Guilds of medieval England" by H.F. Westlake.
"English Gilds" by J. Toulmin Smith (Early English Text Society).
"List of Liverymen & Freemen of the City companies 1538" by E. Salisbury.
"Discovering London's Guilds and Liveries" pamphlet by Family History Association.
"Freemen in England" by H. Ward.

Part 8 The Society of Genealogists

37 Harrington Gardens, London SW7 4JX (Tel. 01-373 7054).

The major library and facilities for genealogy in Great Britain. Open to non-members on a fee basis: approx 7,000 members.
(a) *Publications List*, their own series of very useful leaflets, indispensable to all 'beginners' in genealogy, particularly Nos. 2,3,4 and 9.
(b) *P. Boyds Marriage Index*, 532 volumes, 1538-1837 (3000 parishes, 7 million names) unique collection. See "A list of Parishes in Boyds Marriage Index". P. Boyds "Inhabitants of London" mainly 16th and 17th century.
(c) *The Great Card Index*, 800 boxes contain several million slips sorted under surnames.
(d) *Bernau's Index*, compiled by C.A. Bernau now on microfilm of 4½ million slips of unindexed material in the PRO, mainly

7440D

1842 ... St. Saviours ... the Parish Church
Parish St Saviour Southwark ... County of Surrey

No.	When married	Name	Age	Condition	Rank or profession	Residence	Father's name	Rank or profession of father
271	26th August 1842	John Fleurriet Delaforce	full age	Bachelor	Merchant	Wellington Street	John Delaforce	Gentleman
		Phoebe Wheattall	Minor	Spinster	—	Mansel street Whitechapel	Benjamin Wheattall	Gentleman

Parish Church ... rites and ceremonies ... Established church by Licence by me
John Fleurriet Delaforce ... Benjamin Wheattal ... Samuel Benson
Phoebe Wheattall ... Elizabeth Wheattal

15th January 81

15|1|81

Marriage Certificate of John Fleurriet Delaforce 1842

Chancery and Exchequer depositions and pleadings. A unique source of family history.

(e) *Document Collection*, for about 11,000 different names.

(f) *Parish Register Copies*. The society houses the largest collection in UK.

Computer File Index, *a microfiche collection purchased from the Genealogical Society of Utah (Mormons), 1981 edition for the whole of UK. Booking essential for time on 'readers'.*

(h) *Wills*. Many indexes kept inc. British Record Society's Index library series.

(i) *Trades and Apprentices*. Two major indexes 1710-1762, 1762-1774 of apprentice name, his father's name and the name and trade of the master.

(j) *Poll Books and Trade Directories*. Excellent collection of both.

(k) Local regional collections of unique manuscripts and family histories.

Read "Using the library of the Society of Genealogists".

Part 9 The British Museum Library

The Reading and Map rooms are at the British Museum, Great Russell Street, London WC1B 3DG (Tel. 01-363 1544). A reader's ticket is required. The British Museum Library Catalogue can be consulted at major libraries (the Guildhall etc.). Although an author catalogue it does include many subjects. Supplements are printed regularly and inserted at the end of each author reference index. Supplements are printed regularly to the main index. This is arguably the first library in the world. Amongst many other claims to fame it probably has the finest collection of specialised French and Spanish reference/history books not only outside the countries concerned, but as good or better than the equivalent library in Paris or Madrid. Authors to be consulted are T.C. Skeat, J.P. Gibson, A.J. Willis and A.J.K. Esdaile.

The Department of Printed Books produce a series of free useful Reader Guides (No.6 English Places; No.8 Family and Personal Names; No.10 British Family History, etc.) to material available in the library.

Part 10 The Guildhall Library (01-606 3030)

See "A Guide to Genealogical Sources in Guildhall Library" Corporation of London. The library, situated in the heart of the City of London, has a unique collection of books and manuscripts relating to London and Middlesex. Its collection of wills (Commissary Court of London from 1374, Archdeaconry Court of London, Royal Peculiar of St. Katherine by the Tower), Parish Registers (a national Computer File Index (Mormon Church)), with London and Middlesex on the ground floor and the rest of the UK in the basement. Handlists I, II and III available to original registers in the City, Greater London), 106 original parish registers are deposted with the library.

Maps of all ages of the City and environs are available. The original records of most of the livery companies annd Guilds are stored at the Guildhall in the MSS dept.

On the open shelves are to be found the British Museum library catalogues; the Calenders of State Papers, Patent Rolls, Treasury Books; the complete collection of Huguenot Society; the Harleian Society publications etc.

It is a marvellous collection of historial and genealogical data.

Part 11 The Huguenot Society

This small dedicated society has about 750 members or fellows. their library (for members only) is housed at University College, Gower Street, London WC1, but the postal address is 54 Knatchbull Road, London SE5. Many of their books are noted elsewhere, under Aliens Immigrants, French Sources, Ireland etc. and available at major libraries. Any reader with a French name or suspected Huguenot background should apply for membership.

Other Family History Sources

A.

Achievements Ltd., major genealogical publishers/researchers: Northgate, Canterbury, Kent.

Act Books of Bishops and Archdeacons Courts — consult local County Record Office.

Administrations, Letters of Wills; consult Principal Probate Registry, Somerset House.

Admiralty Records, see under Navy, also ADM records at PRO Kew.

Advocates, consult Law List from 1787, Guildhall; BML; Soc. of Genealogists.

Aldermen, London, consult the Guildhall; regionally local CRO.

Allegations, see Marriage Licences.

Aliens, see part 6 of this chapter.

Almanach de Gotha: European nobility records at major libraries.

Air Force Lists at Soc. of Genealogists; PRO Kew (Air Force records)

America, see USA chapter 21 for source.

Ancient Monuments Soc: Mr M. Saunders, St. Andrews by the Wardrobe, Queen Victoria Street, London EC4.

Ancient Deeds, Exchequer, catalogue of. Treasury of Receipt. 7 volumes published by PRO. (BML 2182 open shelves). Thousands of land transactions between 1200-1500. A mine of genealogical information. Well indexed. A rare and unusual source.

Apothecaries Act of 1815; register of licenciates at Guildhall library.

Apprentices, see Guilds, part 7 of this chapter.

Archdeaconry Court of London, index of wills at Guildhall library.

Archives, see County Record Offices.

Architects, consult Society of Genealogist records.

Arms, see Heraldry.

Army, consult leaflet No.9 by PRO: excellent reading, also specialist books by G. Hamilton-Edwards: Smith and Gardner; R. Higham; C. Dalton (various), J. Kane, T.W. Connoly; M.E. Laws; Harts Army List from 1840; C.T. Watts, A.S. White, "Army

Lists" at Soc. of Geneagogists, major libraries, Guildhall ref. 923.5. War Office records (WO) are at PRO Kew. "London Gazette" at Guildhall, major libraries. Militia, Trained Bands — consult H.A.C. records Finsbury Square, London: Guildhall library. Muster Rolls see WO 10/11/12/13/16 and 25 at PRO Kew. National Army Museum, Royal Hospital Road, London SW3.

Army Ancestry of World Wars by Norman Holding, from Federation of Family History Societies.

Army, British, Operational Records 1660-1914, see PRO Kew leaflet No.58.

Army: Roll of the Great War — very rare — Imperial War Museum, London, have 5 out of 14 volumes. The British Museum Library has a complete set.

Army War Graves, Ministry of Defence, PS12 (CAS) Lansdowne Ho. Berkeley Sq. London W1.

Assoc. of Genealogists & Record Agents, consult secretary, Mrs M.C. Gandy, "Oakdene", 64 Oakleigh Park North, London N20 for AGRA membership lists.

Assession Rolls, recorded in local Manor Court rolls and Court Leet Rolls; consult local County Record Office: assessments of rural rentals from 1500.

Australia, see chapter 20 for sources.

Archeological Societies, consult works in your local library/local studies library, and CRO's.

B.

BACSA: British Association for Cemeteries in S. Asia: Theon Wilkinson, 76 Chartfield Avenue, Putney, London SW15.

Banns, marriage bonds. Since 1753 Banns books/registers must be kept either as separate registers, or combined with marriage registers. Consult the Harleian Society, the Greater London Record Office, Guildhall library and W.P.H. Phillimore have all published books on Banns and marriage bonds/licences — see British Record Society vols 62 and 66.

Baptisms, see Parish Registers, part 1 of this chapter.

Barber-Surgeons, Guild: the Guildhall library has records see Surgeons.

Bankruptcy, Court of, PRO Chancery Lane has records (B).

Baronetages, see Peerages.

Barristers, consult Law Lists: "Calender of Inner Temple Records" Inderwick/Roberts at Guildhall library and Society of Genealogists.

Battle Abbey, roll of, see version by Hollingshed.

Bernau Index, Chancery Proceedings Index: invaluable: at Society of Genealogists Part 8 of this chapter.

Bishops Transcripts/Diocesan Transcripts, "Guide to" by J.S.W. Gibson: Guildhall MS9531.

Birth Certificates, from PRO St. Catherine's House, Aldwych: consult indexes there.

Biographical Records: Dict. of Nat. Biography, Oxford Univ. Press: consult B.M. library, also books by D. Steel, J.A. Venn, J. Foster, W. Matthews, see indexes of The Times: The Gentleman's Magazine 1731-1868.

Black Death devastated population in 1348/9.

British Transport Historical Records at PRO Kew (Rail).

Boyds Marriage Index, invaluable: complete collection at Society of Genealogists. Certain local libraries have copies of parts of the Index; i.e. the Guildhall library: check with local CRO or Family History Society.

Boyds Burial Index 1538-1853 for London and Middlesex at Society of Genealogists.

Boyds London Citizens, 238 volumes at Society of Genealogists; Guildhall library (London).

Boyds, "a list of parishes in Boyds Marriage Index" by R.W. Massey.

Brazil: Mormon CFI library at c/o Wayne Metcalfe, Genealogical Service Centre, 3rd Floor Tower, Church Office Building, Sao Paulo.

British Library, see part 9 of this chapter: consult catalogue available major libraries.

British Nationals Abroad, see Overseas.

"British Family Histories", "held in Scottish Public Libraries" by J.P.S. Ferguson, also by T.R. Thomson, at major libraries.

British Record Society, Hon. Sec. P.L. Dickinson MA c/o College of Arms, Queen Victoria Street, London EC4.

"British Surnames," "a dictionary of" by P.H. Reaney, at

major libraries. Very important book giving original derivations, 10,000 names.

British Telecom Library, Baynard House, 135 Queen Victoria Street, London EC4V 4AT. Tel. 01-248 7444. Directories from 1880.

Brokers/Stockbrokers, records kept at CLRO in the Guildhall and Guildhall Library.

Burial Grounds/Public Cemeteries, started in London with Bunhill Fields, see Guildhall Library Interment Order Books 1789-1854: read "Return of burial grounds in the County of London" by I.M. Holmes: also books by P.C Rushen, A.J. Jewers. Consult local library, local record office, Soc. of Genealogists for records of 'monumental inscriptions' from tombstones. Certainly the local Family History Society should have all available records copied.

Burial Registers, consult PRO St. Catherine's House, Aldwych, London for post 1840 see Parish Registers part 1 of this chapter.

Burkes, "Landed Gentry", "Peerage" "General Armory" "Family Index" "Extinct Peerage", major publishers of 'noble' genealogical works.

British Museum Library. It is certain that every book mentioned in Sources is available at BML; see part 9 of this chapter.

C.

Calender of Patent Rolls, State Papers, Colonial, Treasury Books and Papers, Venetian Papers: the Nation's historical background; well indexed indispensable to the family historian interested in the period 1513-1745, chapters 4-19 are largely derived from these historical records, on the open shelves at BM library, Guildhall and major libraries.

Camden Society/Series. Interesting collection of historical articles: major libraries.

Canada, see chapter 22 for sources.

Canterbury, Prerogative Court of: see Wills part 4 of this chapter.

Catholic, "Sources for genealogy and family history" by D. Steel and E.R. Samuel. Church registers c/o the Archivist, Archbishops House, Westminster, London SW1; Record Society, c/o Miss R. Rendell, Flat 5, 24 Lennox Gardens, London SW1;

Record Society Library at 114 Mount Street, London W1; Registers at PRO, Chancery Lane, London; also Soc. of Genealogists; "London and Middlesex Published records" by J.W. Sims, p.5. Marriages, "Index of" by Fr. Godfrey Anstruther, Church Shop, 222 Leigh Road, Leigh-on-Sea, Essex.

Capewell, Janice. Index of non-conformist registers mainly London; 7 Mytton Grove, Copthorne, Shrewsbury (with S.A.E.).

Card, Great Index, see at Soc. of Genealogists — magnificent Lucky Dip.

Cemeteries, see Burial Grounds.

Census, see part 3 of this chapter.

Central Bureau Voor Genealogie, Mr C.W. Delforterie, PO Box 11755, 2502 The Hague, Netherlands.

Chamberlains Court, see part 7 of this chapter.

Chancery Proceedings, see PRO leaflet No.32 at PRO Chancery Lane, see Bernau Index: originals at PRO Chancery Lane, London "Abstracts of documents" by P. Norman (London Topological Society). Books by J. Unett; R.E.F. Garrett; M.H. Hughes; P.W. Coldham.

Channel Islands: Registrar General, States Office, Royal Sq. Jersey. Societé Jersiase, The Library, The Museum, 9 Pier Road, Jersey. Registrar General, Greffe, St. Peters Port, Guernsey.

Challen W.H. Transcripts of many S.E. England registers at the Guildhall Library or Soc. of Genealogists.

Change of Name: see PRO Leaflet No.5: all relevant information. "Index to Changes of Name" by W.P.W. Phillimore and E.A. Fry.

Christian Names "Oxford dictionary of English Christian names" O.U.P.

Church of Jesus Christ of Latter Day Saints, see part 5 of this chapter.

Churchwardens accounts/Vestry minutes: most Parish Churches keep these records: consult local CRO..

Civil Registration, see parts 1 and 2 of this chapter.

Clergy, Crockfords clerical directory from 1858, Soc. of Genealogists and major libraries: Ordination Registers 1550-1628; 1657-1809 at the Guildhall Library: Fawcett Index at Soc. of Genealogists: Ordination Papers at the Guildhall Library and

Lambeth Palace Library; read Fosters "Index Ecclesiasticus 1800-1840" and "Fasti Ecclesiae Scoticanae" at Soc. of Genealogists. Other books by G. Hennessey, R. Newcourt at the Guildhall.

Clockmakers, see excellent records at Guildhall Library.

College of Arms, read Harleian Society publications "Heralds Visitations," "Records and collections of.." Sir A.R. Wagner: the College is at Queen Victoria Street, London EC4.

Colonial Office records at PRO Kew (CO).

Colonial Records Index by N. Currer-Briggs, 7 High St., Saffron Walden, Essex.

Commissary Court of London, Wills at Guildhall Library.

Commonwealth War Graves Commission, 2 Marlow Road, Maidenhead, Berkshire SL6 7DX.

Convicts & Transportation, "English convicts in colonial America" P.W. Coldham. "The crimes of the first fleet convicts to Australia" John Cobley. See PRO leaflet No.7 "Emigrants"; HO 10,11,26,27 at Chancery Lane.

Court of Common Pleas, "Calender to the feet of Fines for London and Middlesex" by W.J. Hardy, W. Page.

Court of Common Pleas, PRO Chancery Lane, London (CP).

Court of Husting (Wills), at CLRO; also see "Calender" by R.R. Sharpe, Guildhall.

Court of Orphans, records at CLRO, and at Guildhall Library.

County Directories, Society of Genealogists has excellent collection.

County Record Offices "Record Repositories in GB" HMSO Federation of Family History Societies has list. Consult local telephone directory, local Family History Society. Book by F.G. Emmision/I. Gray.

County Courts, records at PRO Chancery Lane ref (AK).

"Coroners Rolls", City of London 1300-1378 by R.R. Sharpe.

County Histories, read "Victoria C.H.", useful for landed families: see Walford's "County Families".

Crown Estate Commissioners, records at PRO Chancery Lane (CRES).

Crests "Book of" by Fairbairn.

Corporation of London Records Office (CLRO) in Guildhall, keeps "Marriage Assessments" "Court of Hustings" "Court of

Orphans" "Freeman Index" etc.

Crime & Punishment "Guide to Middlesex Sessions Records" by G.L.R.O. Prison Commission, records at PRO Kew (PCOM) Home Office, records at PRO Kew (HO). "Calender to the feet of Fines for London & Middlesex" W.J. Hardy & W. Page.

D.

Death Certificates, from PRO Alexandra House, Aldwych, London.

Death Duty Registers at PRO Chancery Lane, Wills room, leaflet No.34.

Deaths Overseas, Records held at GRO St. Catherine's House inc. 'Overseas Consular returns from 1849.' 'Service records' — Army from 1881, RAF from 1920, etc. 'Births & Deaths at sea from 1837.'

Deeds, property, see PRO leaflet No.25, no central source: try local history libraries: CROs: local Family History Societies (Southwark LS has 10,000 deeds; Tower Hamlets, London have 7,000 deeds indexed). See 'Ancient Deeds'.

Denization, letters of, see Aliens part 6 of this chapter: see "Naturalisation".

Dentists, Register of 1888-1922 at Soc. of Genealogists.

Debrett, publishers of books on the nobility.

Diocesan transcripts, see Bishops Transcripts: also transcripts by W.H. Challen and C.R. Webb.

"Dictionary of National Biography" by O.U.P.

Directories, Baileys Northern (1721), Kents (1734), Barfoots (1790), Boyles Street (1792), Holdens (1796), Post Office (1799), Pigots Commercial (1814), Johnstones London (1817), Whites (1826), Kellys (1800). Read "Guide to the national and provincial directories of England & Wales", J.E. Norton. "Universal British Directory" Barfoot & Wilkes. "City of London Directory 1871-1915". "Fashionable Court Guide" by Boyle 1792. Soc. of Genealogists Collection of Directories & Poll Books, J.M. Sims, "The London Directories" by C.W.F. Goss. Directories are an excellent source of information, at major libraries, Soc. of Genealogists, local CRO's.

District Probate Offices & Registries — copies of wills kept at

Somerset House.

Divorces, Register at Somerset House in Probate and Divorce dept: staff will search for a fee.

Doctors, Medical Directory from 1845 at Soc. of Genealogists, Guildhall. Register from 1859 at Soc. of Genealogists, Guildhall. Roll of the Royal College of Physicians 1815-1925, by Munk. Medical Practitioners in London 1529-1725 by J.H. Bloom, R.R. James, Ministry of Health (MH), Dep. Health & Social Security (BN) records PRO Kew.

Domesday Book, see at BM Library (readers ticket), "Domesday Book" by John Morris, published by Phillimore.

E.

East India Company, "Register" at Soc. of Genealogists. Percy Smith Collection at Soc. of Genealogists. Hudson Index of Offices at National Army Museum, London.

Educational Records see Schools.

Eire, see Ireland.

Electoral Registers at local CROs from 1834, see Poll Books. British Museum library from 1832; Guildhall for London records.

Emigrants, see PRO leaflet No.7 — excellent summary: Books by A.H. Lancour; P.W. Coldham, G. Donaldson; D. Whyte; D. Hill; W.A. Carrothers; T. Coleman; J.C. Hotten; P.S. King. Check List by Francis Leeson. Vol XXIV of Huguenot Soc. pub: Passenger lists from English ports can be seen PRO Kew: "Foreign parish registers" are held by PRO Chancery lane: Guildhall has other records on Anglicans abroad, BM library also has collection.

F.

Faculty Office of Archbishop of Canterbury see Banns of Marriage: also Harleian Soc. pub 25/26. See Guildhall manuscripts ref L77:32: Brit. Rec. Soc. vols 62 & 66. See Soc. of Genealogists "Calenders of Licences up to 1837" on microfilm.

Family History News & Digest pub. by Federation of Family History Societies. Quarterly publication with excellent summaries of regional events and discoveries.

"Family History" magazine, pub. by Achievements Ltd, Northgate, Canterbury, Kent.

Family Trees. A genealogical study usually ends up with the composition tree(s) or ancestry charts. Don Steel "Discovering Family History pp 109/110; Soc. of Genealogists pamphlet No.3; give excellent advice. In this book of Family History, the many family trees have been placed discreetly at the back. Every family should have such a family tree, duplicated or copied, particularly for the younger members of the family.

Families, 'County f. of UK' by Walford. 'landed', see Victoria county histories, BML Guildhall, Soc. of Genealogists etc. "catalogue of British Family Histories" by T.R. Thomson. "names in Britain" by H.B. Guppy. Document collection at Soc. of Genealogists.

Far East, 'A brief guide to biographical sources' by Ian Baxter, India Office Library & Records, London.

Fleet Registers, registers of clandestine marriages near Fleet Prison from 1667: records at PRO.

Federation of Family History Societies, Sec. Mrs A. Chiswell, 96 Beaumont Street, Millhouse, Plymouth, Devon. HQ of 100 regional FH Societies.

Feet of Fines, see Crime & Punishment.

Foreign Registers at PRO Chancery Lane and Guildhall.

Foreigners, see Aliens part 6 of this chapter.

Foreign Telephone Book, useful source of possible contacts: GPO, major libraries.

Freedom Registers. "City of London" by M.T. Medlycott; originals at the Chamberlain's Court, Guildhall, London EC2.

Friends, Society of, Friends House, Euston Road, London NW1 (Quaker Records) see "Nonconformist and foreign registers" by Norman Graham.

G.

Galbraith, V.H. "Tower (of London) as Exchequer Records", useful medieval source.

Gazeteers, genealogical have been published by Gardner/Harland/Smith. Inst. Heraldic Studies in Canterbury; Harley/Phillips;

Rodger and S. Lewis see at most major libraries and Soc. of Genealogists.

Genealogy, The Society of Genealogists in London publish a series of interesting pamphlets, beginners guides, courses etc. Joining a local Family History Society is equally rewarding.

Genealogical Periodicals, by local archeological societies (Sussex is an excellent example): the Surtees Society is another: the 'Genealogists Magazine' by the Soc. of Genealogists: "Family History" from Achievements of Canterbury: "Notes and Queries", the "Gentlemans Magazine". Many Family History Society quarterly magazines can be found at the Society of Genealogists.

Genealogical Books, "American & British Gen. & Heraldry" by P.W. Filby. "Genealogical research in England & Wales", D. Gardner/F. Smith. "Guide to printed books & mss. relating to English & foreign heraldry and genealogy". G. Gatfield. "A guide to genealogical sources in Guildhall Library" Corporation of London. "A select bibliography of English genealogy" H.G Harrison. "A genealogists bibliography" C. Humphery-Smith. "An introduction to medieval genealogy" C. Humphery-Smith (very interesting).

General Register Offices at St. Catherine's House, 10 Kingsway, London WC2 (01-242 0262) (Reg. Births/Marriages). Alexander House, Kingsway, (Register of Deaths).

Greater London Record Office, County hall, South Bank, London (moving to 40 Northampton Road, Clerkenwell, London EC1 (also GLC library).

Gentlemans Magazine 1731-1868 excellent source of informaton: at Guildhall, Soc. of Genealogists, major libraries: Indexes 1753-1821. "Index to Biographical & Obituary Notices 1731-80" by R.H. Farrat. "Index to Marriages 1731-1786" by E.A. Fry. Vol I/II Index by S. Aysclough: Vol III/IV Index by J. Nickols Vol V Index by Charles St. Barbe: The magazine was started by Edward Cave in 1731 and lasted until 1908.

Germany W, "How to find German ancestors & relatives" Family History Association, Mormon genealogical libraries in Frankfurt, Hamburg, Kaiserlautern.

Gibson, J.S.W. Author of vital modern genealogical guides:

"Census Returns", "Probate Jurisdictions", "Bishops Transcripts and Marriage Licences", "Marriage Indexes", "Record Offices". Address Harts Cottage, Church Hanborough, Oxford OX7 2AB.

Graham, N.H. Author of vital modern genealogical guides "Cons. guide to Parish Registers (a) Inner London (b) Outer London (c) Nonconformist & Foreign Registers". Address N.H. Graham, 69 Crest View Drive, Petts Wood, Kent BR5 1BX.

Grays Inn/Lincolns Inn/Middle Temple — legal records at Guildhall: read "A calender of the Inner Temple records 1505-1800" F.A. Inderwick & R.A. Roberts.

Guildhall Library, major library and genealogical source. Very knowledgeable, helpful and patient staff, Aldermanbury, London EC2 (01-606 3030).

H.

Harleian Society, major publisher of genealogical books. Their Register section of Parish Registers: Marriage licences: and above all Heralds Visitations: Bedfordshire 19; Berkshire 56-7; Buckinghamshire 58; Cambridgeshire 41; Cheshire 18,59,93; Cornwall 9; Cumberland 7; Devon 6; Dorset 20; Essex 13-14; Gloucestershire 21; Hampshire 64; Herts 22; Kent 42,54,74-75; Leicestershire 2; Lincolnshire 50-52,55; London & Middlesex 1,15,17,65,92,109-110; Norfolk 32,85-86,91; Northants 87; Nottinghamshire 4; Oxford 5; Rutland 3,73; Shropshire 28-29; Somerset 11; Staffordshire 63; Suffolk 61,91; Surrey 43,60; Sussex 53,89; Warwickshire 12,62; Wiltshire 105-106; Worcester 27,90; Yorkshire 16, 94-96. The pedigrees in all these works are indexed in 3 volumes by Marshall, Whitmore and Barrow: see also "Visitation Pedigrees & the Genealogist" G.D. Squibb. Harleian Soc. volumes at Guildhall, BM library, major libraries and Soc. of Genealogists.

Hearth Tax Return, for 1662/4 returns at PRO. All householders were taxed by the number of hearths they had — see Tax returns.

Herald's College, College of Arms, Queen Victoria Street, London EC4. "Records and collections of the college of Arms" by Sir A.R. Wagner.

Heralds visitations, by Officers of College of Arms 1530-1687. Pedigrees of people who had a right to Arms. See College of

Arms: see Harleian Soc. publications.

Heraldry, see collection at Soc. of Genealogists. See Harleian Society Vol 66-68. See Guildhall Library ref. 929 7206. MS 14288 and L77.1. Consult College of Arms above. Read "Discovering Heraldry" Fed. of F.H. Societies: Heraldry Society c/o Mrs J.C.G. George, 28 Museum Street, London WC1.

History, social. All major libraries have collections of works. All good local libraries should also have local historical studies; "Writing local history" pub. by Bedford Square Press: consult books by Authors — G.M. Trevelyan, W.G. Hoskins "Local History in England". Publishers Penguin, Batsford and Longmans have produced many social histories. See Phillimore List of Local History Books. Consult too the nearest County Records Office and Family History Society.

History, Military, society. Duke of Yorks Road, Chelsea, London SW3 (postal only).

Historical Association, produces pamphlets about genealogical sources, 59A Kennington Park Rd., London SE11..

Historical Manuscripts Commission, Quality House, Chancery Lane, London WC2.

"Historical Review", English: also "History To-Day" specialist magazines.

Historical Society, Royal, at University College, Gower Street, London WC1.

Historical Research, "Bulletin of Institute", Senate House, University of London, WC1 (01-219 3000).

Historical Research, Institute of, Senate House, Russell Square, London WC1. 01-636 0272. Open access library of printed historical data.

House of Lords, Record Office, Westminster, London SW1A: Protestation returns etc. cases in House of Lords; see Naylor collection at Guildhall.

Hudsons Bay Company; PRO Records at Kew on microfilm (BH).

Huguenots Soc. of London c/o Mrs I. Scouloudi, 67 Victoria Road, London W8 see part 11 of this chapter.

Humphery-Smith, C. author of specialist genealogical books.

I.

Immigrants, see Aliens part 6 of this chapter.

Index Society/library British Record, published series of local wills etc. see collection at Soc. of Genealogists, BM library and major libraries.

India, Records at office and Library, 197 Blackfriars road, London SE1 enquire for expatriate births, deaths and marriages. "Guide to the India Office Records 1600-1858" by Sir William Foster. "India office Records" by Major V.C.P.. Hodson. Society of Genealogists has card index by Col. Percy-Smith. Hodson Index of Hon. East India Company officers at National Army Museum. Indian Army List at Soc. of Geneaologists, also directories. Consult "Miscellaneous Records" at PRO, St. Catherine's House, Kingsway, London.

Inns of Court, registers, at Guildhall library.

Insolvent Debtors Accounts Books — ask for at local Record office or Reference Library.

Institute of Heraldic & Genealogical Studies, Northgate, Canterbury, Kent. Major publishers of "Family History", County maps, Pallot Index, Index to Irish Wills, Guide to Marriage Licences, Introduction to medieval genealogy, Census district maps, etc. Tel. 0227-68664.

Inland Revenue, PRO Kew have IR records of interest and PRO Chancery Lane for estate duty registers (IR 26/27).

Ireland, General Registry Offices, Customs House, Dublin 1, records from 1845. Public Record Office, Four Courts, Dublin 1, census data parish records from 1901, "A Handbook of Irish Genealogy" by Heraldic Artists Ltd, Trinity, Dublin (ref. 929-1). "Family History Records in Ireland" by Robert Brown. "Irish ancestral research" by M.D. Falley. Huguenot Society publications VII, XIV, XIX, XVIII, XXVII, XLI for Huguenot Church records, pensioners and aliens. "Irish Protestant Rolls" by C.R. Webb. Irish Genealogical Society of G.B. Challoner Club, 59/61 Pont Street, London SW1. Irish wills, indexes at Soc. of Genealogists. County/Parish histories at Soc. of Genealogists. "Bibliography of Irish Family History & Genealogy" Brian de Breffny. Directories at Soc. of Genealogists. A simple guide to Irish genealogy by R. Ffolliott. See Soc. of Genealogists directories.

Istituto Storico Famiglie Italiane, Prof A.C. D'Ardea, 50129, Firenze, Via Cavour 31, Italy; consult for family history problems in Italy.

J.

Jews. Anglo-Jewish Archives, Mocatta library, University College, Gower Street, London WC1. Jewish Historical Society of England, London. Offices of the Chief Rabbi, Adler House, Tavistock Square, London WC1 hold archives of United Synagogue. Jewish Museum, Woburn House, Upper Woburn House, London WC1. Read transactions of Jewish Historical Society of England. Consult N.H. Grahams "Nonconformist and Foreign registers 1537-1837". Consult Spanish & Portuguese Jews congregation: Archivist, 2 Ashworth Rd, London W9. Read "London & Middlesex published records" by J.W. Sims p.52. Read "Appearance of persons coming from foreign parts 1651" by S.W. Samuel. See list of Jewish brokers at Guildhall Library. Read "Sources for R.C. and Jewish genealogy and family history" D.J. Steel/E.R. Samuel.

Judges, see Society of Genealogists records, see PRO Chancery lane (Just and J).

Journals, "Genealogists Magazine" by Soc. of Genealogists. "Family History" by Institute of Heraldic & Genealogical Studies. "The local historian" from Standing Conference for Local History. "Family History News & Digest" from Federation of Family HistorySocieties. Every Family History Society produces a journal, usually quarterly.

K.

Kellys Directories Ltd., Neville House, Eden Street, Kingston-upon-Thames, Surrey.

Knights, see College of Arms: read "the Complete Peerage", Burkes "Peerage" etc.

Kraus-Thomson Organisation Ltd., Millwood, New York 10546 USA. Major publishers of printed archive material, Commissions Reports to the Crown: Huguenot Society; etc.

L.

Land. Revenue Record Office, PRO Chancery Lane (LRRO):

Land Registry at PRO Kew (LAR): "Return of owners of land" (pub 1873), at PRO or BM official publications library.

Land Tax, see Taxes. Tenure, see Manorial Records/Rolls.

Land Confiscations, Crown & Royalist 1642-1660, see PRO Kew leaflet No.54.

Lambeth Palace, library and archives, Lambeth, London: important source of London history.

Lawyers/Barristers, consult "Law List" major libraries, Soc. of Genealogists. "Men at the Bar" by Foster. "Admissions to Grays Inn, Middle Temple, Inns of Court" at Soc. of Genealogists, Guildhall library, BML.

Latter-Day Saints, Mormons; see part 5 of this chapter.

Letters of Administration, see Wills part 4 of this chapter.

Leeson, F. author of "War Office Musters" in Soc. of Genealogists journal, and "Records at PRO Kew" Emigrant Check List. Surname Archive, 108 Sea Lane, Ferring, West Sussex.

Libraries, British Museum Library: Guildhall: Bodleain Oxford: Cambridge University, Soc. of Genealogists: Lambeth Palace: GLRO History Library at County Hall: House of Lords: all Local Studies Libraries.

Livery Companies, see Guilds part 7 of this chapter.

Local Registrar, see Registration of Births, Deaths, Marriages in local telephone book.

Local Histories, Phillimore have published the Darwen county histories: "Victorian history of the counties of England" - major libraries. Local History Societies, 26 Bedford Square, London WC1. Consult British Museum Library catalogue under appropriate place name. "Sources for Engish local history" by W.B. Stephens.

Local Studies Libraries. Vital source for family historians, for directories, ratebooks, property deeds, electoral registers, local census returns, oral history records, maps, prints and photographs, early schools, local government records, press cuttings, tradesmens hand bills, old local newspapers, local histories, early public health records. Every family historian should make a beeline for his nearest local studies libraries.

London Record Society c/o Leicester University Library, University road,, Leicester who publish transcripts, indexes of wills, assizes, surveys etc.

"London Gazette" for naturalisations, change of name, awards etc., at major libraries.

London "Inhabitants of 1638" by T.C. Dale.

"London & Middlesex Published Records" by J.M. Sims (London Record Society).

"London & Middlesex Genealogical Directory" by combined London Family History societies.

London, "Calender of Letter Books A-L 1275-1497" by R.R. Sharpe.

"London, Chronicle" by John Stow (Harleian publication).

London, "Guide to Genealogical Research in Victorian" by C. Webb, Surrey Family History Society.

London, Directories at Guildhall, GLRO library, major libraries.

London, "Index of Wills before 1700" by M. Fitch pub. by Brtish Record Society.

London, City of London Record Office located in the Guildhall building near library.

London, City of London Freedom Registers; Guild freedoms and original indentures at Chamberlain's Court in the Guildhall.

M.

Magazines, see Journals.

Man, Isle of, General Registry, Finch Road, Douglas. Tel. 3358: Manx Museum library, Kingswood Road, Douglas.

Manor Court Rolls, see Taxes.

Manorial Records, books by J. West, W.G. Hoskins, N.J. Hone. Early records are held in PROs. See excellent summary by D. Steel "Discovering Family History" inc Assession rolls, Manor Court Rolls, Court Leet Rolls for early medieval land records: chapters 9, XX in particular. Consult Index at National Register of Archives, Quality Ct. Chancery Lane, London WC2. Consult County Record offices, BM Library, local Archeological Societies.

Maps, County by Soc. of Genealogists: Phillimore: Inst. Heraldic & Gen. Studies.

Manuscript Pedigrees, at Soc. of Genealogists, British Museum Library, College of Arms.

Marines, Royal, see excellent PRO leaflet No.28.

Marriage, Assessments for 1694 kept at City of London Record Office, Guildhall Licences, see Harleian vols 25/26: GLRO; Soc. of Genealogists. Boyds marriage Index at Soc. of Genealogists; Guildhall Library. "Guide to Location" by J.S.W. Gibson. "Allegations for Marriage licences" by G.J. Armytage. "Licences" by C.R. Humphery-Smith in "Family History". "Indexes" by M. Walcot & J.S.W. Gibson. Certificates after 1837 at GRO, St. Catherine's House, Aldwych, London. CFI/IGI Mormon microfiche 1550-1837. Local family history societies for county marriage indexes.

Medicine, "Medical Directory" "Medical Register" at major libraries. Munks "Roll of College of Physicians". Royal College of Surgeons; Guildhall library has Mss. & Indexes

Merchant Navy, excellent PRO leaflet No.8: books by C.T. Watts & M. Mander. See Lloyds Merchant Captains registers at Soc. of Genealogists.

Medieval Sources, Books by C.R. Humphery-Smith; J. Unett; J. West; K.C. Newton. Consult BM library and Guildhall library.

Memorial Tablets, see Monumental Inscriptions.

Merchant Taylors, records with Guild in London: microfilm at Guildhall library.

Methodists, National Archives; Connexional Archivist, c/o Property Division, Central Buildings, Oldham St. Manchester M1 1QJ.

Middlesex Sessions Records 1549-1889, GLRO publication.

Microfilms/Microfiche used for CFI, many Parish records and census data.

Midwives, licences by Bishops: Guildhall MS 10116.

Mexico, Mormon genealogical library in Mexico City and Chihuahua.

Military, see PRO leaflet No.9; and Army; Soc. for Army Historical Research, The Library, Old War Office Building, Whitehall, London SW1.

Migrants, see Emigrants.

Members of Parliament, see major libraries or Soc. of Genealogists. Dods or Vachers Parliamentary Companion.

Monumental Inscriptiions, see Burial Grounds: Society of Genealogists has excellent collection of local records and notes by H.L. White. "Notes on recording" by J.L. Rayment. "Monumental Brasses in the British Isles" by M. Stephenson.

Mormon Church, see part 5 of this chapter: 64 Exhibition Road, London SW7. Library open Wednesday afternoon only.

Mottoes, "Hand-Book of Mottoes" by C.N.Elvin.

Mullins E.L.C., "A guide to the historical and archeological publications of societies in England and Wales 1901-1933". "Texts and calenders" pub. by Royal Historical Society. Vital books.

Museums, National Army Museum, Royal Hospital Road, London SW3. Imperial War, Lambeth Road, London SE1. National Maritime, Greenwich, London SE10.

N.

National Register of Archives, Quality House, Chancery Lane, London (01-242 1198). Set up in 1945 to act as central collection point for information about Manuscript sources for British History *outside* the Public Records.

National Genealogical Directory, pub. from 4/33 Sussex Square, Brighton. An Index of 30,000 families being researched in UK.

Naturalisation, until 1844 a letter Patent of Denization had to be granted or an Act of naturalisation promoted. After 1844 the Home Secretary issued a system of certificates. Sources include the Huguenot Society publications; House of Lords Record Office; "Papers of the House of Commons", London Gazette from 1886; Patent and Parliament Rolls; Camden Society Vol 82; Home Office (HO) records at PRO Kew. See Aliens section 6 of this chapter.

Navy, see PRO leaflet 18 "the Admiralty"; original records at PRO Kew; National Maritime Museum, Greenwich, London SE10; publications Navy Records Society, Royal Naval College, Greenwich, London SE10; Directories by Charnock; Marshall: O'Byrne at Soc. of Genealogists. Collection at Soc. of Genealogists of naval records. "Navy List" at Guildhall and major libraries including Soc. of Genealogists.

Naval Historical Library, Empress State Building, Lillie Rd. Fulham, London SW11.

Netherlands, consult Central Bureau voor Genealogie, Nassaulaan 18, Den Haag: Huguneot Society has Parish Register book for Netherlands: see Huguenot publications Vol I, IV, V, XII, XXXVI; for anyone with ancestors from Holland, these books are indispensable.

New Zealand, Society of Genealogists, PO Box 8795, Auckland 3: Armorial & Genealogical Institute of New Zealand, PO Box 13-301, Armach, Christchurch, N.Z. Mormon Genealogical libraries in Takapuna, Manurewa, Mt Raskill in Auckland; in Christchurch, Hamilton & Wellington. Collection at Soc. of Genealogists of NZ data, directories.

Newspapers, consult Newspaper library, Colindale Avenue, London NW9 (01-205 6039): Newspaper Room at Guildhall library: BM library. Consult local libraries, particularly Local Studies libraries: also local family history societies.

Nonconformist Sources, PRO Chancery Lane has many Parish Registers, consult Norman Graham's "Nonconformist & Foreign Registers". Also Society of Friends (see Quakers); Dr Williams library at 14 Gordon Square, London WC1: Catholics (see Roman Catholics): Huguenot Society: Presbyterian Historial Soc. of England, 86 Tavistock Place, London WC1 has registers. Congregational library, Memorial Hall, Farringdon St., London EC4; Baptist Historical Society, Baptist Union Library, 4 Southampton Row, London WC1: Weslyan Archives at John Rylands Library, Manchester University: See 'Jews'. Consult Janice Capewell Index for East End Register Indexes, at 7 Mytton Grove, Copthorne, Shrewsbury SY3 8UF (with S.A.E.); consult local County Record Offices, local Family History Society, see Guildhall for many original nonconformist registers: PRO has Dr Williams General Registry, births 1742-1837. Read "Nonconfirmst Registers" by Edwin Welch in Journal of Society of Archivists.

Northern Ireland/Ulster: Gen. Reg. Office, Oxford House, 49-55 Chichester Street, Belfast BT1 4HC. Register General, Fermanagh House, Ormeau Avenue, Belfast BT2 8HX. Public Record Office, 66 Balmoral Avenue, Belfast BT9 6NY. Presbyterian Hist. Soc. of N.I., Church House, Fisherwick Pl. Belfast BT1 6DO. Royal Irish Constabulary: PRO leaflet No.30. Mormon genealogical Library in Holywood, Belfast.

"Notes and queries", source of genealogical material at major libraries.

O.

Obituaries, "from the Times" by F.C. Roberts. "prior to 1800" by Sir William Musgrave. See the "Gentlemans Magazine" at major libraries. BM library, Guildhall have printed sources of obituaries. Consult local FHS for source of obituaries in newspapers.

Official Publications library, Dept. Printed Books, British Museum Library, Bloomsbury, London.

One Name Societies, consult F.M. Filby, 15 Cavendish Gdns, Ilford, Essex. (S.A.E.). Over 1000 family names have been fully researched.

Ordination Registers, diocesan records of London 1550-1628, 1675-1809 held at Guildhall also Ordination papers 1676-1764, 1811-1976.

Overseers of the Poor, see Poor Law Records.

Oral evidence, some enterprising local studies libraries have taped 'local' histories. D. Steel has excellent chapter II in his book "Family History".

Overseas, Anglicans see *separate* registers at G.R.O. St Catherine's House, Aldwych: see Guildhall library MS 15,061/1-2 mainly for English communities in France, Portugal and Russia: also Diocesan registers MS 10,926/1/13: Marriages on board HM ships MS 11, 531, Baptisms and burials at sea MS 11,827. PRO records at Kew for Colonial & Foreign Service (CO, DO, FO and BT 158/160, Rg 43): PRO records in Long Room PRO Chancery Lane: Lambeth Palace library also has records.

P.

Pallot Index (1780-1837) covers vital half century before General Registration started, of London, Middlesex marriages in 101 of 103 ancient parishes within the square mile of City of London: also most of Kent, Surrey and Essex. A fee is payable to Institute of Heraldic and Genealogical Studies, 82 Northgate, Canterbury, Kent.

Parish *Histories:* see local Family History Society; local County Record Office; "Victorian County" publications: local studies library. *Maps:* purchase from Soc. of Genealogists; Phillimore: Institute of Her. and Gen. Studies. *Registers:* see Section 1 of this chapter. *Records:* 'the Parish Chest' C.V. Press: information of church seating plans; churchwardens accounts: poor law records. The local Family History Society should have catalogues. *Books:* "Original parish registers in record offices and libraries" by LPS, Tawney House, Matlock, Derbyshire. "Parish & vital records listings" LDS Church/Mormons. "Parish register copies"Soc. of Genealogists collection. "Registers in London" — 3 volumes by Norman Graham. "List of Parishes in Boyds marriage index" Soc. of Genealogists. "Parish Registers London & Middlesex" by Guildhall library. Harleian Society publications. "Middlesex Parish Registers" by W.P. Phillimore. "Contemporary index to printed parish registers" by G.F. Matthews.

Paleography, the study of old writing: works by D. Iredale: F.G. Emmison; H. Grieve; L.C. Hector; W.S.B. Buck and others.

Parliament "Guide to the records of Parliament" M. Bond, HMSO. "Pocket Companion" and "Parliamentary Companion".

Passenger Lists, see Emigrants.

Parochial Records measure, a recent law to enforce deposit of church records in County Record Offices for safer keeping and preservation.

Pawnbrokers, Societies in 18th century London: Bouverie: Holborn: Queens head of Southwark: Halfmoon Inn of Borough: Eastern Society.

Patentees, Index of, kept at Science Reference library, 25 Southampton Buildings, London WC2. Index to old patents 1617-1852 in one volume, thereafter yearly indexes.

Pedigrees, "Index to printed British" by G.B. Barrow: other books by T.R. Thompson, J.B. Whitmore, G.W. Marshall, D. Steel. See College of Arms: see Heralds Visitations. See manuscrips at Soc. of Genealogists.

Peerages, "The Complete.." by G.E. Cokayne. Burkes "Peerage" and "Extinct Peerage". Debretts books all at major libraries, Soc. of Genealogists.

Pension Records at PRO Kew, Ministry of Pensions & National

Insurance (PIN).

Periodicals, see Journals.

Phillimores, marriage indexes. Domesday county series. Publishers & suppliers of all genealogical books, maps etc. at Shopwyke Hall, Chichester, Sussex. PO20 6BQ. Tel. 0243-787636.

Pipe Rolls, early government expenditure records, available at British Museum library, PRO, major libraries. Well indexed and useful source mainly for 11th and 12th century.

Plague, 1626 and 1665 were the two worst years in England, London in particular, later cholera epidemics occurred in 1831/2 and even worse in 1849, with consequent increase in deaths.

Poll Books/Register of Electors. Guildhall library. British Library, Bodleian and Soc. of Genealogists both hold good collections, they have produced their own handlist of what records they have. All County Record Offfices and most Family History Societies will have information about local Poll books.

Poor Law Records. By an Act passed in 1598 each parish was responsible for its own poor members. A Poor Rate was levied on landowners and the parish 'vestry' members and overseers kept records and tables of payments to paupers. In 1834 the law was changed and responsibility was then transferred to Board of Guardians elected by the parish ratepayers.

Poor Law Union Papers, see PRO Kew, Ministry of Health records MH 12,15. London records are at the GLRO and the Guildhall.

Poor Accounts. The overseer of records, kept by local County Record Office and local studies libraries. Poor rate books recorded the collection of the Poor Rate (Samuel Delaforce contribued to Poor Rate, Blackfryars Road, Southwark, London in 1790).

Post Office HQ record office is at Room SG28, PHQ Building, St. Martin-le-Grand, London EC1. Employment registers of staff employed are from 1737.

Post Office Directories. Indispensable for locating current relatives in UK or elsewhere. There are few depositories in UK of overseas telephone diretories. A thoughtful, well-written letter to a possible relative giving information and politely requesting specific information can produce enormous dividends.

Prerogative Court of Canterbury (PCC) had over-riding jurisdiction in England and Wales for Wills and Letters of Administration. See part 4 of this chapter.

Probate, see Wills, part 4 of this chapter.

Principal Probate Office, Somerset House, The Strand, London WC2.

Probate Jurisdiction, see part 4 of this chapter.

Protestant Returns of 1641/2: pub. by Royal Commission on Historical Manuscripts. Originals held at House of Lords: effectively a national census for males over 18 required to sign a declaration of belief in the Protestant Religion, allegiance to the King and support for the rights and privileges of parliament. The Society of Genealogists, leaflet No.8 lists Printed Returns and Other Sources by county and more importantly, exactly where to find the local 'census'. This is a most important survey for readers researching ancestors of 1641/2. See books by L.W.L. Edwards; A.J.C. Guimaraens; S.A.J. McVeigh.

Public Records Offices. The researcher should consult the 3 volume "Guide to the Contents of the Public Record Office" HMSO. Vol 1 is legal records, Vol 2 State papers and departmental records, Vol 3 Accessions 1960-66. Also "An introduction to the use of public records" by O.U.P. The three buildings are at Chancery Lane, WC2 (01-405 0741), Portugal Street, WC2 (01-405 3488) census data only, and Kew Repository, Ruskin Avenue, Kew, Richmond, Surrey (01-876 3444). A readers ticket is required.

Q.

Quakers, Society of Friends, Friends House, Euston Road, London NW1: original register at PRO Chancery Lane. "Encyclopedia of American Quaker Genealogy" by H.I.N. Saw.

Quarter Sessions Records, see book by J. West: visit County Record Office. Excellent national summary by J.S.W. Gibson.

R.

Rate Books, Guildhall has a collection for London. "London rate assessments and inhabitants lists in Guildhall library and CLRO". GLRO also has collection. Every County Record Office, Local Studies Library should have Rate Book records.

Record Offices. Every County has a Record Office which

should hold parish registers, wills, marriage licences, and bishops transcripts. It is worth visiting your local record office and finding out exactly what they do have. Every Family History Society should know where all local records are kept. Most County Record Offices publish a list of records held. See "Record Repositories in GB" HMSO pub. by Royal Commission on Historical Manuscripts and "Enjoying archives" by D. Iredale. "How to find them" by J. Gibson and Pamela Peskett.

Record Societies, check with CRO or FHS if there is one locally.

Record Agents, see A.G.R.A. list of accredited agents.

Record Society of London have published specialist books by H.M. Chew, D.V. Glass, I. Darlington, F.W. Steer, D.J. Rowe,, J.M. Sims. see London Record Society.

Registers, transcripts of by Harleian Society: W.H. Challen: C.R. Webb. Major collection at Soc. of Genealogists.

Return of Owners of Lands, 1783 — House of Commons papers.

Roman Catholics: Record Society, Society of Jesus, 114 Mount Street, London W1. Parish Registers, N.H. Graham "Nonconfirmist & Foreign Registers" in Inner London. Original registers at PRO Chancery Lane. Consult D.J. Steel Index of parish Registers Vol III. See collection at Soc. of Genealogists. Read "Catholic mass-houses and chapels in London Reformation" at Guildhall library.

Royalist Composition papers — 17th century records of Royalist supporters at BM library and other major libraries.

S.

Schools, Guildhall has records of many London schools including Merchant Taylors, Christs Hopsital (L77,34: 373.42): CLRO and Soc. of Genealogists have other school records. Local County Record Offices should have school records (log books, registers). Read "Alumns Cantabrigienses" by J.A. Venn; "A biographical register of the University of Cambridge to 1500" cover Cambridge University and "A biographical register of the University of Oxford to 1500" by A.B. Emden and subsequent volume "1501-1540" by the same author. "Alumns Oxonienses" by J. Foster covers Oxford University. "Family History in Schools" by D. Steel and L. Taylor. "Registers of the Universities,

Colleges and Schools of GB and Ireland" by P.M. Jacobs. Guildhall material on other English universities ref 378.42.

Scotland. National Register of Archives, West Register House, Charlotte Square, Edinburgh EH2 4DF. General Register Office for Scotland New Register House, Princes Street, Edinburgh EH1 3YT — ask for "Ancestry Leaflet". The Scottish Record Office, General Register House, Princes Street, Edinburgh EH1 3YT. National Library of Scotland, George IV Bridge, Edinburgh EH1. "The surnames of Scotland" by George Black. "Scottish Family Histories" by Margaret Stuart. "Introducing Scottish Genealogical Research" by D. Whyte. "In search of Scottish Ancestry" by G. Hamilton-Edwards. "Sources for Scottish genealogy and family history" D. Steel: Vol 12 Soc. of Genealogists. "Scottish History Society" volumes at Soc. of Genealogists. Scottish Genealogical Society c/o Miss J. Ferguson, 21 Howard Place, Edinburgh EH3 5JY. Scots Ancestry Research Society, 20 Yorks Place, Edinburgh EH1 3EP. Aberdeen and N.E. Scotland FHS, c/o Miss Cowper, 31 Bloomfield Place, Aberdeen. Soc. of Genealogists holds a microfilm of 1855 Scottish registers and indexes 1855-1920: also collections by Macleod and Campbell-Young.

Selon Index, by Mrs C.C. Powell, 21 Marlborough Avenue, Ruislip, Middlesex for S.E. London: Parish Registers, Poor Rates, Census data, wills etc.

Service Records, see PRO Kew records (WO).

Settlement, law of 1662 resulted in 'examination passes' and 'removed orders' by which parishes were bound to maintain only those who had gained a legal settlement in the parish. See Poor Laws.

Sharpe, R.R., edited excellent "Calender letter books of London A-L, 1275-1497" and "Rolls of Court of Husting".

Shetlands, "Tracing Ancestors" by A. Sandison.

Ship Passenger Lists to USA (1528-1825) by Carl Boyer, PO Box 333, Newhall, CA 91322, USA, available larger libraries.

Subsidy Rolls, London see books by E. Exwall, M. Curtis, J.C.L. Stahlschmidt, S.L. Thrupp.

Soc. of Genealogists, one of the largest sources of material in UK, see part 8 of this chapter.

Somerset House, Strand WC2. Principal Probate Registry for UK for examination of wills.

Steel, D. Major author of genealogical books, parish registers, nonconformists etc.

Surgeons, Guildhall library has records from 1745 of Royal College of Surgeons.

Standing Conference for Local History, 26 Bedford Square, London WC1.

Stockbrokers, register with CLRO in Guildhall, London.

Surnames, see Soc. of Genealogy leaflet No.7: books by P.H. Reaney, F.K. & S. Hitching. Reaney book gives many original derivations.

South Africa, Human Sciences Research Council: Dr. R. Leonard, Private Bag X41, Pretoria 0001, RSA. Mormon genealogical library in Jeppeston, Johannesburg. Directories at Soc. of Genealogists.

Switzerland, Mormon genealogical library in Zurich.

T.

Tax Returns. Hearth tax for 1662 and 1664 returns at PRO (first national census). Poll taxes levied in 1641, 1660, 1666 and 1667 at PRO. Subsidy taxes of 1524-7 at PRO. Lay Subsidy from 1320: at PRO. Legacy duty/death duty registers see PRO leaflet No.34. Main Inland Revenue records at PRO Kew (IR). Window taxes of 1696-1798 at PRO. Marriage assessment tax of 1694/5 at PRO. London rate assessments, CLRO and Guildhall Library. See books by D. Iredale; J. West; W.R. Ward.

Telephone Directories. Major collections at Guildhall; British Telecom Museum; Bodleian library, Oxford.

Tenure, copyhold and conventionary, see D. Steel Family History Chapter 9.

Templars, "record of in 12th century" by B.A. Lees.

Times, the, "Obituaries from" by F.C. Roberts. Index at BM library, Newspaper library and Guildhall library.

Titled, see Kelly handbook to the titled, landed and official classes. See Peerage.

Tombstones, see Cemeteries, Monumental Inscriptions, books by J.L. Rayment; H.L.White.

Topographical Dictionaries by Lewis; Phillimore.

Tower of London, "as Exchequer Records" by Galbraith: "History & antiquities" by J. Bayley.

Trade Directories, see Catalogue of Directories at Soc. of Genealogists also major libraries, CROs and local studies libraries see Directories.

Transportation, books by A.H. Lancour; P.W. Coldham; J. Cobley. See 'Convicts'; read 'Emigrants' by J.M. Sims.

Trials, Old Bailey sessions papers 1684-1913 at Guildhall library. See "Guide to Middlesex Sessions".

Trinity House, Petitions; merchant mariners requesting charity from 1780-1854 at Soc. of Genealogists.

U.

Ulster Genealogical & Historial Guild: Mrs K. Neill, 66 Balmoral Avenue, Belfast BT9.

Undergraduates, see schools.

Universities, see schools.

"Unrelated Certificates" from Mr John Beach, 21 Larkswood Drive, Sedgley, W.Midlands, from Mrs B. Baker, 270 Clarence Rd. Sutton Coldfield, W.Midlands.

USA, see chapter 21 for sources.

V.

Vestry minutes, parish church councils 'vestry' responsible for election of Overseers of the Poor who raised the Poor Rate on owners and occupiers of lands and buildings.

"Victoria County" Histories: invaluable source of local history at major libraries.

"Victorian London" "Guide to Research to" by C.R. Webb.

Victorian Ordnance Survey Maps by J.B. Harley, published by David & Charles, Newton Abbott.

"Village Records" by J. West (Macmillan).

Visitations, Heralds see Harleian Society publications by H.J. Howard & F.A. Crisp.

"Visitation Pedigrees & the Genealogist" by G.D. Squibb.

"Visitation", Crisps see at Soc. of Genealogists.

W.

Wales. Soc. of Genealogists have collections by Williams, Swinnerton-Hughes, Morris, Watson etc. Welsh genealogy handbook at Soc. of Genealogists. national Library of Wales, Aberystwyth, Dyfed SY23 3BU hold all deposited parish registers and bishops transcripts: wills pre 1858. CROs at Llangerfri, Caernarfon, Aberystwyth, Carmarthan, Clwyd, Deeside, Cardiff, Dolgellau, Cwmbran, Haverfordwest. "An approach to Welsh genealogy" by F. Jones: Hon. Soc. of Cymmrodorion, 118 Newgate Street, London EC1.

West Indies, see Mrs V.T.C. Smith collection 43 vols at Soc. of Genealogists. Trade directories at Soc. of Genealogists.

W. Germany, "How to find German ancestors" by Dr. Heinz Friederichs (in English), from Verlag Degener & Co., Inh Gerhard Gessner, D8530 Neustadt, PO Box 1340 Aisch.

Webb, C.R. author, indexer, transcriber of London, SE England genealogical works: 8 Heather Close, New Haw, Weybridge, Surrey.

Wills, see part 4 of this chapter.

"Who Was Who", at Soc. of Genealogists and major libraries.

Y.

York, P.C.C. wills pub. by Yorkshire Archeological Society.

Chapter 2

The Port Wine Shippers

The history of the Port Wine Shippers is the start of the story. John Fleurriet Delaforce 1805-1881 and his younger brother George Frederick Delaforce, originally living in Southwark, decided about 1830 to enter the wine business. They were both sons of John Delaforce born in 1781 in London. So John went in 1834 to Oporto, in the north of Portugal to join, and later to manage Martinez, Gassiot Port Wine shippers (Gassiots being well-known Huguenots). George Frederick stayed in London, and his marriage certificate to his second wife showed him to be a Wine Merchant. Presumably John produced the port wines and George Frederick sold them, from 30 Savile Row, London, as England was the major market at that time. John died in 1881 and George Frederick in 1885. George Henry 1844-1912 was John's second son and in 1868, aged 24, founded the family firm. Before the end of the century three Gold Medals were gained at successive Paris Exhibitions, besides a Royal Warrant to H.M. King Carlos of Portugal and the King of Sweden. In 1903 George Henry's two sons Henry and Reginald were admitted as partners, initially Henry in charge of production in Oporto and Reginald in London. After 10 years the partners changed roles. After Reginald died in 1925 his shares in the business were exchanged for shares in the Eucalyptus Mills Ltd., and at the same time Reginald's two sons George (Wog) and Martin (Bunting) also left the business. George (Wog) then had a distinguished career in the English wine trade, becoming a Director of John Harvey. Henry's two sons became partners, Victor in 1926 and John in 1935. Frank Heath joined the firm in 1916 and became Manager in 1925.

John Delaforce,
founder of the Port Wine shipping family

During and after the First War business increased dramatically and thousands of pipes (534 litres each) of port were shipped to England each year. Sales were mainly to the 'pub' trade, and the label Delaforces' Fine Old Invalid Port became well known until beaurocracy decreed many years later that the label might be misunderstood!

Sales developed steadily and markets were opened in Canada (Royal Palace Port), Ireland, South and Central America and Scandinavia to the State Monopolies.

Portuguese table wines were shipped to Brazil. Portuguese Brandy was developed and now has an excellent market in Portugal itself. During the years of Portuguese African colonies, sweet and dry Vermouths and a Quinine & Port blend called Quinado all had successes.

In 1931 the Delaforces purchased a lovely wine Quinta on the River Douro about 50 miles East of Oporto. The Quinta da Foz de Temilobos is halfway between Regoa and Pinhao, the two leading small towns in the Port wine growing area. Besides growing vines on the terraces, olives and oranges are grown on the estate run by the 'caseiro'.

The Delaforce wine lodges have always been sited in Villanova de Gaia, on the south side of the river Douro, where thousands of pipes of port are being matured either in casks or vats. Until 1955 the emphasis was on exporting in oak casks which were returnable for the efficient cooperage to repair and renew. The bottling department has grown in importance each year and now well over 90% of all production is exported in a beautiful original bottle designed by Victor Delaforce after World War II, which has the Portuguese Royal coat of arms embossed on it.

During the Second World War Victor and his son Patrick were in the British Army and John in the SOE Intelligence Corps. All the European markets were, of course, closed for five years and Henry in London and Frank Heath in Oporto kept the business alive, with occasional 'bonanza' large orders from the NAAFI or US Army procurement.

After the second war Patrick Delaforce and Trevor Heath (Frank's son) joined the firm. The old markets slowly re-opened again, including many European markets. John Delaforce appoin-

Three generations of Port Wine Shippers, Henry (centre), sons Victor and John, grandsons Patrick and David.

ted excellent distributors in W. Germany and Delaforce port wines have a substantial business there.

Romantic labels such as Trocadero and Casino were replaced. Now the business is dominated by Paramount at the lower price range and His Eminence's Choice at the top quality level for an old Tawnny Port. Every few years a Vintage Port (a single selected unblended port) is 'declared' and shipped in small quantities to selected markets. The standard range consist of ruby, tawny and white port wines.

Late each autumn the new wine is vintaged. The grapes are picked by hand, loaded into straw baskets and taken laboriously to 'lagares' or tanks for pressing. Now usually pressed mechanically, originally the grapes were trampled by foot, which was picturesque for the onlookers, but cold and tiring for the tramplers, who needed and enjoyed brandy to keep their spirits up. Flat bottomed boats used to take the wine down the river to Oporto, but the mundane railway has now taken over. Special ships were developed.to take Port to England, again with flat bottoms to cross the dangerous 'bar' at the mouth of the river Douro. Now huge road tankers and trucks take the exports on their way to any one of a hundred markets.

Victor and John retired as Partners in the 1970s and the business was bought initially by International Distillers and Vintners, who became part of Watneys, who in turn were taken over by Grand Metropolitan. However the business is still managed personally by John's two sons David and Richard, who both live and work in Oporto. Over six million bottles of Delaforce Port are sold each year to all the European markets, Australia and USA.

The Delaforces are members, of course, of the famous old Factory House or British Association — the British port wine shippers private club. John Delaforce has recently written a book about the Factory House, which has had a long and romantic history and another book about the history of St James Anglican Church in Oporto.

The family tree of the Delaforce family in Oporto is shown amongst the charts at the end of this book.

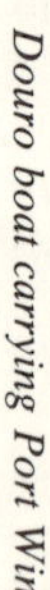

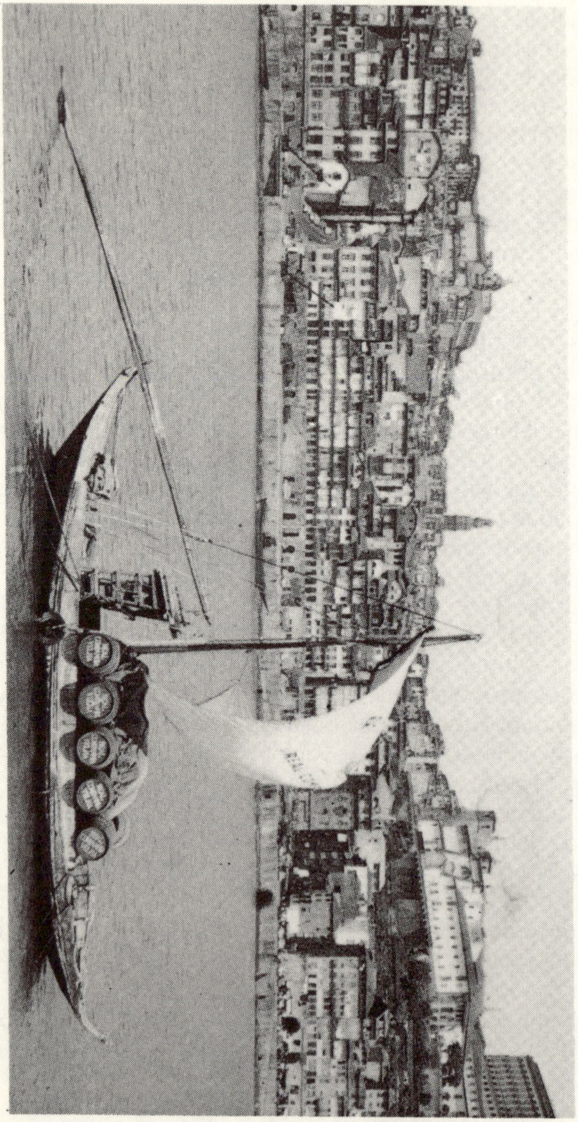

Douro boat carrying Port Wine

Chapter 3

The Fishmongers of London — the Delforce family

The Delforce family started their fishmongering business in Billingsgate, London in 1820. It was founded by John Delaforce born in 1780 who married Jane Starmer in 1802 and then Mary Morris (a widow) in 1807. John William Delforce was born about 1807 and married Mary Maria Doughty in 1835. The three main partners in the middle and late 19th century were John William's sons — George, Charles and Henry.

There are two possible reasons for the change of name from Delaforce to Delforce. One was that here might have been a clash of interests with the Port Wine business and the London wine merchants run by George Frederick. The other (and more likely) reason is or was a good old-fashioned Victorian family row! The John Delaforce born in 1780 was a son of the second marriage of John's (the Card, see chapter 7) second marriage to Sarah Wilmor when she was very young and he was distinctly middle-aged. Possibly a scenario for a family row.

With the arrival of a good railway system the fish business prospered. A main warehouse was set up at No.23 Looe Lane (later renamed Lovat Lane) in Eastcheap. Soon market stalls, stands and retail shops were set up in Stamford Hill, Enfield and Surbiton (south of the river). By the turn of the century between 80 to 100 people were employed and the business was then mainly wholesale — buying fish in bulk and supplying retail fishmongers daily on a 'country order' basis by rail to Kent, Surrey, Sussex, Hants, Wilts, Dorset, Somerset and Gloucestershire — even the Channel Islands by railway-steamers.

It was, and is, hard work. Certainly at the deep sea end and

John Delforce,
founder of the London Fishmonger family

certainly at the distribution points. It meant getting fresh fish to London by four o'clock in the morning for repacking and reshipment by rail to reach the retailers by 8-9 a.m. perhaps a 100 or more miles away.

Hundreds of retail shops bought fish daily from Delforce Brothers. Retail fishmongers with open stone or marble counters with straw hats and blue aprons served fresh fish throughout London, the Southern and Western regions. Cod, mackerel, hake, herring, whitebait, kippers, large quantities of salmon, and trout from Lord Lovat's estates.

George's son was called George Blake who married Constance Baily in 1912. Their only son is Colonel Cedric Delforce now Administrator to Lord Devon at Powderham Castle. Charles married twice, to Fanny, and later, on her death, to her sister Adelaide. The family bought shares in various fishing trawlers. They had agents and buyers in Oban, Fleetwood, Milford Haven, Newlyn, Brixham, Ramsgate, Hull, Filey, Scarborough, North & South Shields, Dundee, Aberdeen, Lossiemouth & Wick — practically every fishing port in the United Kingdom. Fish came into the country from Esbjerg and Ijmuiden.

Delforce brothers prospered for about 100 years. But a chain of related problems arrived. Modern deep freezing techniques were ignored. Alternative methods of transportation by truck and lorry were not tried out. Tastes were changing and cooking habits too.

In 1939 the Emergency Defence Regulations closed the firm down and George Blake Delforce became a Government fish distribution unit based at Watford. After the last world war two new developments helped to kill the business. The frozen prepacked fish (finger) business developed for or by the grocery and supermarket chains eliminated the retail fishonger. The final straw was the new Billingsgate market which opened only at 6 a.m. (not 4 a.m. as formerly) and the early express railway delivery services were cancelled — all in the magic name of progress.

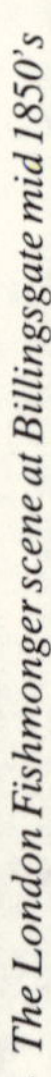

The London Fishmonger scene at Billingsgate mid 1850's

Chapter 4

"People will not look forward to posterity,
who never look backward to their ancestors"
Edmond Burke 1729-1797.

The main objective was to establish if there had been other Delaforces living in England in the 19th and 20th centuries. If there were, how might they have been related to the Port Wine shipper family in Portugal.

Quite frequently in the quality press and magazines there appear sensible articles on basic genealogy and family history fact finding. In the last few years well over a hundred local family history societies have sprung up all over the UK with ever increasing membership. The author is a member of five of them. Their quarterly magazines are source of great interest and extra knowledge.

The genealogical experts quite rightly state that initally all sources within the family should be probed, considered documented and analysed. The family bible, wills, school reports, deeds, marriage and birth certificates, old photograph albums, old letters and above all 'interviews' with the oldest members of the family. The end of this chapter shows a checklist of some of the possible sources of information.

In the case of the Delaforces living in Portugal there was a little evidence available of the English scene. Nevertheless the basic research had almost to be started from scratch.

These were the clues available:

(1) John Fleurriet Delaforce who was born 8th September 1807 in Tooley Street, Southwark had married Phoebe Wheatall, daughter of Benjamin & Elizabeth Wheatall of Baddeley House, Blackheath on 26 August 1842 at St. Saviours Church, Southwark. John was known to be a son of John Delaforce born in 1781 in London.

(2) Edwin Francis Delaforce, son of George Henry (1844-1912) born in Oporto in 1870 spent most of his life in the British Army, married twice in 1895 and 1917 in England and retired after a distinguished service record as Brigadier-general in 1920. He had two sons, Charles Newland Nesbitt and Michael (who died at school in 1932) and a daughter Beryl Blanche Selous.

(3) Albert Lionel, son of George Henry, born in Oporto in 1872, lived most of his life in England, married Margaret Amy Lyndon in 1936. They had no issue.

(4) Reginald Stanley, son of George Henry, born in Oporto 1874, lived most of his life in England. His two sons George Reginald and Martin Woodville, born respectively 1900 and 1907 spent much of their lives in England and married there in 1929 and 1943.

The Public records offices in London are the first prime target for any family historian. An excellent purchase is "Record Offices: how to find them" by Jeremy Gibson and Pamela Peskelt. There are 41 pages of Do's and Dont's, 70 maps of record offices and archive departments which show details of location and transportation. (See also chapter 1 for further details of PROs in the UK).

The key PROs are in the Aldwych, London WC2. They house all United Kingdom birth and marriage records at St.Catherines House, 10 Kingsway (Tel. 01-242 0262, open 8.30am to 4.30pm five days a week). Across the road at Alexandra House is the register room for deaths in the UK.

English Civil Registration started in July 1837. It is essential to consult these records in the Aldwych. A free leaflet PSR 12 gives useful notes and advice. Entrance is free. The space is however limited. For many years there are four quarterly books of Indexes per year, arranged alphabetically. The Indexes give limited information. From them a copy of the original certificate can be ordered and purchased. The code numbering of the parish districts is vital. The births index give the surname in the first column, the given christian names in the second, the town in the third and the reference number in the fourth column. The marriage certificates give an indication of the ages of the bridegroom and bride and the names of their fathers, as well as addresses. The death certificates are less helpful, but the age of the person and witnesses are important. The address where he dies is helpful. It is more economical to order, pay for and collect the copy of the original certificate on the spot rather than by post, although the cost of transport to Aldwych must be taken into account.

For the initial study of the Delaforce family over 1700 volumes had to be consulted. This is an excellent job for a conscientious, well built teenage son or daughter! It is essential for Nil returns to be included in their report. All possible name variations should be included (Delforce, Dellforce, Dalforce, Dulforce etc.).

The results of several days labour were astonishing and exciting. For the period of nearly 150 years, no less than 130 births were recorded, 192 deaths and 138 marriages. Approximately half of the marriages were girls. The average of two births per family was to be expected. But the number of deaths implied that 19th century families were quite numerous.

The vast majority of all references were in the London area. (The Indexes of course cover all of the UK.)

A card file index was purchased to log the nearly 500 pieces of new information. A card for each married couple starts with the marriage date, place and church. Names of witnesses should be noted. A date of birth can be estimated by taking 20 years from the brideroom or bride's age, marked ± to show it is an estimate. later on additional information about their children, addresses, occupations etc. can be added on the back of the card. Certain information can be marked in ink and conjecture marked in pencil.

Cross references can be made backwards by the date of death. A John Delaforce who died in May 1844, a mariner, aged 81 was thus born in 1763. He might have been married when he was about 20 in 1783. If he was the eldest son, then his father too might have been called John and born about 1743. Conjecture and thus marked in pencil. His death certificate showed he died in the district of St Mary Newington, Surrey in the New Kent Road. No relatives were present at his death.

Since the Indexes at the General Register Office (GRO) at St. Catherine's House show basic data only, there comes a time when either a specific certificate is purchased (approximately £5-£8) or further detective work is needed. With a total of nearly 500 certificates involved the answer is obvious. A few key certificates were purchased to unlock certain parentages.

The detective work also involves writing or telephoning the few 'modern' relatives whose names appear in the GPO telephone books. This was of course done with limited results.

The check list was again consulted and two promising avenues of work selected.

Wills All UK wills proved after January 1858 can be consulted at Somerset House, Principal Registry of the Family Division, in the Strand, London WC2. Postal applications for copies, provided the date of death is known, can be obtained for a small fee, from the Record Keeper, Correspondence Dept. Examination of the summary of the Wills is however free. The author's teenage daughter was briefed and set to work and summaries of 35 wills emerged. This was a great help because the legatees were mentioned and usually their relationships explained. (See chapter 23).

Census Another Public Record Office in Portugal Street (Land Registry Office, London WC2A) holds all the UK Census records. The main census years were 1841 (limited)), 1851, 1861 and 1871 and 1881. Details from the 1891 and 1901 censuses can be supplied for a fee to direct descendants on application to the General Register Office.

The census results are on microfilm which is tiring to read. It is essential therefore to know the topographical details of the family before the search commences. The returns list all the occupants of each household, giving names, ages, occupations and relationships to the head of the household and place of birth.

Many local libraries and record offices have acquired local census returns. There are as yet very few Indexes. J.W.S. Gibson's book "Census returns on microfilm, a directory to local holdings" Culliver Press 1979 is therefore a great help for researchers. Also "Census Indexes and Indexing" by J.W.S. Gibson & C. Chapman, published by the Federation of Family History Societies.

The 1841 census showed a substantial Delaforce family living in Bethnal Green, London. The father, Augustus Edward was a silk weaver — a significant clue for further research. He was born in 1785 and married Mary Ann Vandome in 1815. His sons Augustus Edward, Augustus N, George Frederick, Charles, Edward James and Henry all produced families who continued throughout the 19th and to some extent the 20th century, living in London. Their daughters were named Mary, Ann, Mary Jane, Jane Sarah and Harriet Jane. The eldest son, Augustus Edward who married Catherine Franey in 1837 was shown separately with his young family — Augustus (of course), Edward James, George, Henry and Eliza.

There were four other families shown in the 1841 census. Charles Delaforce aged 15 was a milk delivery lad, lived in Pooles Place, Spitalfields (weaver country). William, Ellen his wife, both in their 40s, lived with their daughter Hanna and son William aged 3, in George St., Bethnal Green. George Delafors aged 41 lived at 9 Rose Lane, Bethnal Green, and made 'quality fittings', and John Delaforce, 72, a labourer, lived with Jane his wife aged 46, at 126 Prince Street, Mile End New Town. Altogether 6 weaver-connected families were found living in the Bethnal Green/Spitalfields/Mile End New Town area in the 1841 census (without knowing beforehand where precisely their homes were.)

Huguenot Society of London

With a French name and a Church of England religious denomination it was a probability that some Delaforces were originally immigrant religious refugees from France during the religious wars of 1550-1685 when the Revocation of the Edict of Nantes produced a last final flood of refugees.

Membership of the Society is open to everyone who has reasonable belief that their ancestors were Huguenots. Their published records over the years are invaluable to researchers. Although most of their volumes cover the period 1550-1750 one volume (L11 and L111) covers the long history of the French Protestant Hospital up until the 20th century and thirteen extracts are shown now. Most related to silk weavers. Despite the various names of Force, Delfosse, most of them were relatives.

Several members of the Delaforce family in London were admitted to this famous hospital, provided they were Huguenots or of proved Huguenot extraction. Their records are well documented, and give a considerable amount of information. (Item 13 refers to the French charity school).

(1) Augustus Edward Delaforce entered in December 1893, died 1900, buried in Ilford Cemetery by his sister and son. He lived at 112 Wynford Road, near St. Silas, Islington, son of Augustus Edward Delaforce and Mary Ann (née Vendome) who lived at Old Ford Road, Bethnal Green. He was born in 1816 at Parsons Green, Shoreditch, his parents being married on 16th September 1815 at St. Leonards, Shoreditch. Augustus Edward, the son, married Catherine Franey in December 1837. At that time he lived at Sidney Street, Shadwell and both father and son were silk weavers. He left sons Edward and George and a daughter Kattie/Katherine who married a Mr John Long.

(2) Agnes Dinah Delaforce entered 1916, left 1919 'to live with a friend'. Born 1852 at Hoxton, she lived at 119 Wick Road, Homerton, London N.E., parish of St. Lukes, was the daughter of Charles and Lavinia Delaforce, 17 Chisnall Road, Bow, East London. Charles was the son of Augustus Delaforce, brother of Augustus Edward, so Agnes had a father *and* uncle called Augustus.

(3) George William Delaforce entered 1915, died 1924, buried Illford Cemetery by his son. He had lived at 4 Norton Street, Green Street, Bethnal Green, son of George Frederick Delaforce and Harriet (née Wells). He was born in June 1848 at 32 Cambridge Road, Bethnal Green. He was nephew to Augustus Edward (see 1.). He worked as a bricklayer and house decorator and received 4 shillings per week from the Hearts of Oak Benefit Society. His father George Frederick was born February 1818, son of Augustus Edward and Mary Ann. George William married Elizabeth Pellexfen, South Hackney parish church June 1868. Elizabeth died in 1901 aged 64 and was buried in Bow Cemetery. They left a son Harry Delaforce of 26 Alfred Street, Islington.

(4) James Delaforce entered in July 1899 but died in September. He was given 10 shillings per month from the Poor box.

(5) Jacques Delaforce entered October 17790, died September 1792. A slight mystery here — the entry says "Jean Delaforce (des Petittes maisons) est decedée. 'when entered Jacques'.". "Jaques Delaforce, natif de Londres, petit fils (grandson) d'Etienne (Stephen) Delaforce de la Picardie. Le suppliant agé de 63 ans (born 1727) à la vue si foible (poor sight) qu'il se trouve incapable de gagner sa vie. La cas certifié par L. Mercier, Pastor."

(6) Judith Delaforce entered 1820, left 1821. She was born in 1755, née Le Bouleux, worked as a silk weaver. Both parents were Protestant refugees. Married about 1775.

(7) Mary Delaforce entered 1855, died 1868. She was widow of Augustus Edward, and born in 1785 (née Vendome). Augustus died in 1847 aged 62. Mary was a weaveress and lived at 29 John Street, Green Street, Bethnal Green.

(8) Thomas William Delaforce entered in 1897, died 1914, buried in Ilford Cemetery. He lived at 144 Chatham Avenue, Hoxton near Shoreditch, son of Thomas and Rebecca (née White) of Slater Street, Bethnal Green. He was born in June 1830 at 3 Turville Street, Boundry Street, Bethnal Green. He worked as a carver and wood carver. Thomas Delaforce, a silkweaver, married Rebecca White at Christ Church, Middlesex, December 1809. Thomas William was apprenticed aged 15 in December 1849. He was baptised in June 1830 at St. Leonards, Shoreditch and lived originally with his parents at Old Cock Lane.

(9) Augustus Force died March 1894, son of Pierre Michel Force and Catherine Bandon. His grandfather Francois left France early in the last century in partnership with M. de l'Arbre in the silk trade. He then went to Canada!

(10) Jean Delfosse died in 1781, natif d'Amiens en Picardie, age 70, petit fils of Etienne, suffered from asthma — lived with M. Hude, weaver of Pelham Street, Spitalfields.

(11) Judit Delfosse died 22nd April 1762, native d'Amiens, age 84.

(12) Charles Du Fosse, cabinet maker, died March 1898, aged 43, ill for 2 years. £1 from Poor box.

(13) Emily Blanche and Lavinia Rebecca (who married Albert Botley) were born in 1895 and 1890 respectively. They went to the Ecole de Charite Francaise, Westminster, and they were daughters of Charles Delaforce and Emily Ann (Holt).

* * * *

At the end of many days spent cross referencing the births, marriages and deaths for the period 1837-1982 including the Census data, Somerset House Wills and the Huguenot Hospital School data, a clear picture emerged.

(A) There was and is a 'George Frederick' family — complicated since George Frederick born in 1811 married three times: to Aurelia Mary Cooper in 1837; later when she died, he remarried to her sister Mary Ann Cooper, and then when she died, remarried again in 1861 to Emma Batteley. He was shown on his marriage certificates to be a Wine Merchant and son of the John Delaforce (born in 1781) and thus his family are linked to the Port Wine Shippers in Portugal.

This family produced three more generations of George Fredericks, all connected with the railways. A corporal of a military train (1862); accountant railway clearing house: railway clerk. They also helped found the Canadian family (see chapter 22).

(B) There was and is a 'Delforce' family. From 1820 they were Billingsgate wholesale fish merchants until the middle 1950s. The present Australian family of Delforces descended from John William Delforce born in 1807 and son of John Delaforce. (see chapter 3).

(C) There were and are Delaforce families descended from the Silk Weavers (see chapter 10) mainly based on Bethnal Green, London. Augustus Edward 1785-1847, the patriarch, with his ten children has direct family ancestors alive today living in London.

(D) William and Mary Ann from 1797 who were Calenderers and Clothpressers in Shoreditch have also produced a long line of Williams and Josephs still living in London.

To sum up the position at this stage. For the cost of approximately a dozen certificates of marriages and births (£60), payments to a teenage daughter for research at the Aldwych and Somerset House (£30), subscription to the Huguenot Society (£7.50) an immense amount of information had been gathered for the period 1837-1982 spanning six generations. The family trees are shown in the Appendix at the end.

* * * *

A basic check list of genealogical sources

1. Family records and papers

Family Bible, family pedigree, notes, memoranda, diaries. Photograph albums, birthday books, family portraits, wedding photographs. Account books, purchase/sale of shares, annuities, bank books. Property deeds, rent books, life assurance policies. Marriage/divorce contracts and certificates, baptism and death certificates. School and university records, reports, certificates. Passport, driving licence, wartime identity cards. Work testimonials, references, apprentice indentures. Athletic or sporting records, programmes. Trade union cards, club or professional membership records. Armed service records, decorations, discharge papers. Medical records, certificates. Family solicitor's correspondence.

2. Public Records (see PRO leaflet No.1, 37 and PSR 12),

Public Record Offices — General Register Offices — County Record Offices. Parish Records — see PRO leaflet No.1. Census Records — see PRO leaflet No.2. Wills at Somerset House, London — see PRO leaflet 4 and 34. Genealogical guides from local library. Reference books, trade directories, telephone directories. Local and national directories.

3. Other Major Records

Mormon Computer File Index. Society of Genealogists "Using the library of the Society". British (Museum) library, leaflet No.10 "British Family History". Guildhall library "A guide to Genealogical Sources in...". Local Family History Society (see Federation of LFHS leaflet). Guild of One-name Studies.

Chapter 5

"How many saucy airs we meet
from Temple Bar to Aldgate Street"
John Gay 1685-1732.

18th Century English Families

This chapter covers the period 1700-1840. From 1840 the Public Records Offices, with their efficient index system, make life relatively easy for the family researcher. Before 1840 is altogether another matter. One needs, like a good detective, to consult very many totally different sources and then piece all the fragments together. Luck of course is necessary too!

The clues to be followed were (1) John Delaforce born somewhere in London in 1781 and (2) the significance of the Silk Weavers (which is covered in chapter 10).

The Mormon Church of Jesus Christ Latter-Day Saints of Salt Lake City, Utah have produced a marvellous source of information for family historians. Over the last two decades they have spent large sums of money in many European countries (whose emigrants sailed over the centuries to America in search of safety and work). Their research into baptismal and marriage records are mainly for the period 1600-1840. Their coverage varies enormously from country to country, and from county to county. The Mormons encourage people to trace their ancestors so that they can be posthumously baptised into the faith. Their records now on microfiche, are known as the CFI or International Genealogical Index and covers worldwide 68 million names (see chapter 1 for UK sources). There are 6 Mormon Genealogical libraries in the

UK. In addition such libraries as the Guildhall in the City of London and the Society of Genealogists (members only) have total coverage of the UK. Certain enterprising Family History Societies have also made local arrangements for viewing with local libraries. This is one of the most important sources for all family history researchers.

Consultation of the CFI Index produced 230 names of baptisms and about 25 marriages for the ever increasing permutation of names — Delforce, Dellforce, Dalforce, Dulforce, Delafosse, Delfosse being also recorded because of the likelihood of these names being related. In the 17th century a family of seven Delaforces had seven different spellings to contend with! All the references were in the London area. Searches in other counties were fruitless. Many earlier names in the 17th century were French, Jean, Jacques, Etienne (Stephen), Antoine, Marie etc. The location of the churches was interesting. They were mainly grouped together in the East End of London and the City. The two exceptions were St. Martins in the Fields and St. Saviours, Southwark, south of the river Thames.

The Index produced several entries for John Delaforce — a baptism of 7 March 1778, another of 9 December 1781, both at St. Saviours, Southwark. In neither case were the names of the parents mentioned (this is most unusual on the CFI Index). Norman Graham's excellent booklets on the whereabouts of all London parish registers showed the Southwark registers to be available at the Greater London Record Office, then at County Hall on the South Bank, now moved to Clerkenwell. The microfilm registers of the original parish records showed that both Johns were the sons of Samuel, a cabinet-maker and Elizabeth Fleurriet. The first son evidently died young before 1781. The second was undoubtedly the original John of the Port Wine family. The name Fleurriet has been used by many generations (including the author, his father and uncle) as a given 'middle' name. Now the mystery of the derivation of this unusual name had been cleared up. (Subsequently it was discovered that Elizabeth's father, John was a silk weaver and was a witness at Samuel's grandfather's death in 1779).

It was then easy to track down (1) Samuel's marriage date in

Last Will & Testament of John Delaforce, alias Delafors 1702-1779
Courtesy of the Public Record Office, London S PROB 11/1057 1C/411

This is the Last Will and Testament
of me John Delaforce of the Parish of Saint Botolph
Bishopsgate in the County of Middlesex Pawnbroker
made this thirty first day of August in the year of our
Lord one thousand seven hundred and seventy nine.
I give to my Grandson Samuel Delaforce his Executors
Administrators and Assigns all my Estate and Effects
whatsoever upon Trust to sell and convert the same
into Money and to lay out the same in Government
Funds at Interest and by and out of such Interest
to pay the Sum of five Shillings per week to Mary
Delaforce my Wife for her Life and the Residue I
give as follows to my Son John Delaforce the
Sum of five Pounds and to my Son William
Delaforce the Sum of twenty Pounds and to my
Sister Susan Delaforce the Sum of five Pounds
and to Ann Hire the Sum of five Pounds and to
Mary Coffee the Sum of ten Pounds and as to the
whole of my Effects so given to my said Grandson and
the Money arising therefrom upon Trust after
payment of the said Annuity or Sum of five Shillings
per week to my said Wife and payment of the
aforesaid Legacys the Residue I give to my aforesaid
Sons John and William Delaforce equal [illegible]
share alike. Likewise at the Death of my said Wife
equally [illegible] share alike And I do appoint the
aforesaid Samuel Delaforce and James Delaforce
Goldwriter Executors of this my Will In Witness
whereof I have hereunto set my hand and Seal the
day and year abovewritten Likewise I give unto the
aforesaid Samuel Delaforce and James Delaforce
the Sum of ten Pounds each and to Thomas Delaforce
and Daniel Delaforce and Mary Walker the Sum of
five Pounds each — John Delafors — L.S. — Signed Sealed
published and declared by the said John Delaforce as
and for his last Will and Testament in the presence of
us who in his presence and at his request and in the
presence of each other have subscribed our names as
Witnesses, Witness John Fleurriet, James Harrison.

This Will was proved at London the fifth day of October in the year of our Lord one thousand seven hundred and seventy nine before the Worshipful Thomas Bever Doctor of Laws Surrogate of the Right Worshipful Peter Calvert Doctor of Laws Master Keeper or Commissary of the Prerogative Court of Canterbury lawfully constituted by the Oaths of Samuel Delaforce and James Delaforce the Executors named in the said Will to whom Administration of all and singular the Goods Chattels and Credits of the deceased was granted having been first sworn duly to administer.

Ex.

On the twenty second day of November in the year of our Lord one thousand seven hundred and seventy nine the Will of John Delaforce otherwise Delafors late of the parish of Saint Botolph Bishopsgate London deceased was proved by the Oaths of Samuel Delaforce and James Delaforce the Executors named in the said Will to whom Administration of all and singular the Goods Chattels and Credits of the said deceased was granted they having been first sworn duly to administer a Probate of the said Will of the said deceased granted in the last month to the said Executors by the Names of John Delaforce only having been first voluntarily brought in and declared null and void.

Ex.

1770 and baptism by his parents John & Elizabeth on 24 April 1749 at St. Leonard's Church, Shoreditch. The excellent (2) John Harvard library in Southwark has a special section dedicated to Southwark's history. They produced evidence that Samuel was a man of property, died wealthy and endowed a Delaforce Charitable Foundation in Southwark based originally on the church of St. George's. (3) As a cabinet-maker he was found to be a member of the Carpenters Guild (records at the Guildhall library) and made Free in 1770 when he was probably aged 21. His father who sponsored him was shown to be John Delaforce, Musicianer of St. Botolphs, Bishopsgate. (4) His will of 1805 was tracked down at the PRO Chancery Lane and showed him to be a Stockbroker when he died. (5) The Corporation of London Records Office in the Guildhall building maintains early records of stockbrokers, showing Samuel's partnership and dates. (6) later on his grandfather's will of 1779 showed Samuel to be the favourite grandchild and inherited money and a pawnbroking business. (7) The St. Savours parish register also recorded the birth to Samuel and Elizabeth of an older son called Samuel born in 1770/1 who in turn became a cabinet-maker and pawnbroker.

To summarise the sources used — CFI Index; parish registers; local (archive) library; two Wills; a Guild reference; the association of Stockbrokers (they were not a Guild).

Samuel's father John the Musicianer was initially traced through his membership of the Musicians Guild kept at the Guildhall library. He was a fascinating man (the Card) and his short biography (and that of Daniel his great uncle and Samuel his son) have been in included in chapter 7.

The Card's father, John, died in 1779 and left a will which is a family historians dream and left a plethora of splendid clues!

(1) His will gives two alternative spellings of his name "John Delaforce alias De La Fors".

(2) It mentions his trade — that of pawnbroker.

(3) It mentions where he lived — the parish of St. Botolphs, Bishopsgate.

(4) It mentions his wife's name — Mary who gets five shillings per week for life.

(5) It mentions his sister Susan who gets a legacy and was thus alive

in 1779.
(6) It mentions his elder son John (legacy of £5) and younger son William (legacy of £20).
(7) It mentions many grandchildren (legacies of £5 each); his favourite Samuel was left the business and money to run it. Others named were James (co-executor with Samuel), Thomas, Daniel, Mary (Walker), Mary (Coffee) William's wife and Ann (Quanion). His will was witnessed by John Fleurriet, Samuel's father-in-law.

It does show how valueable wills can be for the researcher! (See chapter 1 on sources). With these various clues it was again possible to track down John's father (1702-1779). It was not easy because by a quirk of fate there were four silk weaver John Delaforces alive in the period 1700-1725 and living within the proverbial square mile of the City (see chapter 10 — silk weavers).

Other clues were **(8)** his son John was also a tailor, a dealer in coals, a soldier, a pawnbroker as well as being a Musicianer! **(9)** William the younger son, who married Anne Bowers in 1750 at St. Peters Le Poer church was a jeweller working in Broad Street in the City. Although there were pawnbroker societies in London there do not seem to be the equivalent of Guild records. The Goldsmiths Guild mention John Delaforce the Card. It looked as though there was a money-making-lending strain in the family which in the event proved correct in the next search.

The next table covers the sources used to discover John's father's name, marriage, trade etc. To clarify the various Johns they have been coded as follows: The Card 1728-1788 is shown as John (4). His father as John (3) 1702-1779. His grandfather and great-grandfather are discovered to be John (2) and John (1). There is a little overlap with chapter 13 as the emphasis shifts to France.
(1) March 1685 Sieur (Sir) De La Force (1) was witness at death of Mr Thomas Coxe, "Docteur en Medecine" in Guines, near Calais.
(2) In 1702 Sieur (Sir) Jean Delafous (2) jeweller of St. Martins in the Fields married Suzanne Massienne of Paris at Crispin Street French Church in Stepney. Jean was shown to derive from Chatel Heraud (modern Chattelrault).
(3) 29 November 1703 John Delafons or Delafors (3) baptised to John (2) and Susanna, St. Martins in the Fields church. A daughter Susanne was baptised in 1711 but evidently died before

1716 when a second daughter was baptised (and likely to be still alive in 1779). Other children were Peter Paul and Mary Anne who probably died Young.

(4) 16 December 1705 Daniel Deforce baptised to Daniel and Susanna at the same church of St. Martins in the Fields. The Daniels were son and grandson of Daniel De La Force (Le Beau Chevalier, chapter 7).

(5) 1712 London trade directory shows 'Lafosse a jeweller in Broad Street in the City' probably Jean (2).

(6) 1714 John Delafours (2) jeweller of St. Martin in the Fields was Master to Robert Charles Guillet, gentleman for the fee of £16 (a large sum in those days). It seems that John (2) lived and worshipped at St. Martins in the Lane but practised his trade of jeweller in Broad Street.

(7) 22 October 1726 John Delafous (3) was married to Hester Gales of Dunestable by Mr Dubourdienne. John lived at 'St. Marteins in ye Fields'. The church was St. Vedast, Foster lane.

(8) In 1730, Chancery Lane proceedings C11/2035/6 showed John de la Fous or Fons (2) Jeweller in the Parish of St. Martins in the Fields as executor for Charles Barbe, 'a French minister of the Holy Gospel' and for his wife Margaret Barbe (then Margaret Martell, a widow), concessing a 61 year leasehold messuage (property in Litchfield Street, Parish of St. Annes, Westminster. Barbe did not behave at all well, cheated Margaret out of her possessions and money and returned to France.

(9) In 1731 John Delafous (3) married again to Mary Dory in Chelsea, probably at St. Lukes. She would have been alive in 1779 to receive 5 shillings a week for the rest of her life.

(10) In 1741-49 John Delaforce (3) lived in the parish of St. Dunstans in the West.

(11) The Gentlemans Magazine records, sadly, that in Sept. 1743, John Delafors, Jeweller, of Westminster, was made bankrupt, and presumably took up pawnbroking.

(12) In 1744 and much later in 1793 William Lafosse was a jeweller at 52 Old Broad Street, City. This was likely to be John (4)s brother.

(13) In 1756 John Delaforce (4) owned the Golden Bell pawnshop in Widegate Street, Bishopsgate but lived most of his life at 39 Norton Folgate nearbye.

(14) In 1779 John (2) died aged about 78, alias De la Fors.
(15) It is possible that Samuel De La Fosse married to Dinah Beosu in 1690, was a brother of Sieur Jean (1). Samuel was an Orloguer of Faubourg St. Antoine, Paris (a clock-maker) who lived at Riders Court, St. Annes, Westminster. He worked in Spitalfields, Stepney. Parents of Samuel, Elisabeth, Jacob, Jeanne and Anne. In 1698 a mysterious news snippet says "Three cousins named Delfosse were left money in a will": one or more was a goldsmith. Why did John (4) the Card call his first son Samuel? Perhaps after an uncle of that name.
(16) 9 April 1699 Francis de La Fosse married Susann Buoys at St. Martin in the Fields church. Perhaps the three cousins were John, Samuel & Francis.
(17) St. Martins in the Fields, Poor Laws Rate Books (Victoria Library, Buckingham Palce Rd.) reveal more movements of the grandfather, father and son John Delaforces. In 1691 'John Laforce poore' lived in Salisbury Court, was assesed at 0-10-0 but was unable to pay. A wealthy man in France in 1685 living in Guines near Calais, a few years later he was a penniless immigrant living in London. His cousin Stephen lived in Long Acre and paid 0-12-0, and his cousin Daniel lived in Hewetts Court. In 1694 John was living in Exchange Court (a suitable name for a jeweller and pawnbroker), and was joined by his father John Fossa, or Laffors, who lived in the Strand and Exchange Court. Their rates went up (inevitably). In 1707 John Delafour of Charing Cross East paid two guineas in rates. The Duke of Buckingham in the same parish paid £15-0-0 (but was totally in arrears). The Duke of Queensbury was rated at £10-0-0 (but was £7-10-0 in arrears). The Earl of Peterborough paid his £4-0-0 promptly. About 1725 John senior died and his widow Mary continued to live in Exchange Court and pay rates. The John Delaforce born in 1702 was living off St. Martin's Lane in 1722 and paid £1-0-0 a year in rates. Each year's rate books balance income from the relatively affluent who pay rates, with expenditure in the back of the book which is itemised by individual recipient and specific payment. From the family historian's point of view these books show a wealth of interesting material, from 1598 when the original Act was passed. Each parish was responsible for its own poor and the vestry elected Overseers

of the Poor. In this forty year span three generations of John Delaforce were shown arriving in the parish of St. Martins in the Fields from France.

This tableau of clues derives from the (a) Huguenot Society records (b) CFI Index (c) Wills (d) Chancery Lane proceedings at PRO in Chancery Lane (e) local London trade directories (f) Society of Genealogists Apprentice Index (g) Boyds Marriage registers (h) Parish registers, (i) the Gentlemans Magazine, (j) Poor Law Rate Books – ten different sources.

It was an exciting moment when the links with France were proved. No-one in the family had had any idea of when or whence the Huguenot connection would appear.

The 18th century produced a score of Delaforce families who were mainly silkweavers (chapter 10) and a few members of other Guilds (chapter 9) and linked by their churches (chapter 12). Towards the end of the 18th century, weavers as a trade fell on hard times for a variety of reasons. Many became despondent and then desperate. The weaver Delaforces were well-off. The Huguenot volume LV has a survey on 1739-1741 listing the Spitalfield weavers in dire straits. There were no members of the family amongst them.

Nevertheless a Stephen, father and son, were transported in 1718 to America as convicts. James followed in 1767 and Joseph in 1770. William a young convict was transported to Australia in 1834. Isaac, a fugitive from Dublin in 1776 went to Wood Street prison for 1 year.

In 1817 the respectable James Moses family emigrated to America. Two young Delforce brothers sailed for Australia early in the 19th century for brighter opportunities the other side of the world.

A few news items to end this chapter.

(a) About 1800 Jacob Delaforce kept the Flower Pot in Islington where the Linton Club of Huguenot emigrées met regularly.

(b) Charles and Elizabeth De La Force, grandchildren of Daniel the Chevalier sailed for India and at Fort St. George, Madras married respectively Elizabeth Pain in 1710 and Thomas Bellysis in 1719.

(c) Susanna Delaforce aged 47 lived in Barbadoes BWI with her 5 children in 1715.

(d) Jonathan Delaforce from 1790-1810 was a manufacturer of Straw hats at 1 Lambs Conduit Pass in London.
(e) William Delaforce was a butcher in Mile End New Town in 1788.
(f) James Delaforce kept a shop called the Portobello at 20 St. Martins Lane in 1795-1805.

Chapter 6

A short history of Pawn Broking

Borrowing money with an agreed (however high) rate of interest against a pledge or pawn has been happening for thousands of years. Thc cnd rcsult is the worldwide network of sophisticated retail bankers who operate on the same basis as the original Lombards and the later pawnbrokers. A modern banking overdraft is usually secured to the bank by something of equivalent or higher value.

Part of the Delaforce family were Lombards 'men' and goldsmiths in the 16th. century, and were jewellers, goldsmiths, pawnbrokers and commodity/stock brokers in the 18th and 19th centuries in London

In 1598 Ben Jonson's 'Every Man in his Humour' showed two men about town talking of a third. Matheo 'Lets give him some pawn.' Bobadilla 'Pawn? We have none to the value of his demand.' Matheo 'Oh Lord man, I'll pawn this jewel in my ear and you may pawn your silk stockings and pull up your boots — they will ne'er be missed!'

William Shakespear wrote 'Redeem from broking, pawn the blemished Crown.'

Later Samuel Pepys' description of Lady Peterborough in 1667. 'The woman is a very wise woman, and is very plain in telling me how her plate and jewels are at pawn for money.'

Charles Dickens' Sketches by Boz in 1836 showed in Chapter 23 page 1 a vivid description of pawnbroking in the early 19th century.

William Hogarth's picture of 1751 called Gin Lane is meant to be the first known representation of a British pawnbrokers shop.

Broking of pawn has a long history attached to that trade.

Although the main retail business started with the Lombard goldsmith-brokers in London in the 16th, century and reached its peak in the middle of the 19th century, the custom started at a very early date, at the highest level.

King Henry III about 1240 pledged a valuable 'Image of the Virgin' to obtain money to pay his officers of the Crown. About the same time Robert Grossteste, Chancellor of Oxford University founded the "Oxford Chests". The first one was called the Frideswyde chest. They were charitable loan funds secured by pledges mainly to help support university expenditure on poor students.

In the 13th century King Edward I pawned the customs dues to help pay for expenses of war. In the next century King Edward III, having no dues to pawn, deposited his crown on three seperate occasions and in 1339 pledged his own and his Queen's crown! The next year, in dire financial straits, the whole of his crown jewels followed!

King Henry V pawned his crown to the Bishop of Winchester for 100,000 marks. King Henry VI in 1430 pledged one of the crown jewels, called the Rich Collar, in three pieces, to pay the expenses for his wedding with Margaret of Anjou — and never redeemed it!

When King Richard II married Queen Anne of Bohemia, he pawned large quantities of jewels with the citizens of London. In 1485 the Earl of Richmond, before becoming King Henry VII, borrowed money from the French King, leaving two live pledges (the Marquis of Dorset and Sir Thomas Boucher). He won the crown at Bosworth Field, borrowed 6,000 marks from the patient citizens of London and then redeemed the two noblemen!

In 1564 a Law was passed to fix at ten percent the legal rate of interest and in 1603 James I passed comprehensive legislation 'An act against brokers'.

Charles I in 1638 granted the citizens of London a Charter called 'Fees to be taken by the Register for Brokers — for the Bond to be entered into by every Broaker, Brogger & Huckster to the Chamber — Eightpence.' 'For every bargain, contract & pawn for and upon which shall be lent or given one shilling or above and under five shillings — one farthing.'. The rate for transactions of 5 to 20 shillings — a fee of one halfpenny: 20-40 shillings a fee of one penny.

A London Pawnbroker mid 1850's

Charles II passed three Acts in 1673, 1674 and 1680 containing clauses against unlawful pawning by Silk Throwsters.

In the early years of the 18th century many goldsmiths gave up pawnbroking, threatened by the giant 'Charitable Corporation for Lending Money to the Industrious but Necessitous Poor.' The Corporation had a capital of £600,000 — a huge amount at that time. After 24 years it went out of business in 1731 charged with receiving stolen goods. The Corporation had 294 pawnbroker members at the time.

In 1745 a committee representing the larger and more reputable pawnbrokers introduced a Parliamentary Bill to protect themselves against "Divers persons of ill Fame & Repute who live in Garrets, Cellars and other obscure places taking upon themselves the Names of Pawnbrokers, who charged 6d in the pound per week or 130 percent interest, selling pledges within 3 months."

The greatest growth in pawnbroking occurred in the hundred year period 1750-1850. There were in 1750, 250 large London pawnbrokers and double that of smaller establishments. In 1830 there were 1537 licenced pawnbrokers in the UK, of which 380 were in London. By 1864 there were 2500 pawnbrokers in the UK. London had 375, Manchester 200, Liverpool 130 and Birmingham 100. Their capital averaged about £5,000 and they accepted and redeemed about 60,000 pledges each a year.

The Pawnbrokers Act of 1756 licenced pawnbrokers to charge 20 percent, a fifth of which was to go to support hospitals and workhouses. Another Act in 1785 compelled all pawnbrokers to register and in 1800 another Act limited charges to 20 percent up to a pawn of £2, 15 percent on two guineas to ten pounds. As important was legislation to ensure pledges could only be forfeited after a year.

The usual family pawnbroker establishment consisted of three people. One to value the pawn, one to make out a ticket, and one more to put the article away in store. In the 19th century there were trade groupings. In 1821 it was the Pawnbrokers Institution. In 1836 the Pawnbrokers Association, which in 1847 merged with the Metropolitan United Pawnbrokers Protection Society. The Manchester and Salford Association founded in 1810 was said to be the oldest in the UK, followed by the Liverpool Association. In

London the Northern Friendly Society met at Holborn, also called the Queens Head or Holborn Society. The Bouverie Society was another group. the Local Society of Pawnbrokers of Southwark met at the Half Moon Inn, Borough in 1812. The Eastern Society met at the Laurel Tree in Brick Lane in 1813.

The famous sign of three balls indicating a pawnbroker establishment to show their trade derived from the Lombard goldsmiths who came originally from the Medicis in Italy. Part of the coat of arms of the Medicis were three blue circular discs. To show the association with goldsmiths the blue discs subsequently became gold balls.

References

Mr W.A.H. Hows 'History of pawnbroking' 1847. Alfred Hardaker ' A brief history of pawnbroking' 1880. S.W. Levine 'The business of pawnbroking'. Kenneth Hudson 'Pawnbroking' 1982.

Chapter 7

"Le beau Chevalier, the Card and the Philanthropist"

Three unusual members of the family have been included in this chapter: Daniel 1644-1719 'le beau Chevalier', John 1729-1788 the Card and Samuel 1748-1805 the Philanthropist. Samuel was John's oldest son. Daniel was John's grand-uncle, i.e. his grandfather John's brother.

William Browne 1591-1643 "well languag'd Daniel"

Daniel de la Force, le beau chevalier

Daniel was born in 1644 to Jean de la Force and Judith de Boucqoi. Jean, Claude and Abraham were his brothers and Judith his sister. He was born either in Calais or in neighbouring Guisne and came

to England as a young man and became intimately connected with the Huguenot counts and nobles fighting for England against the Catholic armies of France. He was particularly linked with two eminent nobles: de Duras and de Miremont from 1662 onwards.

It is tempting to believe the comment in Huguenot Society Proceedings No.17 page 446, which states "Daniel Laforce 1686-89, another resident of St. James, is recorded as burying a child at St. James Church. He was probably a relative of Duchesse de la Force, also buried at St. James", but that was not the case.

Daniel quickly joined the French émigré army and became a captain of a Troop of Horse in Ireland. Later he was made secretary to the first Earl of Feversham who was the inefficient Commander in Chief of the British Army in the 1680s. In 1672

Feversham went to Paris with Peace Papers between Charles II and Louis XIV. The Earl was Lewis/Louis de Duras, a Huguenot Count and nephew of Marshall Turenne, who lived close to Daniel in Soho Square, In 1688 King James took the advice of his French General Feversham/de Duras and resolved to fall back on London and the Thames. Daniel was also for a time in 1687 until 3rd January 1688 a Major-General with Marquis de Miremont's regiment, when it was disbanded. De Miremont (or De Mauriac) came from the Haute Auvergne and were neighbours of the De la Forces and possibly intermarried. In 1701 De Miremont was put on trial in effect for embezzling state funds. "Appellant first brought a bill against the Marquis and his agent Monsieur de la Force as well as against Respondent, whether the troops were well supplied with equipment — received 1000L from King James to raise troop of 59 men but only obtained 36". The faithful Daniel made various Town Depositions in July 1699 and again in 1709. In 1706 the La force regiment under De Miremont had fought at the disaster of the Almanza. It is clear that the Huguenot commanders possessed courage, élan, but perhaps not skills in either administration or military tactics!

In 1694 three other members of the family were noted in the War Office records as serving officers in the Irish campaign: Pierre du Foussat was a lieutenant in the Comte de Martins' Regiment of Foot, the Sieur du Fosset (possibly Daniel's son) was lieutenant in the Marquis de Miremont's Regiment of French Dragoons, and Francis de La Force was a Captain in Colonel Robert Byer Leys' Regiment of Horse.

In 1687 Daniel was granted a Royal Warrant and Bounty for services in Ireland from Windsor Castle. On 9th September 1689 he obtained a pass to go to Holland and also visited his family in Calais. On 20th November 1712 he got another Royal Warrant from Windsor Castle to the Lord Lieutenant of Ireland "nominated a pension of 3 shillings a day to Daniel de la Force who has served long in public employment and is now reduced to low circumstances having lost a son in her majesty's service". Later on he received a pension of 45 guineas for services in Ireland.

Daniel was also a friend of Lord and Lady Arlington, Secretary of State from 1665. In 1699 The Vice Chamberlain Sir John Coke notes a list of lodgings at Somerset House in Fleet Street, St. Clemence Danes' parish.

	Rooms	**Closets**	**Garrets**
Lady Arlington	9	6	1
M. Meremont (Marquis)	4	1	1
Lord Clarendon	12	4	1
M. La Force	3	1	1
Mr and Mrs Killigrew	5	4	—

Feversham was Chamberlain to the Queen and Henry Killigrew was page of the Bedchamber. King Charles II walked frequently in Arlington Gardens and inevitably Daniel would have met the King before Charles death in 1685.

In 1680 aged 36 he married Catherine Coseri, his second wife, and son Daniel was born in June the same year. Charles D'fforce was baptised 15th December 1687, St. James Piccadilly, to Daniel and Catherine. It may have been Charles who was killed in action before 1712, as the Daniel born about 1680 (died 2nd May 1716 St. Edmunds, Lombard Street) married Susanna (names given as Delaforce, Deforce, lafosle, laforce) St. Martins in the Fields. Daniel was born in 1705, Anne 1707, Margaret 1708, Mary 1710 and another Daniel in 1712; the first presumably having died in infancy.

Daniel twice wrote to the King, Charles II, in 1677 and 17th December 1683. "Petition praying an order to the Minister at the French Court to endeavour to obtain leave for the petitioner's brother, a merchant in Calais, who desires to settle in his Majesty's dominions to transport himself and with his estate accordingly." A copy was sent to Lord Preston. State Papers Domestic CAR 11 435 No. 59.

He died in August 1719 aged 75 and left his estate to Katherine, his widow.

Nearly all of the information about Daniel comes from published State Papers and Chancelry Proceedings viewed at PRO Chancery Lane.

Charles Dickens 1812-1870
"Eccentricities of genius"

The Card — John Delaforce 1728-1788

Despite the difficulties of research some 250 years back, there seems little doubt that John Delaforce was indeed a Card — an eccentric, a man of talent, immense energy and an appetite — in all senses — for life. That is why, out of the many dozens of Delaforces whose lives have been glimpsed from libraries, books and museums, John seemms to stand out with his exuberance.

"John Delaforce, son of John Delaforce of the Parish of St. Dunstans in the West, London, by and with the licence & consent of the Governors of the Hospital of Bridewell, London, apprenticed to Thomas Roay citizen and musician 11th September 1741. Made Free 17 November 1749".

Bridewell Chapel, Hospital and Precinct Church were later united with St. Brides, Fleet Street.

John's (the father) permission was needed so that as an apprentice musician the son could start his apprenticeship at the age of 12 rather than the customary 14.

When he became an apprentice to the Musicians Guild in 1741 he gave his initial occupation as a Taylor living in Bride Lane (many tailors lived and practised at St. Brides). He also gave an alternative occupation as a Dealer in Coals. So at the age of 20 he was involved in at least three activities. The pity is that there is no knowledge of his skill as a musician, no record of the instruments he played. An alternative address is given as Bordes Lane (although this might be a misprint of Brides lane). In fact he lived most of his life at No.39 Norton Folgate, the continuation of Bishopsgate Street, heading north.

About 1749 he married Elizabeth. their children were Samuel born in 1749, Daniel 14th October 1750, Joseph 30th May 1752, Benjamin 1754, Mary 1st February 1756, Jeremiah 5th February 1758 and Sarah Jane 12th July 1761.

John married again to Mary Willby 18 August 1765 at Saint Leonards Church, Shoreditch.

John also must have helped his father John with the pawnbroking business, Golden Ball at Widegate Street, Bishopsgate, but the indications are that John (and William his brother) were thought to be very capable of supporting themselves (as shown in the father's will).

From 1759 to 1782 John was a lieutenant, then captain in the Honourable Artillery Company in Finsbury. He probably joined them before 1759 when he was 30. He was also an Ensign in the Orange Trained Bands, organised as the militia to defend London from mobs and attackers.

From 1770-1776 he was a Liveried Member of the Musicians Guild. His first wife Elizabeth must have died (possibly in childbirth) in the late 1760s. Several children died young — Benjamin age 2, Jeremiah age 2, Sarah Jane age 6. John's father died in late 1779 and left him £5! It may be that John was so prosperous with all his various activities — musician, tailor, coal dealer, pawnbroker and stockbroker — that his father felt he had no need of any more money He left £20 to his son William, modest legacies to his grandchildren, but the bulk of his estate, including the pawnbroking business, to his favourite grandson Samuel, John's eldest son.

On 28th May 1780 he married yet again, to Sarah Willmott, a minor — given away by her father Sam — and their son John was baptised at St. Botolphs, Bishopsgate, but Joshua, 13th June 1784 and Isaac, 1st July 1787, were baptised at St. Leonards, Shoreditch, and finally William, 12th October 1789, at St. Botolphs without Aldgate.

On the 13th June 1782, in the reign of King George the Third, John became a City of London Stockbroker, in partnership with Joseph Bond, citizen and blacksmith, each with a £500 bond.

On the 18th December 1788 John died, leaving in his will everything to his wife Sarah. His addresses at this time were Peters Court, Cartwright Square and also Darby Street, Rosemary Lane.

It is interesting that John Delaforce 1781-1855, Samuel's younger son, was a Taylor of Mile End, as shown in Samuel's will of 1805. John had followed his grandfather's first declared trade of tailoring.

John and Sarah's first son John, born 1780, was the founder of the Delforce family who in 1820 became Billingsgate wholesale fish merchants. It is possible there was ill-feeling in the family about John's third marriage to Sarah, which may have prompted a later generation to change their name to Delforce.

The information about John came from various Guilds, including brokers, from the Honourable Artillery Company, from Parish Registers, the Chamberlain's Court, and the IGI Index.

Psalms "That most excellent gift of charity"

Samuel Delaforce — the Philanthropist

The Delaforce Educational Foundation — Southwark

Samuel Delaforce 1749-1805 was the eldest son of John the Musicaner of St. Botolphs, Bishopsgate (and Elizabeth Delaforce,). His Guild and that of his son Samuel, was the Carpenters, of which he was made Free on 4th September 1770 and he became a skilled cabinet maker. In 1770 he married Elizabeth Fleurriet from a well-known Weaver family, at St Saviours, Southwark. Like his father John, Samuel had several commercial interests: pawnbroking, mainly in connection with his grandfather's Golden Ball in Bishopsgate; stockbroking; and possibly commodity broking like his father. In fact in partnership with Samuel Robinson, auctioneer, of Christchurch, Surrey — both putting up bonds for £500 in 1793 (a large sum in those days), he must have made a lot of money. (His estate was however less than £17,500). He conducted his stockbroking business from his own coffee shop, the Magdalene in Southwark.

He owned many houses in Southwark, on Blackfriars Road, also No.25 Queen Street, Park and also Ratcliffe Highway in Stepney. (Ref. PROB 10-3729 XP001388 Dec.1805). On his death on 10th November 1805 he left £3,000 each to Samuel and John, his sons and £3,000 to his wife Elizabeth which reverted on her death to St. George the Martyr Church, Southwark. His will is quite specific and is shown below.

Delaforce's Charity — St. George the Martyr, Southwark

Samuel Delaforce, by will dated 10 November 1805 gave to his wife Elizabeth, the interest of £3000L 3 per cents for life; after her death, £500L for instructing poor children in reading in the Poor House of St. George, Southwark for ever. The interest of £1,000 for the nourishment of poor people in a poor, weak, sickly way in the poor house of St. George Southwark for ever. The interest of £500 for the support & eduction of poor boys and girls in the Charity Schools of said Parish. The interest of £1,000 to be given away yearly to such poor decayed families as had lived as good housekeepers, and had borne a good character and were then of the Parish of St. George, to each family two bushels of coal, 5s in money, and a quartern loaf which were to be distributed yearly by the churchwardens & overseers at their discretion for ever. The Testators widow is still living.

1879 20 October. Transferred to 3000 New Consols, Divs £82-10. Trustees Robert Drewitt Hilton, Alexander Hawkins, Thomas Emary & James Chubb.

There is no doubt that Samuel and Elizabeth were deeply attached and committed to help the Southwark poor. Samuel was buried in the crypt at St. George the Martyr.

The Rector wrote in April 1981 "The Samuel Delaforce Educational Fund is administered from the Town Hall (Southwark) taken over at the time when the Borough Councils were, established at the turn of the century. I know of a number of grants made to assist local children."

Information about Samuel came from Parish Registers, Wills, John Harvard Library, Brokers Guild, and the IGI Index.

Chapter 8

Oxford Book of Ballards
"They sent him up to fair London,
an apprentice for to bind"

The Delaforces in 17th Century London

Although there were many Delaforces living in London at the end of the 16th century mainly in Tower Warde, the main emphasis for most of the next 50 years was on Jacques and Mary De La Force, who produced a large well-documented family, nearly all of whom were silk weavers, whose descendants live in London today.

Jacques was the fourth generation of this name, and was born about 1570. He married (as "James Le Fort") his wife, Mary, about 1591, when she was 18, probably in London. The John Fosse, Yeoman, St. Clemence Danes, who died in 1625 and left a will (PCC 144 Clarke) was probably Jacques' younger brother, born about 1572.

1595-8 Jacques was a business merchant spending part of his time in London, and then for another 20 years or so, most of his time in Valenciennes, northern France. He was in partnership with Anthony de Liniall and the arrangement, which lasted for 21 years, ended with Anthony's death in October 1616.

Jacques bought "Lawns and fine cambrics to be purchased in Valentienna of Lyonesse in the Province of Flanders and woolen clothes bought in England by Anthony." Each purchased the others goods and sold them respectively in northern France and England. Almost certainly Jacques' brother John in Lille also sold the woolen textiles in his area, and possibly the other merchant Delaforces in Calais traded as well.

The partnership was successful, profitable and amicable. It was continued with Anthony's widow Rachel de Liniall (née de Bavoy), who took her husband's share of the partnership on his death. Jacques visited London frequently on business but many of his children were born in or near Valenciennes (and therefore needed to be naturalised English later on). He was in London in 1620 as Church witness at the Chambeau family wedding.

On his death on 24th August 1626, aged about 56, his widow Mary de La Force continued the business, but unfortunately the two widows fell out and litigation followed, with Rachel suing Mary for loss of profits! (Chancery Proceedings of Charles I D13/72 233).

Each widow was assisted — Mary de la Force by her son Francis and her son-in-law John Fountaine, and Rachel by her nephew Paul de Bavoy and a friend Robert Thiery. Rachel claimed that for 6 years Jacques "had kept all the profits and did a great trade for himself overseas during which time Rachel sent him moneys, as her factor, for goods. After Jacques' death Mary de la Fosse his relict and executrix took all the whole estate and did not give Rachel her share estimated at L1600" — a large sum at that time. Mary, in her turn, counterclaimed for moneys due to her in the accounts. (Chancery Proceedings C24/574 Pt.I). Her son Francis also made a Town Deposition when he was aged 30 living in Coleman Street (between St. Olaves, Hart Street and St. Katherines Cree and Close to St. Botolphs without Aldgate and Threadneedle Street Church).

Mary de La Force died 7th February 1645 aged 67 in St. Botolphs, Bishopsgate parish (probably in Coleman Street) leaving a substantial family behind. The Court proceedings showed that she had two children born in Valenciennes about 1617-1618.

(A) James Fosse was probably born — the 5th James in line — about 1595, and died about 24th January 1625/6. Probably he and his wife died in the plague of that year. In his will he left £50 each to Catherine Waterton (aunt on father's side to look after the three children — Jas (James), John and Thomazin Fosse, a daughter, who were each also left £50. James was a Yeoman in the City of Westminster when he died. As the eldest son he probably retained links with diplomatic circles because of James, his grandfather, who also lived in Chelsea and Westminster.

(B) John Dellforce, the second son, was born in 1599, probably in

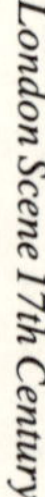

London Scene 17th Century

Valenciennes, married Marie Jacqueline Cuvelier (Caullier) in 1619, a sister of Elisabeth Caullier who married John's younger brother Francis in 1627. Marie died on 3rd February 1659 in Kent. John helped in his father's business in Valenciennes, but as John Delforto, was admitted in London as a foreign weaver member (by certificate of the French Church) on 25th May 1635.

John and Marie had a son John, born about 1620 (a tailor, who married Anne Lewis), and a daughter, Jenne/Jane, who married in 1634, John Le Threvillier, a merchant of London. John De La Fforte was then living in Coleman Street, London, probably with Francis and their widowed mother, Mary. Other children were Jacques baptised 1624, Pierre baptised 1622 and possibly Thomas, baptised 11th November 1629. Also Francis Laffosh baptised 1623, died 12th January 1635, aged 12. John died in 1664 aged 65 in St. Botolphs parish, Bishopsgate.

(C) Francis Dellafoss was born in 1602 and married twice: initially to Elizabeth, shown in the Church Records as "Franchhoys, fils de feu Jaques, native de Valenciennes, et Ellysbet, fille de Barthlemyeu Caullye, natyve de Canterbury", on 6th February 1627. As Frances Defours, stranger, he was made Free as a Weaver member on 28th November 1627. He was naturalised as Francis de la Fosse on 11th January 1637.

His son Bertholomé was baptised 18th November 1628, and daughter, Mary, on 20th August 1629 at St.Botolphs without Aldgate. But Mary and her mother both died in August 1629 possibly from Childbirth (Guildhall MSS 9233). Their names in the Register were Deleforce and Dellforce. Almost certainly young Bertholomé died in infancy.

He remarried on 29th March 1630 as "ffraunces Delefosse to Hellin Cressoone" (Cresson) at St. Stephens Church, Coleman Street. The Caullier family were also present at this wedding and obviously had a longstanding friendship with the Delaforces.

In 1643 Elaine De la Force and Marye Caullier were witnesses at the same wedding. Francis and Elaine, to give her correct name, (which included Eline, Ellen, Helen and some others) had a large family.

1. Jacques was baptised 9th January 1631, St. Dunstans, Stepney He was alive in 1662.

2. Marie 25th March 1632 but died 20th October 1634 St. Botolphs without Aldgate.
3. Elisabeth February 1633 St. Stephens, Coleman Street died 5th January 1634 St. Botolphs without Aldgate.
4. Bartholomew baptised 1634, but died in 1654 and left a will to his father Francis. His grandfather Bertelemy Caulier, who died 19th October 1653, left money to his grandson.
5. Elisabeth (again) 12th November 1635 Threadneedle Street.
6. John 21st December 1638 St. Botolphs, died 1666, left a will to his widowed mother, Helaine.
7. Francis Fortey baptised 1641 — died 1st April 1643.
8. Estienne/Stephen 6th June 1641 Threadneedle Street married Mary Largilee 1666.
9. Pierre 19th November 1643, as Peter Delaforse died 1645 aged 2½.
10. Pierre 20th February 1648 Threadneedle Street, alive in 1662 aged 14.
11. Jenne/Jane 14th December 1645 Threadneedle Street.
12. Marie (again) 7th October 1649 Threadneedle Street.
13. Benjamin February 1651 St. Botolphs, Bishopsgate, but "a still-born son of Francis Delforce died 1651 St. Botolphs.".

In 1630 Francis and brother John and probably mother Mary were living in Coleman Street. In 1638 Francis De Le Fore of St. Botolphs paid £10 rent per annum, Gunn Alley, Cock Yard. In 1651 Francis and Elene were wedding witnesses in Canterbury.

A Francis Defore baptised 1643 was apprenticed silk weaver 18th February 1657 to Phillip Defore. This might have been another Francis' son apprenticed to his Uncle Phillip.

When Francis died in 1662, aged 60, he left a will benefitting his widow Helaine and surviving children, Elisabeth, 27; John 24; Jane, 17; and Peter, 14. The children each got 1/- and Helaine his estate.

(D) Antoine Lafosse, born 1612, married Jeane Farbu(t) 29th August 1633, Threadneedle Street Church. A son Antoine, was born 1634, and Marie in 1635, then James/Jacques about 1636 (admitted a forraigne weaver in 1664). Anthony lived in Stenheath, Middlesex. Francois, his brother, was a witness at Marie's baptism. Marie married David Mund in 1666 at St. Botolphs, Bishopsgate — her name spelt Deleforce. Antoine died

15th August 1636, aged 24.

(E) Phillipe baptised 1609, married Mary de Rante, a widow of Mathieu Renier, when he was 35 and his wife about 30, on 7th May or 12th April 1646 at Threadneedle Street Church. He might have had an earlier marriage because a Phillipe was born 1633, a weaver, died 1684, age 51. Phillipe's name was shown as de la Fosse and Du Fore. In 1640 Phillip del Fose visited Amsterdam Huguenot Church as a Temoin (witness).

Phillipe died 7th November 1689, aged 80. He certainly fathered a Phillipe alive about 1647.

(F) Marguerite de la Fosse, "fille de feu (the late) Jaques," married Balthazar de Marc, son of Jean de Marc(k) of Valenciennes on 13th November 1628. She was probably born about 1610.

(G) Marie de la Fosse, daughter of Jacques married Jaques Mangon on 28th January 1630, at Threadneedle Street Church. SHe was probably born about 1612.

(H) Collette de la Fosse married Peter Mershe February 1638/9. She was probably born about 1618 in Valenciennes.

This was a large, prosperous family, and Mary, who outlived her husband by 19 years was obviously a strongminded matriarch, which was needed in the days of the Gunpowder Plot 1605, Shakespeare in his prime, the massacre of Protestants in Ireland, the outbreak in 1642 of the English Civil War, all during the reigns of James I and Charles I.

The trend from merchanting to becoming individual weavers started with this family, with most of the sons being admitted as foreign weavers.

The next generation of Jaques' and Mary's grandchildren takes the family into the late-17th century.

The sources for the 17th century depend mainly on Huguenot Society publications, on the CFI index of baptisms, on silk weaver records at the Guildhall library, on Chancery Proceedings (Bernau index at the Society of Genealogists) and on wills located at the PRO Chancery Lane. The Threadneedle Street French church records are invaluable. So indeed are the records of Aliens published by the Huguenot Society (see chapter 1). Poor Law rate books for appropriate areas are also useful data sources. All the original name varieties are shown as printed in the reference books.

Chapter 9

Jonathon Swift 1667-1745
"Find out if you can, Who's Master, Who's Man."

The Money Men and the London Guilds and Trades

Apprenticehsip was one of the principal means of learning and gaining admission in medieval times to a trade or profession. Guilds of traders and craftsmen originated in the early Middle Ages both as social institutions and as a means of regulating admission to trades and crafts, and maintaining standards of workmanship and trading

In the 16th and 17th centuries the power of the Guilds was considerable, but started to wane during the 18th and by the 19th had virtually disappeared. By 1900 in the City of London there were still 77 livery companies. Many Delaforces belonged to the Silkweavers Guild as shown in the next chapter.

The Freedom of the Guild was obtained in three ways:–

(a) By Servitude. Usually the young apprentice started his indentures at the age of 14 and achieved his freedom after seven years, at the age of 21.

(b) By Redemption — the payment of a fee, usually £2.6s.8d. in the 17th and 18th centuries.

(c) By Patrimony, by which every child born in lawful wedlock to a freeman after admission to the freedom had a right to the freedom by patrimony.

The rules of behaviour between Master and Apprentice were clearly spelt out as this extract from Indenture of apprenticeship shows "during which term the said apprentice his said Master

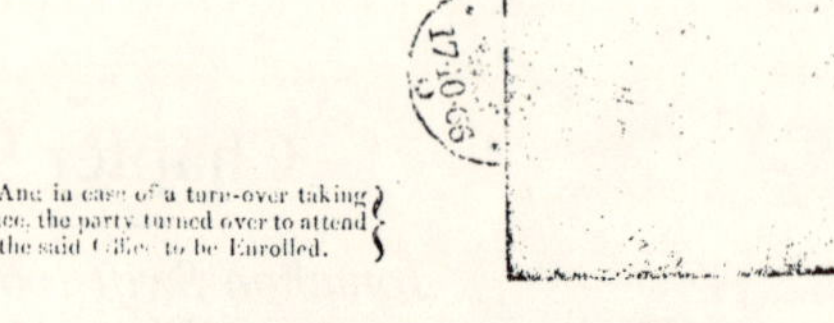

This Indenture Witnesseth, That Thomas Alfred Delforce son of William Delforce of 31 Warner Street ... Road in the County of Surrey Fish Salesman

doth put himself apprentice to Thomas Durbidge Moore of 70 Lower Thames Street in the City of London Citizen and CLOTHWORKER of LONDON, to learn his Art of a Lighterman

and with him (after the manner of an Apprentice) to serve from the Day of the Date hereof unto the full End and Term of SEVEN Years from thence next following, to be fully complete and ended. During which Term, the said Apprentice his said Master faithfully shall serve, his Secrets keep, his lawful Commands every where gladly do. He shall do no damage to his said Master, nor see it to be done of others; but that he to his Power shall let or forthwith give Warning to his said Master of the same. He shall not waste the Goods of his said Master, nor lend them unlawfully to any. He shall not commit Fornication, nor contract Matrimony, within the said Term. He shall not play at Cards, Dice, Tables, or any other unlawful Games, whereby his said Master may have any Loss. With his own Goods or others, during the said Term, without Licence of his said Master, he shall neither buy nor sell. He shall not haunt Taverns or Play-houses, nor absent himself from his said Master's Service Day nor Night, unlawfully. But in all Things as a faithful Apprentice he shall behave himself towards his said Master and all his, during the said Term. And the said Master, in consideration of the Premises, and

in consideration of faithful service

his said Apprentice in the same Art which he useth, by the best Means that he can, shall teach and instruct, or cause to be taught and instructed: finding unto his said Apprentice, Meat, Drink, Apparel, Lodging, and all other Necessaries, according to the Custom of the City of LONDON, during the said Term. And for the true Performance of all and every the said Covenants and Agreements, either of the said Parties bindeth himself unto the other by these Presents. *In Witness* whereof the Parties above named to these Indentures interchangeably have put their Hands and Seals, the Twelfth Day of August in the thirty second Year of the Reign of our Sovereign Lady VICTORIA, by the Grace of God, of the United Kingdom of *Great Britain* and *Ireland*, Queen, Defender of the Faith, and in the Year of our Lord One Thousand Eight Hundred and sixty eight.

Sealed and Delivered (being first duly stamped) in the Presence of

Geo. Robert ... Clerk

T. D. Moore

Note. This Indenture must bear Date the Day it is executed: and what Money or other Thing is given or contracted for with the Clerk or Apprentice, must be inserted in Words at Length; otherwise the Indenture will be void, the Master or Mistress forfeit Fifty Pounds, and another Penalty, and the Apprentice be disabled to follow his Trade, or be made Free.

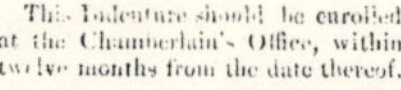

This Indenture should be enrolled at the Chamberlain's Office, within twelve months from the date thereof.

And in case of a turn-over taking place, the party turned over to attend at the said Office to be Enrolled.

Indenture of Thomas Alfred Delforce, lighterman 1868

faithfully shall serve — his secrets keep — and his lawful commands gladly do. He shall do no damage to his said Master, nor see it done by others, but that he, to his power shall hinder, or forthwith give warning to his said Master of the same. He shall not commmit fornication, nor contract matrimony within the said terms. He shall not play cards, dice, tables, nor any other unlawful games, whereby His said Master may have any loss. With his own goods or others during the said term, without licence of his said Master, he shall neither buy nor sell. He shall not haunt taverns, nor playhouses, nor absent himself from his said Masters service day or night unlawfully, but in all things, as a faithful Apprentice, he shall behave himself towards his said Master, and all his, during the said term. And the said Master — his said Apprentice in the same art and mystery which he useth, by the best means that he can, shall teach and instruct, or cause to be taught and instructed".

The first recorded Delaforce Guild members were three or four Master Cutlers in the period 1274-1310 with a Raymond, William and a John classed as 'Cotelers' or 'taillandiers' and in 1288 when Peter de Fors was a Master to John atte Gate for 70s. In Dowgate ward in London. Peter and his brothers were merchants of wine from Cahors and leather shoes from Spain.

Later a long but intermittent line of Goldsmiths, Silversmiths, Lombard bankers, Pawnbrokers and Stockbrokers was originated by Pierre de la Fosse/Force, elder son of Sir Bernard (1472-1523) who was a Goldsmith of Faversham, Kent. As Peter Force he left a will at Canterbury, and paid taxes for 3 years.

James Le Forsey/De La Fore/Fossé, a 'Lombardes man' of 1551 in London, in St. Olaves, Hart Street was Pierres grandson or grand-nephew. Bernard Deforse, a 'Sylversmith' of St. Katherines Free Church, near St. Helens Bishopsgate, 1540-1613, was a grandson or grand-nephew of Peter Force.

In 1583 John Desfort, 'Duch', was a Goldsmith of Aldersgate.

Edward Delves or Force, the Goldsmith at the Mermaid in Lombard St. 1570-1638,who married Maria Balser in 1592, was a great grand-son of Pierre/Peter.

Edward Deffors 1590-1651, who died in St. James, Clerkenwell, may have continued his father, Edward's, business. Oliver, his son, died in 1631. The "Golden Ball" shop existed in Winchester

No. 16

MARINERS, SOLDIERS, AND MARINES.

Whereas, in and by an Act of Parliament made in the fifty-sixth year of the reign of His late Majesty King GEORGE the Third, intituled *An Act to enable such Officers, Mariners, and Soldiers as have been in the Land or Sea Service, or in the Marines, or in the Militia, or any corps of Fencible Men, since the forty-second year of His present Majesty's reign, to exercise Trades*, it is enacted "that all such Officers, Mariners, Soldiers, and Marines as have been at any time employed in "the service of His Majesty since the twenty-second day of *June*, One thousand eight hundred and two, and have not since "deserted the said service, and also the Wives and Children of such Officers, Mariners, Soldiers, and Marines, may set up and "exercise such Trades as they are apt and able for, in any City, Town, or Place within this Kingdom, without any let, suit, "or molestation of any person or persons whatsoever for or by reason of the using of such Trade:" And whereas it appears to me, by Certificate under the hand of T. R. Walcot Esq, Principal Clerk, H. M. Admiralty Somerset House,

That William Delaforce —— hath served His late Majesty King GEORGE the Third since the said twenty-second day of *June*, One thousand eight hundred and two, as a Boy 3rd Class on Board H. M. Ship L'Achille whereby Joseph Delaforce, Son of the said William, is duly entitled to the benefit of the said Act: These are therefore to will and require all and singular the Serjeants of the Chamber, and all other persons whatsoever, not to molest or hinder the said Joseph Delaforce —— in exercising such his Trade within this City or the Liberties thereof, according to the said Act.

Given under my hand, and sealed with the Seal of the Office of Chamberlain of the City of *London*, in the Guildhall of the said City, this 21st day of June. in the year of our Lord 1842.

Freedom of City of London for Joseph Delaforce, 1842

Street, off Broad Street in 1673, which John owned in 1740 or earlier.

Then comes a long gap of traceable activity until John Delaforce 1702-1779, his son John, his grandson Samuel, his great grandson Samuel who were Pawnbrokers, Stockbrokers and Brokers (perhaps of commodities) of Bishopsgate, Norton Folgate and Southwark, until well into the 19th century.

John Delaforce 1729-1788 was a Member of the City List of Brokers on 2nd July 1782, in partnership with Joseph Bond, Citizen and Blacksmith, with each paying a £500 Bond (Ref. CCRO Fr 163(4). His son Samuel 1750-1805 also became a Stockbroker (Book Q3) on the London Stock Exchange in 1793 in partnership with Samuel Robinson, Auctioneer, of Christchurch, Surrey. Both paid a Bond of £500. Samuel's son Samuel, baptised 1773 was also a Broker and a Pawnbroker.

Tailors

(1) The tailors in the family were first represented by Michel/Michael Forsse/de Fort/Le Faux in the tailors trade in Langbourne Ward, a 'Dutchman'. In 1567 he was living in Billingsgate in Tower Ward. As Michel Del Foar of Beauvois (N.W. of Paris) he was in Middlebourg at the Huguenot church in 1576. His son married 1585 Marie from Cambri and had a daughter Marguerite.
(2) John Delforce 1599-1664.
(3) John De Forse/Delforce 1620-1670 who married Anne Lewis was a Tailor.
(4) Jean Delfos in London 1679-81, arriving from Sedan, was a Tailor.
(5) Peter Delaforce baptised 1701 was a Tailor of Bethnal Green.
(6) John Delaforce the Musician in 1749 described his original trade as a Tailor of St. Brides.
(7) John Delaforce 1781-1855 was described in his father samuel's will, as being a Taylor of Mile End.

It has not been possible to trace continuity of this trade. None of the Delaforces were members of the Merchant Tailors Guild.

Cooks

The original records in the London Guildhall show:
1695 Daniel Laffonds app. to Samuel Ruffoil.
1697 Stephen Lafforse admitted to Freedom in 1714.
1700 William Lafforse held apprenticeship of Stephen Lafforse (his father).
1710 Stephen Laforce a master (Guildhall MS L35/31).
1716 William Laforce was master @ 2/6d. to J. Marriott.
1720-55 William is master to John Dunddis and several others.
1722 William in Cooks Guild MS L35/31.
1725 William Doarfo... apprenticed 2/6d. p.a.
1735 John William Lafolo app. William Lafosse.
1737 Thomas Fowse app. to Francis Briggs.
1740 John Martin app. to William Laforsse.
1755 William Legatt app. to William Laforce.

Other Guild members included:

Samuel Delaforce 1749-1805 was Apprenticed 5th July 1763 to John Speere and later Mr Bunyard, and on 4th September 1770 was made a Freeman of the Carpenters Guild. The church registers showed him as a Cabinet Maker. His son Samuel became a member of the Carpenters Guild in 1821.

James Fawcey(?) 1722 was admitted to the Framework Knitters Guild.

John Delaforce 1729-1788 became a Freeman 21st November 1749 of the Musicians Guild, described in church registers as a Musicianer.

Daniel Delaforce baptised 1751 was app. March 1765 to Stephen Skinner and made Free August 1775 as a Barber. His father John paid the £5 fee.

John Delafors baptised 1744 was made Freeman (46/8d.) 2nd September 1766 as a Spectaclemaker.

Joseph Delaforce baptised 1783, app. 1st November 1797, made Free February 1805 as a Clothworker. The fee of £2 was paid by Langbourne Ward Charity School. He was son of Thomas Delaforce, weaver of Mile End New Town.

The Guildhall library has a superb collection of early Guild manuscripts. The City of London Freedom Registers in the office of the Chamberlain of London also have an excellent series of records of Guild memberships from 1784.

Chapter 10

Robert Herrick 1591-1674
"Whereas in silks my Julia goes, then, then (me thinks) how sweetly flows that liquefaction of her clothes."

The Silkweavers of London

The London weavers' first charter was received in 1155 and was the first Royal Charter granted to any London craft. In 1191 the merchant guilds won control of London. They offered King John an annual payment if he would suppress the weavers guild. John did so in 1200. Henry VI in 1446 took the weavers under his personal protection. The influx of highly skilled French silk weavers and throwsters in the 17th century caused a lot of dissension with the existing English weavers.

Apprentices usually started at the age of 14 and were admitted to Guild freedom after 7 years, aged 21. (A very useful guide for genealogists). The 11s.10d. charged as admission included a 'free' silver spoon valued at 5/- or 8/-.

The Guildhall library (manuscripts) keeps nearly all the original weaver records. MS4660, MS4656, MS4657 etc. The nearby Alderman's Court keeps the Freedom indentures for each admission after about 1685. This is most helpful as names of fathers and addresses are usually noted on each indenture form. Lastly the Huguenot Society Volume 33 includes excellent extracts from about 1660 of Huguenot weavers, including details of some of their misdemeanours.

In 1409 Bernard Fort of the Gironde was a Tisserant, 'Oweure' or weaver, the first recorded in the family.

For at least a hundred years, from 1530 to 1630, Delaforces in

London, Calais, Lille, Sedan and Valenciennes in northern France, were engaged in textile trading with wool, and 'fine lawns and cambrics'. At an early stage therefore Delaforces were involved in a kindred trade of silk throwsters and weaving.

The Huguenot silk weavers, refugees from France were much in evidence in London in this century. Apart fro the various Jaques/James there were:

John Delfos 'a Burgundian (i.e. from Burgundy-controlled part of the Low Countries, possibly Bruges) living in London 'for religion' was also shown as John Delfonce/Delfosse' and his wife Katherine (Gergart, see Threadneedle Street capers), daughter Jane 'all burgundians living at St. Martins Ontwiche (in the fields), Parish of Creplegate Without as Dyers, makers and weavers of Threde in the House of Anthony Agagh, public notary, worshipping at the Duche church in London in the period 1566-1571 came into this realme for religion about V years past.'

Later Francis de Fosse/de la Fosse a journey-man weaver in 1582 was living in London and shown as a Master Weaver in 1583 and born in 1560.

In 1592 Gilles, Joc, and son Peter Foyse were silkweavers living in Tooley Street, south of the river Thames.

(A) In MSS 4556 Vol.I of original Weavers Records are shown:
Danyell Defowce, stranger, weaver admitted 10 July 1623
Fraunces de Fours, stranger, made free weaver 28 November 1627. John Delforto admitted for member, cert. of Fr. Church 25 May 1635. Peter de Fallso admitted for member after Denization 25 May 1635. Jaques de Fos/Vos weaver admitted November 1638.

(B) Volume 33 of the Huguenot Society has extracts of early Huguenot Weaver Records.
18 Feb 1657 Francis Defore app. to Phillip Defore his father.
5 Sep 1664 James Delafosse, son of Anthony, of Stenheath, Middlesex admitted a forraigne brother 11s.10d.
17 Dec 1666 John Delafe...named Weaver.
19 Oct 1668 Stephen Delafosse upon certif. from Canterbury

A London silkweaver at work 19th century

admitted a for. weaver.
16 Nov 1668 Ja: Delafosse fined 6s.8d. for reproaching yeomanry and resisting search.
16 Nov 1668 Abra. See brought in John Delfoss.
17 May 1669 Stephen Delafosse a weaver (Master).
18 Jan 1669 Charles Delfoss having been here a year were deemed to be admitted.
13 Jun 1670 Charles Desfosse having served at Valenciennes admitted member.
30 May 1670 James Delafoss admitted for weaver.
20 Jun 1670 John Delafosse had a fortnight to prove his service.
13 Jun 1670 John Desfosse admitted.
28 Feb 1676 James Delafosse app. to Abra: Godowne.
7 May 1676 Isaac Delafosse app. to Fra: Hilder and made free 9 June 1684.
30 Jun 1684 Phillip Delfosse served in Valentian, attested by Anth: Lansee for W(eaver) admitted a for.w.51 (age).
30 Jun 1684 Gosse Gallis served at Valentian, attested by Phillip Delafosse for w. and a member of the Fr. Church is admitted 11s.10d.
5 Jan 1685 Fra(ncis) Noah Delfoss appr. to Phill. Delfoss his father.
31 Mar 1685 He. Hess for. w(eaver) was very sorry for his offence and pretended his ignorance by his not understanding English. he paid a fine of 10s. and promised to conform. John Delfoss for the like offence paid 5s.
2 Mar 1685 John Delaplaus (sic) a master to Peter Flameng.
8 Sep 1685 Alex. Barneville appt. to Cha: Delafosse for .w.
3 Apr 1693 John Delavoer (sic) admitted Master.
1706 Pierre Lefos at weavers baptism.
5 Sep 1711 Peter Delafosse appr. to James, father.
11 Apr 1715 James Fosse Master.
28 Jan 1715 John Delfort a Master to James Carle.
15 Dec 1718 John Delaforce made Free from Robt. Excerbee Citizen.
4 Jun 1722 John Le Fause Master.
11 Mar 1723 Robert Griffin appren. to John Delaforce.
7 Sep 1724 John Delforce appr. to Wm. Norton.
1744 Charles Delafosse weaver without being a Freeman.

(C) Chamberlain's Court Records at the Guildhall (include some non-weavers)

1. Peter Dolforce, son of James of Stepney, apprentice Weaver 1692, became Free June 1699 (i.e. born 1678).

2. John Delaforce, son of John, silkthrower, app. 9 Jan 1704, Free April 1712 (i.e. born 1690).

3. John Delaforce, son of Isaac, weaver, of St. Dunstans Stepney, app. to Robert Excelbee, Jan 1707, Freeman in 1718 (i.e. born 1692).

4. Jacob Delforce, son of James, weaver, app. to John Clary, app. 4 May 1731,Free in mar 1750 (i.e. born 1717).

5. James Delaforce, son of Peter, taylor, of Bethnal Green, app. 1745, as Weavers, Free April 1753 (i.e. born 1731).

6. John Delafors, Freeman of Spectaclemakers (pd. 46/8d.) 2 Sept 1766 (i.e. born 1745).

7. John Delforce, son of James, citizen & weaver of London, was app. to John Clary (see 4) 6 June 1737, Freeman June 1744 (i.e. born 1723) brother of Jacob.

8. John Delaforce, son of John, St. Dunstans in the West, with licence & consent of the Governors of the Hospital of Bridewell, London, app. to Thomas Roay, citizen and Musician 11 Sept 1741. Freeman 17 Nov 1749 (John Dulaforce) Bridewell Chapel & Hospital & Precinct Church, near St. Brides, Fleet St. (born 1728). (Permission might be needed as a Musician to start apprenticeship under age 14).

9. Jas Delfors, son of James, Mile End New Town, weaver, app. Thomas Bampton, 6 Aug 1744 for 7 years but Free only in June 1769 (born 1730).

10. Samuel Delaforce, son of John, Musicianer, of St. Botolphs, Bishopsgate, Carpenter, app. John Speere, then Mr Bunyard, app. 5 July 1763. Freedom Sep 1770 (i.e. born 1749).

11. Daniel Delaforce, son of John Delaforce, St. Botolphs, Bishopsgate, Taylor, app. to Stephen Skinner as Barber. £5 paid by father John 5 Mar 1765, Free Aug 1775 (i.e. born 1751).

12. William Delaforce, son of John Delaforce, weaver, of Castle St. St. Matthew Bethnal Green, app. Oct 1748, Freeman 1752 (i.e. born 1734) weaver.

13. James Delaforce, son of Thomas, weaver, app. 6 Aug 1793, Free Feb 1801 (born 1779) weaver.
14. Joseph Delaforce, son of Thomas, weaver, St. Dunstans, Mile End New Town. £2 fee paid by Langbourne Ward Charity School. app. 1 Nov 1797, Free Feb 1805 (i.e. born 1783) Clothworkers Guild.

(D) At the beginning of the 18th Century there were no less than four John Delaforce silk weavers, practicing at the same time:
(a) son of Isaac & Mary Garnier, b.1692, app. 1707, free 1718 (Delaforce)
(b) son of James & Jane Cooper, b.1701, app. 1715, free 1722 (Le Fause).
(c) son of John & Susanna, b.1710, app. 1724, free 1731 (Delforce)
(d) son of John & Mary, b.1690, app 1704, free 1712 (Delfort/Delfosse).

(E) The Huguenot Society vol. 55 record the saga of the Spitalfields weavers of 1739-41 who were in need of aid. The archives of La Maison de Charité de Spittlefields gives a sad and a serious account of some 543 cases of weaver familes in need, and indeed receiving help. There were no Delaforces amongst them — perhaps surprisingly. This book is a mine of information about the East Enders of this time and should be consulted by researchers with 18th century descendants living in that part of London.

There was a major crisis in the weaving trade in 1811 when America declared war on England. In Manchester 32 out of 38 mills closed. In Glasgow weavers wages fell from 17/6d. weekly to 7/6d weekly. The Luddites broke up hundreds of framework knitting machines.

The decline in prosperity of the silkweaving trade had a profound effect on the Delaforce family. Some emigrated to Australia and America. Most of them entered totally different trades: cab drivers, butchers, milkmen, barbers, straw hat manufacturers, spectacle makers, tailors, cabinet makers etc.

London Silk Weavers in the 17th Century

At the end of the 16th century London's population was about 250,000 including Westminster, Lambeth and Stepney, 'defended' by eight massive gates — Aldgate, Bishopsgate, Moorgate, Cripplegate, Aldersgate, Newgate, Ludgate and Bridgegate. The second and third cities in the country were Norwich, with a population of 29,000 and Bristol with 20,000.

When the epidemics of bubonic plague struck the city the death roll was horrific. In 1603 30,000 died, in 1625 35,000, in 1636 11,000 and in the great plague of 1665 no less than 70,000 people died. It is a wonder that the population of London continued to grow. Amidst the survivors the silk weavers flourished, including many Huguenot immigrants, whose industry was not always appreciated.

1595 Complaint of the Yeoman Weavers against the Immigrant Weavers addressed to the Minister & Elders of the French Church in London.

1. 'Kepe Apprentices and Loomes twyce or thryce as many as they ought whereby such an intollerable multitude of workemen are growne, that nowe one is not able to live by another.
2. They doe not refuse to teache their Countrymen which new come over, the Arte of silke weaveinge, though before they were a Taylor, a Cobler or a Joyner...
3. They sett Wooemen and Maydes at worke, whoe, when they are become perfect...'...

The sumptuary laws of 1597 forbade any man under the rank of Knight's eldest son to wear a velvet jerkin, doublet or hose or to use satin, damask, taffeta, tuftafetty (tufted pile) or grosgrain for cloaks, coats, gowns, or 'uppermost garments'. No woman below the degree of Knight's wife could legally wear velvet or silk embroidery or 'nether stocks of silk'. Under the reign of the Stuart Kings these laws were not observed!

According to the customs of the City of London and the Weavers Company the proper manufacturing procedures were as follows. 'A Merchant Silkman may deliver silk (yarn) or other stuff unto any Master Weaver that is a Freeman, or other which is admitted a Master by the Bailliffs, Wardens and Assistants of the Weavers Company. And the silk or other stuff ought to be delivered by weight and being wrought or fashioned, the owner may receive the same again by weight and pay the weaver for the workmanship or fashioning thereof, either by the pound or by the dozen, as both parties can agree, allowing sufficient waste upon every pound.' Alternatively the merchant or silkman might sell the raw materials to the weaver at a certain price and buy back the woven fabric at a price high enough to recompense the weaver for his work.

The price paid for silk was 3d. or 4. a yard, and silk woven scarves sold at 18d. each. A journeyman weaver's wage was 2s.4d. a week plus food, drink, lodging & washing 'fitting for a journeyman' and new clothing at the beginning and end of his 7 or 8 years servitude. (Apprentices served 7 years — 55 percent, 8 years 35 percent, and over 8 years — 10 percent). Masters paid 20s. to the Weavers Company for journeyman weaver's admission and had to provide 'reasonable fare ... sweet and holdsome for man's bodie.'

There were three distinct grades after Citizen and Weaver of London (i.e. Freeman of the City). These grades were called 'admissioners or foreign brethren'.

1. Foreign masters, whose qualifications were fully approved by the Company and who were allowed to take apprentices.

2. Foreign weavers allowed to work independently but not to set up as 'householders'.

3. Journeymen — weavers who had proved their apprenticeship or capability in the craft, but were not permitted to work except as journeymen.

Moreover the grades of Gild membership were defined commercially in terms of the number of single looms, numbers of journeymen annd apprentices employed.

	Single Looms	No. of Journeymen (max)	Apprentices (max)
Denizens or foreigners			
in 1st year after admission	5	1	1
in 2nd year	5	2	3
in 3rd or subsequent years	5	2	3
Strangers (aliens)			
1st year after admission	4	1	1
2nd and subsequent years	4	2	2
Liverymen of Company	6	unlimited	4
Bailiffs/Wardens of Company	7	unlimited	5

The location of Weavers in London in the 17th Century were 30 percent in Southwark, 20 percent in Cripplegate, 20 percent in Shoreditch and 10 per cent in Whitehall. In 1618 a survey showed the percentage of weavers 'strangers' in London.

	Total		Weavers	
Bishopsgate	190	of which	138	plus 6 throwsters & 4 threadmakers
Portsoken	84		29	2
Coleman Street	31		10	
Southwark				
St. Saviours	13		3	plus 8 dyers
St.Thomas	29		22	
St.George	15		3	
St. Olave	93		30	plus 8 throwsters & 11 dyers
Bermondsey St.Mary Mag.	27		14	plus 1 throwster
TOTAL	482		289	

During this century the Weavers Gild admitted between 8 and 10 strangers/aliens per annum paying £5 fee, and 'forren' admissions, mainly from the provinces, between 11 and 14 per annum paying a £3 fee initially. The livery 'fine' was increased to £6 in 1680. At the end of the century the Gild granted a total of about 150 Freedoms a year (86 percent by servitude, 12 percent by patrimony and 2 percent by redemption). But a hundred years later, in 1790, there were only 12 Freedoms in total granted. The following statistics show the rise and fall of the Gild membership.

1681 grand total of	5,403 members
1692	6,330 members
1701	5,785 members
1730	5,240 members
1750	2,613 members
1790	1,820 members
1820	905 members

London had two main weekly lace markets — one at the George Inn, in Aldersgate Street, and the other at the Bull and Mouth, also by Aldersgate. Some silk weavers specialised in broad weaving, others narrow wares such as ribbons, girdles, garterings, braids, cords and laces. Others in very light delicate fabrics such as cobweb lawns and tiffanies (silk gauze). Others wove black heavy-dyed 'London' silk tufted taffetas, figured satins, fine slight ribands, ferret ribands both black and coloured, and pure silk damasks. The Orris weaving was a lucrative section of the trade – the manufacture of gold & silver lace and braid. Finely drawn gold and silver wire spun upon silk in proportions described by Act of Parliament, was made into lace and braid known as 'statute lace'. Bone Lace, from bone bobbins by lacemakers, or bone pins for pricking out the lace, was mainly fashioned by the out-work trade by large numbers of young children 'and divers ancient people spinners and workers of waste silks ... a very great number' who had no others means of getting a living.

Well might the Gild in 1603 be described as 'Bailiffs, Wardens, Assistants and Commonalty of the Trade, Art & Mystery of Weavers of London' based on Weavers Hall in Basinghall St.

The Weavers company employed their own "Yeomanry" to inspect the work place and warehouses and endeavour to maintain high standards. There were 16-20 of them 'below the Livery' policing the five main districts 'in search of the craft.' They collected 'a search grant (4d)' as a customary contribution towards their travel and charges. This was a longstanding right to collect from those whose premises they searched! They also collected a 'search breakfast' and a 'search supper' at the end of the day!

Samuel Pepys in his Diary tells of a pitched battle in 1664 between the weavers and the butchers, "Great discours of the fray yesterday in Moorfields, now the butchers at first did beat the weavers, but at last the weavers rallied and beat them ... and the butchers were soundly beaten out of the field and some deeply wounded and bruised: till at last the weavers went out tryumphing calling '£100 for a butcher'!"

There were more weaver riots in 1675 when the use of engine looms was introduced to weave silk ribbons.

At the end of the century Strype described "Spitalfields, a great harbour for poor Protestant Strangers, Walloons and French, who as in former Days, so of later, have been forced to become Exiles from their own Country for their Religion & for the avoiding cruel Persecution. Here they have found quiet and security, and settled themselves in their several Trades & Occupations: Weavers especially."

The move by the weavers to the newer communities of Spitalfields and Bethnal Green took place early in the 18th century.

Sources

Frances Consitt 'The London Weavers Company.'
Alfred Plummer 'The London Weavers Co. 1600-1970'.

Chapter 11

"At length they all to merry London came"
Edmund Spenser 1552-99.

The 16th century Huguenot families in London — first arrivals

The historical background of this century is worth summarising as a backdrop to the influx of Huguenot refugees who swarmed into England either directly from France or via the Low Countries (usually Bruges). The Low Countries were not a haven for long as the Spanish Catholic armies and their masters (Alva in particular) made life difficult and dangerous for the Huguenot refugees.

In 1517 Martin Luther nailed up his 95 Theses and the Reformation started.

In 1520 King Henry VIII disported himself on the Field of the Cloth of Gold.

In 1529 the name 'Protestant' originated.

In 1534 Henry VIIIs Act of Supremacy, asserts control over the English Church.

In 1541 John Calvin regained authority in Geneva.

In 1544 Henry VIII invaded northern France. Two brothers 'Captain De Fossé fought gallantly for him' (John and James).

In 1547 Henry VIII died and was succeeded by the boy King Edward VI.

In 1553 Lady Jane Grey briefly became Queen, but Mary succeeded in the same year. Following five years severe persecutions in England by the Catholics of the Protestants.

In 1558 Calais lost to the English: Mary died, succeeded by Elizabeth.

The French Huguenots arrive on the English beaches — 1685

In 1561 Mary Queen of Scots returned to Scotland.

In 1562 First war of religion started in France; the next year the catholic Duke de Guise was assassinated in Paris. First great Plague of London 22,000 people died.

In 1566/7 the Netherlands revolted against their Spanish oppressors.

In 1569 the Huguenots were defeated at the battle of Jarnac and their leader Condé was killed.

In 1572 the Massacre of Saint-Bartholomew in Paris set of massacres throughout France: at least 70,000 Huguenots were killed and emigrés poured into England usually through Dover and Canterbury.

In 1573 The Siege of la Rochelle, bastion of the Huguenots, by the Catholic armies.

In 1579 the Dutch republic of 7 northern provinces founded.

In 1587 Mary Queen of Scots was executed; the next year the second Duc de Guise (Catholic leader) was assassinated in Paris

In 1593 Henry IV at Navarre decided Paris was worth a Mass, became a Catholic and then King of France.

In 1598 the Edict of Nantes was signed guaranteeing protestants liberty of worship and the wars of religion ceased — for the time being.

The beginning of the 17th century was notable for the large families of silk weavers descending from Jaques/James and Marie his wife, with homes in Valenciennes, northern France and in London. His successful textile business ensured that most of his descendants later in the century were relatively well-off.

What is not clear at this stage is the link if any, between the textile traders/silk weavers and the jewellers/brokers deriving from Guines/Calais. The first group of Delaforce families emigrated from France mid-16th century and the second group at the end of the 17th century. The religious war of 1562 produced the James/ Jaques textile family and the revocation of the Edict of Nantes in 1685 the John/Jacques jeweller family.

Luckily there is an amazing amount of information available about the Delaforces in 16th century London. Despite the variety of strange permutations of the name (which is shown as seen in the appropriate records and archives) there seems to be a clear continuity throughout the century. Most of the sources are shown in chapter 1 — Sources under Aliens/Immigrants. In particular the Huguenot Society volumes VIII, X, XVIII, XXVII and XXXV were invaluable. Parish records exist sketchily for the last 30 years of the century. The first part of this chapter concentrates on the saga of the James/Jaques. Since marriages were made earlier — the man being about 20 — one must reckon on five generations to the century and the clues now forthcoming have been numbered 5,4,3,2 and 1 for each James (the earliest being numbered one). James the textile merchant is now shown as James 5. Research of course is not always a neat and tidy operation and clues do not appear always in chronological order! There was a major gold-strike immediately.

The Huguenot Society showed the Denization Rolls, Westminster 36 dated 1st July 1554. The long original parchment Roll can be seen (776a Roll of Queen Mary's reign) at the PRO Chancery Lane.

(1) "Jakys Delafowsse of Dorchester in Dorset. Aged 60 years is stayed for his age: 1 July 1554: came from France".

(2) "James De La Force came to London in 1532. Born in Paris. In 1554 was servant to Robert Snellying Esquire in Westminster".

They both appeared on the same roll with effectively the same name spelling. It is logical to assume they were father and son. So Jakes/James(1) was born about 1494, was alive in 1554, came originally from France and lived or had property in Dorset. James(2) was born in Paris about 1514/15 came to London when he was 18 and was living in Westminster and alive aged 40 in 1554. Subsequent research showed that in 1595 Robert Snelling as Chief Revenue Officer at Chichester had collected that year £1243-14-6¼ in import duties. The implication is that James(2) had been allocated a job with an important revenue officer by an influential trader (which is what James(1) turned out to be).

(3) The next three clues have been linked together since they refer to the same man. On 29 January 1551 James De La For(c)e was on the Denization Rolls 'from Lombardy'. As James Fosse he was shown in 1559 as a 'Lamberdes man, Parish of the Hospital'. In 1571 as "James Le Forsey dennyzein and Frenchman hath byn here twentie yeares.". The Lombards were money-men and James was probably a merchant banker/goldsmith. He lived in St. Olaves, Hart Street parish near the Tower of London. It is probable that he was James(3) born about 1533, but more likely to be grandson of Peter Force a goldsmith 1475-1525 living in Canterbury.

(4) In 1549 Tewes/James Fourse, stranger, servant to Thomas Brydges, pd VIIId tax: possibly James(3) born 1533.

(5) "James De Lafirs, stranger (i.e. foreigner) died 3 November 1573 St. Olaves, Hart Street parish" — from St. Botolphs, Bishopsgate records. This may refer to James(2).

(6) On 7th May 1595 Jaques dell Force was buried at St. Botolphs, Bishopsgate and this refers to a James (3) or (4).

(7) On 14 January 1562 James Fosse was on the Denization Rolls from the Dominion of the King of Spain and paid 6s 8d i.e. came from the Low Countries, but no clue about age or profession.

(8) In 1571 "James Drewriye (Drury) and Elye Fossie parteners, borne in Valencia (Valenciennes) came into this realme about 11J yeares past (i.e. 1568) for religion and live by dressing of flaxe". They worshipped at the French church and lived at St. Nicholas, Acorn, Langbourne Ward in London. Elye/Helie was born perhaps in 1540, married in 1560. (The first Helie appeared in the family in Bordeaux in 1080).

(9) In 1569 "Wa(l)ter Fose and Degyn his wyf borne in Flanders' with daughter Nell, sons Peter and James, dutch persons", were living in Est. Smithfeylde (the sons perhaps born about 1550).

(10) In 1550 James Dewfousse was a 'prentes', St. Clements Ward. Born about 1534 and probably a weaver. Possibly made a first marriage in 1554.

(11) November 1564 Jaques de la Fose/Fosse was already married to Denise, widow of late Pierre le Cuiginier at Threadneedle Street Church. As a widow perhaps of 28, and James about 30, almost certainly he was the 'prentes' of (10) and as an early member of Threadneedle Street congregation, certainly a silk weaver.

(12) In 1569 it was recorded that "Jacques de Fosse, ville (viel/vieux)" was alive and he and younger Jaques would have been born respectively about 1534 and 1554.

(13) James Fesse or Fosse and Jaqueline his wife and 1 servant were living in 1597 in St. Botolphs parish, possibly born 1554 and married 1574.

(14) In 1539, at a major wool sale in Calais, Jaques de Ford(?) and John Deffort/Delufall were buying large quantities of English wools at the Calais Staple. If they were brothers, despite the spelling, then there is a textile link much earlier in the century.

(15) The records at Valenciennes in northern France were carefully checked. "Les Chanteries de Valenciennes", and Pierre Joseph le Boucq's "Troubles à Valenciennes" (both in BM library). Helin Faulset/Fosset was mentioned in both, a John De Fors but no Jaques.

The clues most appropriate to James(5) born about 1574 and a textile merchant are (7), (10) and (11). It looks probable that James(5) was the grandson of the Threadneedle Street Capers Jaques and the widow Denise who thought so little of her father-in-law that she called him a Ruffian and Pimp! It is also probable that Helie/Elyne Fossie of Valenciennes was James(5) uncle.

The clue to Jaques(4) is number 13. James and Mary Delaforce were members of the St. Botolphs, Bishopsgate congregation and so were James and Jaqueline. James(5) obviously had money and capital to finance his merchanting business. James(4) and Jaqueline had a servant so they were not exactly destitute.

There is now no reason why Jakes Delafowsse(1) 1494-1560 and Jakes De La Force(2) of Paris 1514-1573 should not be the originators of the Jaques dynasty in the 16th century.

There were 'money men' in the family in this century — goldsmiths, silversmiths and Lombards men John Des Forts, 'Duch', a Goldsmith was in Aldersgate 1583 from Bruges. Peter (de) Force was the first. Born in 1472 in the Auvergne (elder son of Sir Bernard chapter 18 and brother to Anthony, chapter 17), he was a Goldsmith from 1500-1523 in Feversham and Canterbury and paid taxes for at least 3 years! A Peter Foytz 'stranger' of Norton Folgate/Bishopsgate of 1559 was possibly a son. Peter Du Four(c)e who died on 18 August 1576, St. Annes Blackfriars, Peter Duffoij(s) of Bruges who married Tannekin Backers of

Brussels on 5 May 1590 and lived in Redd Lion Alley, Pierre Du Fosse, a wedding witness in 1607 were probably all related. So too was Peter Force born about 1590 who sailed in the Mayflower as a member of the crew, with the Pilgrim Fathers in 1620.

There were several Edwards. Edward Force(1) lived in London in 1555, Edward Fousse(2) had a large family: Jellyan(Gillian) born 1566, Edward(3) born 1569, Emanuel 1574, William 1576 and Barbara 1572.

There were also Bernards in this century (the first recorded was in 1039 AD). Bernard Le Fors/La Fosse was born about 1540, married 1565 to Margaret Tannekin Van Alselot, lived at Dux or Dukes Place, by the Cree Church near the Tower of London. Their son Bernard was a Sylversmith, born 1566, married Abigail Vrambouts in 1594 and died in 1613 at St. Katherines, Cree Church. His son Bernard was a witness in 1605 at his cousins wedding the De Langhes at the Dutch Austin Friars Church. In 1598-1600 Barnard Le Fort/Laffort was living at Dukes Place with 3 widows. His mother Margaret was one, Tannekin and Jane the others.

In this century Peter, James, Edward and Bernards were all recorded as 'money men' of one kind or another.

At the end of the century in Tower Ward there were six related families. John married to Margaret Smith: Thomas and Jane Wright, William and Margaret Hatterley, William La Force/Le False/Fortin and Mary; Jaques and Mary (the textile merchants), and Michel (the Taylor) and Marie.

There were of course several unexplained oddities.

a. In 1524 Gerard le Fosse a 'Dutchman' was living in Villa West Monastery (Westminster) with a lay subsidy of XL shillings.

b. In 1541 William de Fore from the Duché de Cleves in England 1 year.

c. In 1542 "Gossen" Fosse was living in Tower Ward with lay subsidy of 11Jd.

d. In 1554 John De Foce was a baker from Davern, Picardy in England 30 years married to an Englishwoman.

e. In 1544 Gylys Fowcie of Dorchester, Dorset, Carpenter, aged 30, married to a Frenchwoman, in England 20 years "Impotent in his leg and broken in his bely".

f. In 1544 Guillam Forton a "Helyer" born in Normandy, in England 25 years.

g. In 1571 "Leavan" Fauser and Madeleine his wife 'twister of silkes' Douche, born in England 111J yeares' had 4 servants and lived in Coleman Street Warde (as did Jaques family 35 years later). Leavan might be a permutation of Jehan or John.

h. In 1567 John Forte, Dutchman, lived in Tower Ward.

i. In 1576 Daniell, his wife Judick/Judith de Fore/Force and daughters Lucy and Rebecca, Guy de Force (his son perhaps) and his wife Collette were living in Stone Alley, near St. Clements. Daniel died in 1574 and another Daniel in 1584 — a young son and later the father.

By using all of the sources listed for tracing Aliens and Immigrants a comprehensive picture of the 16th century Delaforces shows that the main family derived from Paris through Jakes/ James father and son. They were amongst the earliest Huguenots to leave France and be naturalised British Citizens in 1554.

Two firm links and bridgeheads with France have now been established: John who arrived in London about 1685 after the Revocation of the Edict of Nantes and James(1) and (2) just before the first French wars of Religion commenced.

Chapter 12

—Thomas Carlyle 1795-1881:
'The three great elements of modern civilisation, Gunpowder, Printing and the Protestant Religion.'

The London Churches and the Threadneedle Street Capers

The London churches were very important to the persecuted Huguenot refugees from France. They were a haven in a very dangerous and hazardous life and maintained a degree of family continuity with baptisms, marriages and the inevitable deaths and burials. Baptisms were frequently recorded not only in the French churches but also in the equivalent neighbourhood family church. The Delaforces, being an Anglo-French family, dutifully recorded their saga in both English and French churches. The London plagues of 1584, 1604, 1625 and 1665/6 took their dreadful toll. Many Delaforces lost their lives and the long lists of burials make sad reading.

Before 1666 the City of London had 97 churches within the wall and 10 without. Some were Saxon, some were Norman. Generally they had small towers with Norman arches and fonts. The Norman churches were built of Caen stone. Those with surviving Roman tiles after 1600 years were showing signs of turning to powder. In the Great Fire of 1666 no fewer than 86 parish churches were gutted. Sir Christopher Wren rebuilt no less than 51! Rebuilding was helped by a tax of three shillings on every ton of coal entering the Port of London. Wren's wife gave a lot of silver candlesticks to hasten the work on certain churches. By 1939 the number of City churches was reduced to 46, of which Wren had built 35.

The main English churches used by the family were St. Botolphs Bishopsgate, St. Leonards Shoreditch, Christchurch Spitalfields,

The original French Huguenot Threadneedle Street Church — 17th century

St. Mary Whitechapel, St. Dunstans Stepney and later St. Matthew Bethnal Green. Most of them have records dating fom 1558. Less frequently used were St. Olave Hart Street, St. Luke Old Street, St. Giles without Cripplegate and St. Martins in the Fields.

St. Botolphs is near the ancient gate dating from the 13th century and maintained by merchants of the Hanseatic League. St. Botolph the Saxon Saint was the patron saint of wayfarers which was appropriate to the early Delaforces. Mr W. Challen has summarised in 3 volumes the St. Botolphs parish registers. Many Delaforces were recorded there in the period 1558-1730 including James/Jaques and Mary's large family of weavers.

St. Leonards Shoreditch is just north of St. Botolphs with excellent records dating from 1558 available in the Guildhall library. Over 30 Delaforce marriages are recorded there in the period 1692-1731, 23 deaths and about 50 baptisms — mostly weavers living nearby in Cock Lane, Black Lion Yard, Holywell Street, Rose Alley, Godderds Rents, Long Alley etc.

Christchurh, Spitalfields Stepney was an important parish from 1729 for the weaver families living in Pearl Street, Browns Lane, Farthing Street, Brick Lane, Quaker Street, Wheeler Street, John Street, Old Artillery Ground and Gun Street. 20 Delaforce families worshiped there for 100 years. The parish bordered with St. Botolphs and St. Mary Whitechapel.

St. Dunstans Stepney was more isolated, about a mile from Bishopsgate and half a mile south of Bethnal Green. 40 Delaforces were married here in the period 1646-1849.

St. Matthews Row Parish of Bethnal Green was built by George Dance in 1746. Until the 18th century Bethnal Green was a small hamlet with the remains of a medieval Bishops hall and a rich mans country house. Silkweaving worked up from Spitalfields into the south west corner and the population of 15,000 in 1742 had increased to 82,000 in 1847. 35 Delaforces died and were buried at St. Matthews and 32 baptisms recorded. There was considerable overlap with St. Dunstans Stepney, St. Mary Whitechapel and Christchurch Spitalfields.

King Edward IV signed a Charter allowing the French Huguenots and Flemish Walloon churches to open in London. During Queen Mary's reign they were dissolved. There were a number of Fench Huguenot churches in London well documented by the Huguenot Society. From 1550 when it was built, the Threadneedle Street church was the most important. In 1846 it moved to St. Martins-le-Grand and finally in 1893 to Soho Square. The original records are kept at the PRO Chancery Lane. As early as 1627 Jacque's and Marie's family were worshipping there. Three other Huguenot families were closely linked to the early Delaforce weavers — the Caulliers, des Carpenteries and the Largilliers. The four families intermarried. Since the Temoins or witnesses were always recorded for each wedding and baptism over a period of a hundred years, one could trace the familiar names in varying patterns.

The last part of this chapter consists of verbatim extracts from the Actes de Consistoires which were the daily or weekly minutes of the deliberations of the Elders of the Fench Threadneedle Street church. The Actes were compiled by Antoine du Ponchel session clerk of St. Anthony's chapel. Huguenot Society volumes 38 and 48 record most of the earlier years from 1550 onwards in diary form. The Elders were very strict and families entered in the records were definitely in disgrace. This seemed to happen to 16th century Delaforces quite frequently.

A. In 1560 Jehan Fortin (Latin version of De Force) was on the mat!

B. In 1564 "Jaques de la Fose, quy a espouse (Denise) la vecue (widow) de feu (late) piere le cuiginier se presenty pour comuniquer à la Cène (Masse) se excusant que de 2 ans ny avoyt point este prometant aire meilleur diligence pour launiere, lui fut a corde de sy presenter. Jeudi dernier de Novembre".

C. In 1564 "ledy jour Jehan Fortin amenyt une fille au consistoire nomme Katerine Gergart. Ledyt Fortin de prendre pour femme ladyte Katerine. Jehan Fortin fut admonesté de ce qu'il ne honte point les sermons ne qu'il ne vient à la Cène..".

D. In 1564 "Ledyt jour fut faiet Raport par Maistre Fichet du scandale adueau a la maison de Jaques de la Fosse et Jaques Chaumois de ce que la femme didyt Jaques a appellé son beau père (father-in-law) "Ruffien", et "Maqueaureau" (Pimp!): il furent tous appellés au Consistoire".

E. In 1571, 12 September "Jan de le Fosse venu de Lille depuis un an. En quis comme desus a dit qu'il na cognu la fille ny comment la chose est venue seullement qu'il a entendu que si l'homme se fut bien gardé il ne fut pas mort et que les voisins (neighbours) disoient que le cop (body) restoit mortel qu'il a cognu le personage et veu aller les rues frequentant les tavernes et yttonnant comme de coustume par lespace de 3 sepmaines (weeks) apres le coup (blow) donne.".

F. 1572 Jan de la Fosse sera manle pour mercredy prochaine par Fontaine (name of the Priest).

G. 2 January 1572 Jaques de le Fosse, sa femme et la femme de Jacques Chermoise ont faict plaincte (complaint) de Jean de Vick disans que ledict de Vick auroit dict que Pierre le Cuisinier estoit ung larron (thief) et qu'il jamais faict autre chose que de rober et quant il estoit trouvé au faict disoit qu'il ne faisoit que jover et dìsent les dìctz plaìndans que ledìct de vick auroìt dìct en presence de Jaques Chermoise et de Pierre Hernet dict Le Pelau. Tout ce different et debat ne procede que dune cedule portant a la somme de 23s 4d sterlin que le dict Jaques de la Fosse demand au dict de Vick (Viguer).

H. 16 January 1572 Jan De La Fosse enquis sil na point baille un soufflet à Anthoine Troielle en plaine vue sil ne la point appelle faux raporteur aiant une fausse lange de serpent (!) un garcon et un Glistre Confesse que ovy se plaindant quil avoit chargé sa femme destre pailarde mesme en ce pays...

I. 30 January 1572: Fontaine (the Minister) a exhibe par escrit les plaintes de Jan de la Fosse on les envoiera a Nordwis (Norwich) et les remains seront ovys pour mercredy prochain...

J. 6 February 1572 Jehan de la Fosse plaintif contre Anthoine Truyelle demovant a Nordwits la produict pour tesoins Jeanne L'homme femme à Hubert Lengle... que A.T. disoit en sa maison que la femme Jehan de la Fosse estoit ribaude (ribald) ce propos furent tenus en Arras plus par le chemin de Nordwits il y a demy an environ...

K. 9 January 1574 Jaques de la Fosse et Jan de Vignes sestant remis pour un different en arbitrage, Robert Huttal, Estienne Le bras et Thomas Hasqvent raportent que Ledyt de Fosse ne veut obtemperer.

L. In 1574 Isabeau Pennis venue au Consistoire remonstrance luy

a este faite des injures dites par elle a Jean Fortin lesquelles elle n'a voulu recognoistre et sa mocquant desdytes admonitions et du Consistoire sen est allée.
M.1574 Remonstrance luy a esté faicte touchant ses rebellions appiniatres et detractemens quil a fait et dict par cyderant tant de leglise (church) du consistoire que des arbittres lesquels sestvient emploies affin de la pacifier avec Jean Fortin. Dont il en a recognu faute en consistoire en la presence desdict arbittres et s'est reconsilié à la compagnie et ausdictz arbittres confessant sa faute en demandant pardon à Dieu et a tons ceux qu'il avoit offer se promettant aussy de vivre plus christienement a lavenir.
N. 1577 Des promesses que Guillaume Fortin auroit faire a la Fremine et quilz ont trouves.

Although the old French is difficult to translate the gist of the capers of John, James and William with their spouses or girlfriends is clear. The Elders obviously thought they were a difficult family to have in the congregation, either because they thought the sermons too boring or because of noisy domestic scenes which were brought to the notice of the Elders. In a foreign land the new churches were on their best behaviour and the Elders were most strict with their sometimes unruly flocks.

The Dutch Walloon church of Austin Friars has records from 1559 and the parish records are published in books by Mr W.J.C. Moens. On 29 August 1594 Bernard de la Fosse of Bruges married Abigail Vrombouts of Sanwits (Sandwich, Kent). 6 daughters were born. In 1619 their son Bernard la Fosse was a wedding witness. Bernard was grandson of Bernard Le Fors/La Fosse who was married to Margaret (nee Tannekin Van Alselot) and born about 1544. They were silversmiths living in Dukes Place near the Cree church in Bishopsgate.

Various Anthonies (Anthoni de Fosse in 1594) were also recorded as being part of the Dutch church congregation during the 16th century. Peter Duffoij(s) of Bruges married Tannekin Backer of Brussels on 5 May 1590 in the Dutch church.

Immigrants from the Low Countries came into England to escape from the Spanish invaders catholic regime. The repressions in the

Low Countries were severe but not on such a scale as in France where major pitched battles were fought between rival armies of Huguenots and Catholics. Members of the French family who as refugees had found refuge in Bruges usually worshipped at the Austin Friars Dutch Walloon church rather than at Threadneedle Street which was dominated by the French silkweavers. The Bernards, Anthonies and Peters in the Dutch church were either 'money men' or politicians and certainly not silk weavers.

The other French Huguenot Churches were La Patente, Spitalfields; Thorney; Bristol; Plymouth; Stonehouse; Thorpe-le-soken; Savoy; Le Carré; Berwick St; Spring Gardens; Les Grecs; Chapel Royal; St. James; Swallow St; the Tabernacle; Glasshouse St; Leicester Fields; Rider Court; Hungerford Market; Le Petit Charenton; West Street; Pearl Street Crispin St; Swallow St; St. Martin Orgars; St. Jean Spitalfields; Artillery Church, Wheeler St; Swanfields, Hoxton; La Patente de Soho; and Rerpertoire Generale.

There were Huguenot churches in Ireland: St. Patrick & St. Mary, Dublin; various French Nonconformist churches in Dublin and Portarlington. Some 40 churches spread over England and Ireland served the spiritual needs of the 100,000 Huguenots who had fled from France. Baptisms and marriages are faithfully recorded and well indexed. These volumes should be considered a prime source for families with Huguenot ancestors.

The main sources for this chapter are the Huguenot Society volumes of Parish Registers of Threadneedle Street church and Moens well researched books containing the registers of the Walloon church at Austin Friars.

Chapter 13

The Book of Common Prayer
"Lord, thou has been our refuge from one generation to another"

The Guisné Delaforces

In chapter 4 Sieur Jean Delafous, jeweller arrived in England after the Revocation of the Edict of Nantes in 1685 and later married Susanne Massienne from Paris. Jean in his records stated that he was 'from Chateau Herault' which is modern Chattellrault close to Poitiers, but 300 km from Paris. It must have been a difficult question for Jean to answer. He could equally correctly have said (a) Guisné near Calais, (b) Paris, (c) Chatellrault, (d) the Auvergne, (e) Gascony, (f) Bordeaux and the Gironde (Bourg, Bazas, La Reole etc.) and (g) Navarre. That was the route which his family had travelled before they reached England. In this chapter he is called Jean(1), his father Jean(2), his grandfather Jean(3) and his great-grandfather Jean(4).

Both Jean (1672-1730) and James (1494-1550) descended from Sir Anthony of Paris, Bordeaux and Gascony (1475-1530). This chapter sets out to prove the line of Jean/Johns from 1600 to 1672. They spent about 70-75 years as merchant traders/secret agents, possibly goldsmiths in Guisné which was the major refuge for Huguenots not only in France but in Europe. Occasionally they took refuge in Bruges. They spent some time in Paris, Orleans Poitiers, Chatellrault area.

The Huguenot temple in Guisné was founded between 1562 and 1568, a few years after the capture of Calais by the Duke of Guisné. At one time 3000 Huguenots, out of a total of 15,000, were worshipping at the largest Huguenot temple in France. It is sad that there is now no vestige of traces of the original temple in Guisné, which was a few miles inland from Calais.

Unfortunately only a small part of the Guisné church records — from 1668-1680 — have survived. The Huguenot Society (Volume 3) have produced an admirable record of this twelve year period. The original records are in the Boulogne archives. In the Oxford Bodleian library the Tanner MSS XCIV p.103 states that 'de la Force is a common Guisné name'. It is true tht from this short period almost 80 years of family history can be traced.

Boulogne was famous for false names and forged documents, as refugees endeavoured to leave the country: The Delaforces adopted an alias. They chose Jennepin. They came from Oleron — Olehain — Allouagne — Lomagne, and perhaps the alias derived from an amalgam of their past. A later version in London was Gillemain. The alias was used in the Calais and Guisné area, and only in this period — perhaps 1600-1680. The church records would say 'Jean Jennepin 'dit' de la Force'. It would have been interesting to know whether they were known overtly and particularly to strangers as 'Jennepins'. The Christian names given were mostly from the Old Testament; Isaac, Daniel, Abraham, even a Solomon are to be found, but John is the name carried through the century.

Jean Delaforce(4) was born in Paris in 1600, probably came to seek refuge in Calais and Guisne after 1610 when Henry IV was assassinated. By 1628 the last bastion of the Protestants — La Rochelle, had fallen to the Catholic armies and the Protestants were on the defensive. In 1640 the French Catholic armies devastated Guisné.

Jean(4) married about 1620. His son Jean(3), a 'marchand', married in 1642 at Guisné to Juditch Boucquoi. This marriage produced four sons: Jean(2) born 1643 (and married in 1671), Abraham born 1644 (and married in 1675), Claude born in 1645, and Daniel born in 1646 who emigrated to England was mentioned in Chapter 7 (le chevalier), and a daughter Judith, baptised in 1656 and married in 1677.

In 1671 Jean de la Force(2) married Madeline Jacob; Abraham his brother and Jean Jennepin de la Force (father) were witnesses. Children born to them were Jean(1), Mary and Isaac.

In 1677 and again 17th December 1683, Daniel de la Force wrote direct to King Charles II to enable his brother "a merchant in Calais who desires to settle in England, to come to England with his effects". Unfortunately the first letter had no affect, and there is no reason to belve that the second letter had either. Now John and Abraham his brother were certainly merchants in 1675, but in 1683/5 it is Isaac who is known to be in England and writing to the Archbishop of Canterbury for help!

In 1677 the Temple records showed Jean(4) Jennepin dit La Force père "Le Dit Jean Dois Etre Enrigitre Dans Le Mois Avril De L'Annee Passes A Ssavoir 1676. Il N'a Pu Estre Enregitre En Son Rang" of Sieur or Sir. On 22nd October 1678 Jean de la Force(4) senior died in Calais aged 78.

Chapter 14 gives some account of the family as secret agents in this period when the family were always uncertain when the Catholic troops would throw them into the Channel.

The State papers of Charles I, William & Mary show some more news item.

(a) 26 Nov 1625 "The Council of Charles I wrote to Monsier la Force at Calais that 'their owners might have their goods, saved from the wreck of various English vessels sunk off Calais' ".

(b) 20 Nov 1647 "My Lord Willoughby arrived at Nantes and lodged att M. Fos an English merchant, his house upon the fosse".

(c) May 1647 the Samuel Pepys letters show that "De la Fosse, a merchant of St Valery en Caux, near Boulogne was dealing in corn and cloth".

(d) 9th May 1648 "Mr Le Force is Master of the Mermaid at Calais."

(e) 1657/58 "M de la Force, the English Government agent at Calais."

(f) 14 Ap 1661 Hester de le Fosse, daughter of Mary Force writes to Lady Arlington for help "Her mother dead in 1659 and family recently over from France". Possibly this was Jean(4)s wife whom he married about 1620.

(g) July 1666 Lord Arlington to the Mayor of Dover "The King is informed of the breaking out of the infection (plague) in M La Force's house in Dover." An account to be returned to him (Charles II State Papers).

THE HUGUENOT SOCIETY OF LONDON

THIS IS TO CERTIFY THAT

Patrick de Fleurriet Delaforce

HAS BEEN ELECTED A FELLOW OF

THE HUGUENOT SOCIETY OF LONDON

having for its objects THE INTERCHANGE AND PUBLICATION OF KNOWLEDGE RELATING TO

The History of the Huguenots in France and adjoining countries;

The Huguenot Emigrations from France;

The Refugee Settlements throughout the world, particularly those in Great Britain, Ireland, and the Channel Islands, and the resulting effects of those Settlements upon the Sciences and Arts, and upon the Economic and Social Life of the several places in which they were made;

Huguenot Genealogy & Heraldry and Huguenot Church and other Registers;

TO FORM A BOND OF FELLOWSHIP *among some of those who inherit or admire the characteristic Huguenot virtues, and who desire to perpetuate the memory of their Huguenot ancestors.*

PRESIDENT

HONORARY SECRETARY

DATE 12th November 1980

Certificate of Fellowship of the Huguenot Society of London

By chance the Huguenot Society volume 3 showed clearly the French connection, with generations of the family perched uneasily in Calais, and occasionally in Dover, waiting perhaps for the blow to fall, as indeed it did in 1685. When Louis Quatorze, under consistent and growing pressure from the Catholic Church, agreed to sign the Revocation of the Edict of Nantes, he had no idea that so many wealthy, skilled artisans and traders would emigrate. France suffered a considerable commercial recession for nearly a century after the Huguenots left the country.

The French civil servants faithfully recorded "Estat des biens (goods) abandonné des fugitifs des Villes & Gouvernment de Calais et Ardres en 1687 — Abraham "Jennepin" de La Force et ester Barizeau, sa femme, maisons et terres à Calais, moulin (mill) à huile (oil), proche de le pont Saint-Pierre".

Abraham had fled the country, and so did his brothers and their families, leaving practically everything they owned behind them.

Chapter 14

Baroness Orczy 1865
"We seek him here, we seek him there,
Those Frenchies seek him everywhere
Is he in Heaven? — Is he in Hell?
That dammed, elusive Pimpernel."

The Secret Agents

The family deriving from Sir Bernard (chapter 18, Sir Anthony (chapter 17) and then the two sons James (chapter 15) and John (chapter 16) were living in turbulent times of political and religious wars. But also they were faced with problems of patriotism and conscience. Where they French or English? They spoke French as their natural tongue but they all spoke English and used it as frequently. For two hundred years they served English, French and Spanish Kings. Anthony's four sons were divided in their religious loyalties; two were fervent early Huguenots and the other two probably stayed Catholic. This made for additional stresses within the family.

There is evidence in the British state papers in the British Library and Guildhall (well indexed) that for another 150 years into the 18th century, Delaforces were secret agents for the British government. Travel between France and England was easy and possible in wartime.

The first scene opens in the middle of the 16th century:

(1) 28 November 1552 Mr Killigrew a senior politician of Chelsea had a discussion about 'the defences of Metz with one De Force, a banished man'. Six years later Calais surrendered and the English had no base in France.

(2) In 1583 the Harleian MSS show "original memorial of the baron of Sance and the Sieur de (la) Fos, agents of Monsieur de Soubize'. This relates to John shown as Jehan Forteau (in Latin) de Soubize, one of the Huguenots condemned to death in 1569 at Bordeaux.
(3) In 1588 the Catholic Duke of Guise was assassinated in Paris, and this was witnessed by a John De la Fosse, the Paris 'curé ligeur.'
(4) The Cecil Papers Vol. V of the Salisbury MSS show some remarkable evidence of the Delaforce involvement in power politics. there are three letters addressed to the Earl of Essex. 14th September 1595 Edmund Wiseman to his Master, the Earl of Essex, "Senor Peres hath showed one of your Lordships first letters to M de la Force and others of the French. He hath not received any crowns of the French. I think crowns can not make him stay. His fear is more than any man that lives. He is lodged in a house that was the Duke of Mercuryes given by this King to the last King's wife. His sister, Madame, is come to this town from St. Jarmanes (probably St. Germain, west of Paris)... useth Senor Perez kindly."

22nd Septmber 1595 Edward Wylton to the Earl of Essex, "The cause why Monsieur de Force courteth him, more than the rest is that hee hopeth the King may be drawn by his counsels to invade Spayne, by way of Navarre, by which course hee promiseth great honor and advauncement to himself, as his followers stick not to affirme by reason of his goverment in those frontiers."

Late September 1595 Edward Wilton to the Earl of Essex, "The King arrived at Paris the last of September. M de la Force and Antonio Perez went to meet him at Fontainbleau. The King used him well and means no doubt to gratify him with many honourable courtesies if he could be content to frame his humours to accept of such as France."

The way the letters are written by two of Queen Elizabeth's envoys to the Earl of Essex suggests that Antonio Perez, a Spanish agent of the English government, and M de la Force were in partnership to persuade the French King to attack Spain (via the French King's own territory of Navarre). France making war on Spain would be to England's advantage. The quotes "he hath not received any crowns of the French, I think crowns can not make him stay" (i.e. in France) indicate that he was pro-English. He was one of the distinguished Anglo-French Delaforces of Paris, Rouen, Dieppe, Calais and London. They had sufficient rank and position to write direct to Queen Elizabeth and Cecil. He was probably therefore a grandson of Anthony called Jean De La Fosse, one of King Henri IVs ministers.

(5) In 1604 there was a major political spy scandal in Paris. An Englishman, or perhaps more accurately, a Welshman called Morgan together with Sieur de Fortan (the same man in league with Antonio Perez in 1595 onwards) were accused of plotting treason against Henri IV. Apparently de Fortan had been in France for about a year and amongst other things was living with Madame la marquise de Verneuil. She not only had a distinguished husband the Sieur d'Antrague, Marquis de Verneuil, but she was also King Henry IV's mistress. For instance in 1601 the King was paying her for favours rendered £1,500 per quarter!

Of course there was the usual Capucin monk lurking in the corridors called P. Archange (believe it or not!) who supplied information to all and sundry.

The lady's husband and her brother the Comte d'Auverge were in the plot. De Fortan's cover was that he was teaching the Spanish language to various nobles including Monsieur de Villeroy for five or six months.

The plot was to encourage the Spaniards to invade France either from south or north for which the rewards would be tremendous. Castles in Portugal were offered to the French nobles in the plot. They were betrayed (of course) and charged with an assassination plot against Henri IV. The nobles De Fortan and Morgan were sent to the Bastille where the latter confessed (Cependant les prisoniers sont fort interrogez afin que par leu declaration l'on puisse connoistre toute la verité de cette action). The plotters had apparently received at various times 'dix mille pistolle du Roy d'Espagne par les mains du Sieur de Fortan, prisonnier détance à la Bastille'. The lady talked herself out of trouble and resumed (a little later) her relationship with the King. Morgan was assuredly on King James I secret service payroll.

It appeared that the French nobles escaped with their lives, perhaps because of the Marquise's undoubted charms (she died in 1633 aged 50). The Sieur de Fortan was Jean De la Fosse, minister of the Army for King Henri IV but temporarily disgraced in the period 1604-1607.

(The source for this story is unusual — 'Receuil de pieces interessantes' published in Amsterdam in 1699 — republished in 'Archives Curient de l'histoire de France', series 1 book 14, P.166 by P. Danjou.).

(6) Now for a mystery. From 1580 to 1599 a Francois le Forte with a brother Jaques appears in the State papers. He corresponded with Sir Robert Cecil. He was a wealthy Huguenot, Married in Antwerp to Mary de Moncheron with 10 children. He was a wily, shrewd merchant who supplied Sir Walter Raleigh and many others. His main business was dealing in white cloths rom Normandy and imported oils. He was on familiar terms with Cecil and the Earl of Essex. He supplied the King of France with Spanish wines (from Navarre). He certainly supplied the English ministers with secret information from France.

(7) 26th May 1606 Captain Ersfield to the Earl of Salisbury "A ship from Bordeaux with 150 soldiers, all Gascoignes, bound to serve the states, all voluntairies, under M de la Force their Captain to Dover." This small force were on their way to the Low Countries to fight the Spanish catholic invaders.

(8) 1614 James de la Forca/Force and Claude de le Fos involved in English-French diplomatic services (Claude de la Fos/Fors married Mary in 1653).

(9) 6th June 1621 M de Fores/de Fos/de Force from La Rochelle visited England to ask King James I for help with the succour of Huguenots besieged at La Rochelle.

(10) 1622 a Daniel and David de Fos wrote to the Duke of Buckingham at Portsmouth from Dover, requiring assistance.

(11) 26th November 1625 M de la Force (John born 1600) was the British Government agent in Calais.

(12) 9th July 1627 letter to John le Force merchant of Lisle near Chatellrault "their friend from Portugal with his man landed in the Downs — had been imprisoned at Dover — hopes for their release and their letters were safe."

(13) 1657/58 M. de la Force (Jean) was the British Agent in Calais.

Certainly John (2) born about 1620.

(14) Isaac Doriflaus, 13 March 1654 wrote to Secretary of State John Thurloe. "One Jeniper (the alias for the Delaforce family in Calais) hath been employed in that place (Calais) for many years and was put in by the Earle of Suffolk, being his servant, the said Earl being then Admiral & the place being at his disposal."

(15) The Clarendon State Papers showed three more news items. Colonel Blampfield wrote to Sir John Hobart from Paris on April 28 with this enclosure for Secretary of State, John Thurloe. "At Callaice (Calais) left some cloth in pawn at Mr De La Force's house where he (Blampfield) lay sick and here owes for meat and lodging and not having had one penny except by pawnning or selling some of his necessaries".

(16) Jan 1658, the year of Cromwell's death. William Thomas, alias Sir J. Grenville writes to Sir Edward Hyde 'Remarks in disguised language upon the King's affairs, his agents annd friends in England. Mention of M. de Fosse and others' (Vol.59).

(17) Aug 1658 'letters sent to Calais à M. Bamfield chez M. de la Force a la Syrenne' (Vol.58).

(18) 28th April 1672 Lord Arlington, another politician, writes "Monsieur La Force junior (this is John(2) of Guisné) a merchant at Calais to be recruited as an agent: M De Foy at Boulogne also a correspondent." John Carlisle writes to Joseph Williamson, Secretary of State "I have again written to Monsieur La Force junior a Merchant of Calais to keep a correspondence with you. If they have any occasion (need) at Whitehall, you will be their friend." The Guisné church registers of 24th April 1673 showed John as "Jean Jennepin (alias) dit de la Force junior".

Joseph Williamson, Secretary of State to Lord Arlington, Clerk to the Kings Council "We shall lodge in Calais at the Golden Dragon, Mr La Force and hope to be there.. shortly." The 'we' referred to were the Navy Commissioners (State Papers Cav II 435 No.59).

(19) 31st October 1689 a curious and funny episode is recorded in the William and Mary State Papers "3 square glass bottles in 2 leather cases were brought from London and delivered to Mrs La Force at the Kings Head in Dover and His Majesty's service requiring that Mrs La Force be shortly searched and transmit the bottles with all speed to me with an account of the proceedings". From Whitehall the Earl of Shrewsbury to Deputy Governor of Dover. We will never know whether the lady was smuggling good French cognac or perfume or whether there were secret papers concealed within the flasks.

(20) 22 August 1691. Admiral Russell to Lord Nottingham "The master of one of these French vessels tells me that they've constant intelligence from England about the fleets. Mr Forty of St. Malo an English merchant with brother merchants in London, well-known by an officer in the Fleet who tells me they are very busy inquisitive men." This can be interpreted in several ways. Disinformation is a modern word. False information is a phrase which may have been more appropriate.

(21) In 1691 Simeon Lafosse, and in 1697 James Defors, a French Protestant, received official passes to go to Holland.

(22) On 21st November 1691 Charles de la Fosse, Elizabeth his wife, Elizabeth his mother, his daughter Margaret and 2 servants received a pass to go to France.

(23)1699-1702. The Historical Manuscripts Commission 8th Report 1881, Vol. 7 P.14 "Other correspondents were French refugees, the chief of whom was M Caillaud and M de la Force. The latter seems to have acted in concert with Hopkins and remittances were sent for division between the two. Caillaud was expected to discover amongst other matters the movements of the French Navy.

(24) 11th January 1701/2. The Earl of Manchester, Secretary of State wrote to M de la Force to divide a sum of 100 Louis 1400 Francs with Mr Hopkins and stimulating him to increased exertions. On 22nd January 1702 he wrote again to M de la Force "expressing esteem for frank and honest manners." An elaborate system of code names was set up in London — Gardiner, Wilton, Peterson and Ford merchants in trade. The Post Master would then deliver the letters from M de la Force direct to the Earl of Manchester. This was probably Sieur John de la Force, whose father was recruited in 1672 — a merchant of Calais.

It is clear that the Anglo-French family were secret agents for about 150 years with frequent visits across the channel on behalf of the English government.

Chapter 15

"Captain or Colonel or Knight in Arms",
Milton 1608-1674.

James and the Queens of Scotland & England

Jacques De la Force was born about 1494 in Paris. He was son of Sir Anthony, grandson of Sir Bernard and greatgrandson of Lord Bernard, killed at the battle of Barnet.

By the time Jacques was a schoolboy his father was a member of the French parliament in Paris, and Jaques De la Fonte/Forte was shown with his father Antoine de Foers/Fours in "Gallia Christiana" chartes of about 1502 (French Ecclesiastical Records).

In Sept. 1524 Jaques/Jacquet de la Fosse was a 'Mesureur de Terre Jure pour le Roi Francois I.' The Fench King ordered Jaques, who lived in Rouen, to make a detailed survey of the new port and town of Le Havre. "Process-verbal de la mesure de divers lieux et places fieffés en la ville du Havre, ordonné par arrest du Parlement de Rouen." The complete survey was for tax reasons, but also to establish Le Havre's potential as a seaport, as shown in Stephanode Merval's book 'Source documents fondation de Havre' pp.240-255. The original survey is in the Archives Seine-Inferieure (Papiers de chapitre de Notre Dame de Rouen). One of the major landowners in Le Havre was Guillaume de Fosse.

In February 1537 Charles de Grave wrote to Lord Lisle "You had given me charge to write by the hand of monsieur Delfault of Gravelines" and in 1538 Sieur Jacques de Fours is seen in Rouen.

On 29 September 1539 Jaques de Ford and his brother John (Deffort and Delufall) were buying large quantities of English wools and textiles at public auction at the Calais Staple.

On 20 December 1539 Sieur Jaques Dufours of Paris is mentioned in Lady Lisle's published letters.

In 1544 two brothers "Capitaines nommés Forces" were fighting bravely for the English in Boulogne during King Henry VIII's invasion of France. (Histoire Boulonnais J. Hector de Rosny vol.3 p.406). This is significant. James and John had obviously, like their grandfather and great-grandfather, come down, like all true Gascons, on the side of the English. John is shown in a separate chapter as an important envoy of King Henry VIII.

On 22 March 1544 Jaques de le Fers and his brother Michel petitioned the English King "for a licence to bring to the Isle of Jersey unarmed ships during the present war with the French King — 1000 tons of canvas, dolas, lokorum, olrons, crestclothe and poldavys and carry away 1000 tons woolen cloth, tin and lead." The next month they requested a smilar form of barter transaction.

In 1553, Jaques owned lands at Colemberg (Boulogne) and Haimicourt (Abbeville).

On 1st July 1554 Jaques Delafowsse and his son Jaques De la Force were both naturalised in Westminster Denization Rolls. Jacques was shown to be about 60 years of age and to have an estate in Dorset at Dorchester.

In July 1555, Jaques, Monsieur de Fors was Lieutenant-General of Dieppe and the provice for King Henri II of France. The King wrote to Jaques 'au chasteau d'icelle ville pour trouver le moien de recouver quelques vaisseaux propres pour le service du Roy". And surprise "et néantmoins que les deniers du Roy ne fussent encoure arriver pour paier les frais". Like many Kings of the middle ages, funds were always slow in arriving. Anyway Jaques received some very nice letters from the King which counted for something. In brief, he expected Monsieur de Fors to sieze a minimum of 6 ships for the Royal Fleet. "Toute fois, M. de Fors, sage et avisé chevalier pour tout cela" set to work and briefed the local admiral and captains (maistres et carsonniers) and quartermasters. What followed was, in effect, a full scale naval battle between the French fleet out of Dieppe and twenty four "hourques' from Flanders. After heavy losses on both sides and after some excursions to Dover (connected with wine-tasting and jollity), M. de Fors was able to report to his royal master that he had achieved a notable victory and obtained some six (probably rather battered) additional ships for the Kings navy. Finally the King sent back to M. de Fors a very nice letter complimenting his lieutenant-general on his victory. Almost certainly 'les deniers' never arrived, nor were they intended to arrive!

(Source: F. Daniou, 'Archives Curieuses de l'histoire de France'. 1st series vol 3 pp 150-170 entitled 'Histoire de la Bataille Navaille les Dieppois & Flamens').

James was converted to Calvinism by M. D'Andelot Francis de Chatillon, brother of the great Admiral Coligny. The French chronicles of Dieppe by M.L. Vitet (Histoire des Anciennes Villes) mention Jaques frequently as M. Force or M. Desfort. In the autumn of 1557 the Scottish parliament approved the marriage of Mary, Queen of Scots, to the young Dauphin of France — Francis. In April 1558 eight commissioners, bishops and lords, including Lord James Stuart, Mary's half-brother, sailed to France as representatives of Scotland. They signed an agreement with France that Scotland was to keep its independence. On their way home to Scotland they were suddenly struck by illness as a result of which four of them died in one night. James Stuart himself fell ill, although he did recover. Mary spoke of this decimation as being God's will, but at the time a more sinister explanation was advanced. Knox murmured of poison, either French or Italian. It was rumoured that the Catholic Guises had determined to poison the commissioners because they had discovered something about the secret treaties which signed away Scotland's birthrights.

The Lord High Treasurer's records vol.10 p.393 of 1558 show three items of expenditure by Queen Mary at her court in Edinburgh, to James De la Force, Admiral of the Fleet including the ship Carrogun. "Item the xj day of October to Monsieur Delaforce Capitaine of Deip & Admirale to the schippis in hamebringing of the lordis fra oure soverane Ladeis marriage ane(one) cheyne of gold weyand ijlij unce wecht (ounces weight) contenand iij crownis of the sone extending to iijjlxxxij Li x s."

"Item, the third day of Occtober to Alexander Forestar Carritee pursevant and John Caldor, messinger passand of Edinburgh witht ane chagre of the Quenis grace to the tounis of Sanct androis,

Dunde(e) and Monrois to inquire for the Admirale of the France schippis laitlie cumin in with the lordis." iiij li xs.

"Item be the Quenis grace charge, deliverit to Rothesay herauld passand of Edinburgh to Dunde witht Monsieur De la Force, Capitane of the Carrogoun that he be sufficientlie furnesit in all his necessaris. xl s."

But on 17 November 1558 Mary, Queen of England, died 'with Calais engraved on her heart'.

In 1558 "Jacobus Forsans thesaurius (hoarder of money!) anno 30 Juli 1558 sententiam obtinuit a praeposito (Prevostship) Paris super justitia plailliace. Thesaurii (treasury) St. Frambaldi of Paris." (Gallia Christiani) It appears that the French court honoured James for his political activities, and had become a wealthy man.

From 1558 to the end of 1562 Jacques was Governor for both Rouen and Dieppe until the French Catholic armies overwhelmed Dieppe in late autumn 1562. For several years M. de Fors/Fosse/Force wrote direct to Secretary of State Cecil and to the Queen 'Mother' Elizabeth I. He was undoubtedly a key figure in the defence of both towns.

In 1560 "M de Fors makes sure that no harm comes to the Lutherans".

Francis Edwards to Lord Cecil 15 December 1560 "Monsieur de Fosse will be new Captain of Dieppe.

On 1 anuary 1561 "M de Fosse governs the town and castle of Dieppe and Rouen again".

In 1562 the State Papers No.881/2/3 show "Edw. Ormesby of Dieppe on 20 October. Montgomery sent to M De Fortz for succours". 'M Du Bois-Denalbout was sent hither with a trumpet for to M. De Fors from the Queen Mother with a letter of credence from her signed by herself only declaring that Rouen had made composition (peace)' 'The Captain De Fors assembled the council of the town with the burgesses of the same and these resolved upon an answer to the Queen Mother..the effect whereof he sends enclosed'.

In 1562 "he praises the liberality of the Queen, and asks Cecil for more troops to defend Rouen." "Some troops are sent by the Queen from Rye to succour the French Protestants."

Jacques tells the Queen "the writer and all the inhabitants of Dieppe are ready to render all due obedience to their lawful Sovereign". The rash and impetuous Earl of Essex challenged the Governor to a duel or a tournament, which James sensibly refused!

Despite the visit of Mr Henry Killigrew, a Government official, and "his wife Madame de Fors came with divers gentlemen and ladies in August 1562", Rouen and Dieppe were doomed. Survivors including M de la Force arrived in Rye, as Mr Young, Mayor of Rye, reports to Secretary of State Cecil. Jacques hastened from Rye to London to see the Queen with the Earl of Warwick. "M de la Force, Capitaine du Chateau de Dieepe se retirent en Angleterre".

The following year, Jacques was back in Le Havre-de-Grace with a gascon captain, Sieur Catteville Malderé, in the Queen's cause. On the 6th October 1562 3,000 English troops occupied Le Havre. (Source State Papers Domestic Elizabeth Vol. XXV Nos 25/35/38/41).

The French author Charles Merk 'History of Dieppe' records the two year events of Jaques in Dieppe.

On the 1st May 1560 Captain Deforts, Captain of the Town, declared himself for the Reformation: his example was followed by the Baillif, Mayor and Aldermen. Admiral Coligny could now claim that Dieppe was Protestant. Cardinal de Bourbon sent a threatening letter to DesForts. The Royal Order forbade the public preachings of the Reform. The Captain replied boldly for the townspeople that they could not cease worshipping nor live as atheists. The Duke de Guise — the Catholic leader — sent the Duke de Bouillon to dismantle the town i.e. sack it. DesForts was arrested and sent to Rouen for trial and M de Ricarville, a Catholic, replaced him. Young King Francis died suddenly and Catherine de Medici assumed the reins of government on behalf of the new King Charles IX. When she passed through Dieppe with Admiral Coligny, Captain DesForts was released from prison and returned in triumph to the Chateau of Dieppe. A Synod of 50 Protestant Ministers was held in Dieppe in May 1561. DesForts found it difficult to control the excessively zealous Protestants. Freedom was a heady drug. The Duke de Bouillon again visited Dieppe and severely reprimanded DesForts. A bitter feud started between the Catholic de Ricarville, Captain of neighbouring

Arques, and Captain DesForts, and many minor battles and skirmishes were fought. DesForts was wounded trying to break down the Church windows at Arques! A few months later the Plague broke out in Dieppe — a punishment of heresy, the Catholics said. War broke out in 1562 on a much larger scale and DesForts wrote to Queen Elizabeth asking for money to raise new militia companies. A fleet of six vessels with 900 men, mostly Scotsmen, and 14 guns arrived. The town garrison was increased to 2000 soldiers plus the 7000 citizens. After savage fighting the Catholic armies won the day and the Huguenot refugees who sailed to England were led by captain Desforts. He and Montgomery, the defenders of Rouen, plotted a return, and DesForts returned in disguise. On 22nd December 1562 his hated rival de Ricarville, who had taken his place, was done to death by the conspirators. The Gascon captain de Catterville and his men siezed the Chateau.

The next year Catherine de Medicii made a state visit to Dieppe, gave a few favours to the Protestants and dismissed Captain DesForts, who almost certainly gave up the unequal struggle and retired to his estates in Dorset (temporarily).

As Jaques de Fossé he reappeared in Dieppe in 1563 as Administrator of Charities and relief funds for the refugees pouring into the Channel ports as a result of the religious wars.

In 1568 the Calender of Cecil papers showed that M de la Force is in the list of noble Huguenot officiers in the Army of Poitou.

In January 1569 M de Fors and M. de Chaumont wrote to Cardinal Chatillon in England to petition him by order of the Queen of Navarre to help with the persecuted Hugenots at La Rochelle.

In 1569 Jaques de Fosse ville (viel or vieux) was living in London with his son James, probably in Tower Ward near his brother John.

James the father died on 3rd November 1573 as James Delafirs, stranger (i.e. a foreigner) St. Olave, Hart St. parish, but registered at St. Botolphs, Bishopsgate records.

Jaques' career was rather unusual. Born and bred in Paris, he had divided loyalties to France and England. His father, grandfather and great grandfather were both English and French. All three generations traded with London, had English titles and served English monarchs or pretenders.

After Jaques' conversion to Protestantism about 1555 his main priorities were to save and succour the Protestant refugees, even though this meant service under the French King. The Wars of religion transcended the old French-English political loyalties, and faith was stronger than patriotism (which in Jaques' case was mainly to England, which is where he retired and eventually died).

Chapter 16

'This golden rigol hath divorc'd so many English Kings'
W.H. Shakespeare 1564-1616

King Henry VIII's troubleshooter — John

Chapters 15-19 deal with five people, five generations who descended from Bernard Lord De la Force (chapter 19) who died at the battle of Barnet. His son Sir Bernard (chapter 18), Ambassador for 4 English Kings to 2 Spanish Kings: his grandson Sir Anthony (chapter 17), who was Perkin Warbeck's faithful companion and a Parliamentary member in Paris and well-known to Emperor Charles VIII and Louis XII: his great grandson John who was King Henry VIII's theological troubleshooter: his great grandson James who was rewarded by two Queens for his services.

John (Anthony's son) was born about 1490, probably in Macon, Burgundy. His father Sir Anthony and Perkin Warbeck (Duke of York) were in Paris in 1496, and in 1498 Anthony received 50 Marcs from the hands of Louis XIV. John's grandfather Sir Bernard is shown as Bertrand de Forcez on 14 January 1490 rendering homage to Louis XIV, King of France and Navarre "Seigneur s'etait acquitte des memes devoirs feodaux en 1494". In 1491 Sir Bernard had repurchased control of the family town of Fources/Forcez in Gascony, and in 1494 rendered homage to King Charles VIII.

John made the news headlines as a student. On 25 Aug. 1503 "Hemon" or "Jehan" de La Fosse went to prison in Paris for defying the Catholic Church. (This was some 50 years before Luther's disciples had spread the gospel of reform in France!)

Jehan or John was a college student at La Sainte Chapelle. He described himself as coming from 'Bourgoyne.' His father Sir Anthony was Archdeacon of Macon in Burgundy at the time. But Jean said also that he derived originally from Abbeville. His powerful father rescued him from the Church and the Law. "Gallia Christiana" noted that 'Johannes de Feurs, seu de Fours', son of Anthony in 'Matifconses' (Macon) was made Prior d'Iregny in 1506 when Jean was about 17. (The modern abbey of Igny is west of Reims). His father shortly afterward became Bishop of Paris in addition to being a member of the Paris Parlement, and Jean's advancement followed at the same time.

The first mention of John is in Gallia Christiania Book 12 p.655. "Antoine de Feurs seu de Fours" 1506 Johannis de Feurs in "Matisconsensis ternforio et Antoine de Sachins, filius Antonius, protonaturius (a first chief notary) apostolicus, prior d'Iregny, abbas Sancti Leonardi Ferrariensis, praefes (magistrate) camerere inquisitionem in parlemento Parisiensi, major archidiacanus Nannetenus & Lugdenensis decanus (dean), episcopus Nivernosis. mai 1505 in Regestis Vaticani (Vatican Registry). Regi fidem juravit Blefis 8 Feb 1505/6/7Ecc."

The Journal de Barillon by P. de Vaisseres records "Jean de Feurcy apres la mort d'anthoine de Coupigny, survenue en mai 1520, le Roi Charles Quint (the Emperor not the King of France) nomma l'office pour Abbé de Mont-Saint-Eloi (near Arras) et St-Jean-au Mont de Therouenne (near St. Omer)", but also he was made "l'un des maitres de son Conseil"; in effect a junior minister but without nominated responsibility. Jean was also in 1520 a landowner 'Bail a rente de Jean de la Fosse de Sainte-Pierre-du Vauvray' was granted by the Rouen parlement.

In the next six years Gallia Christiana (book 111) showed 'Johannes de Feucy, Henniacensis (Hainault) Monasterii praesul, comes consistorianus & magister libellorum supplicum Caroli V imperatur (Emperor Charles Quint), rejecto Phillipo de Marchenelles, quem elegerat, conventus, declaratur abbas a praefate Carolo V qou etiam annente, paulo post Georgium Egmondanum in partem laboris assumsit successorem que designavit', and 'Johannes X de Feucy superioris nepos, adsciscitur conciliis Caroli V imperatoris, ac propterea Petrus

Bouchier, datur ei coadjutor ab eodum principe: et paulo post nempe anno circitur 1521. Johannes fit abbas Montis Eligiani (Mont Saint Eloi) ubi vide.' (Ecclesiastic. Atrebensis/Artois).

The Emperor Charles Quint was the most powerful ruler in Europe, but he did not rule France. Nevertheless John had secured a good patron for his ecclesiastical honours on the Flanders-French frontiers.

During the period 1530-35 John Delaforce was employed on the King's behalf to seek theological advice in Germany and Italy from Martin Luther's 'apostles' which might convince the outside world and the Church that there were grounds for divorce from his Queens Catherine of Aragon and Anne Boleyn.

King Henry VIII wrote "It will be expedient to hire as many Italian Doctors as possible to defend the King's cause against opponents. As theologians are rare here (in England), who do not live in or profess religion, it would be advisable to gain as many provincials of the orders as possible". In 1530 the King spent 5000 crowns obtaining the opinion of German divines.

The State Papers are the source for these quotations. In the cast are Richard Croke, a minor English humanist teaching at Cambridge, previously at Paris, Louvain, Cologne & Leipzig; and Jerome de Ghinucci, Bishop of Worcester, auditor of the Apostolic Chamber.

A. 2 Mar 1530 Croke to Ghinucci (21 Henry VIII) "De La Fossa meantime is miserably in want and cannot insure the help of those whom he has already obtained for the Kings side: has received nothing although messengers arrived from Bologna on Fr, Sa, Sun, Mon with letters from Bernardino. Mostye to John de la Fossa sends a new Hebrew writing of Mark to Ghinucci".

B. 22 Mar 1530 Croke to Ghinucci "John de la Fossa replied tonight that he would give Croke no more money, and had received orders to that effect from Ghinucci's brother Peter. Complains of this and asks how he has offended him. Has always written well of him to the King. Need 70 crowns .. or will perish of hunger .. spent at Milan that Crucinus might gain his friends .. of which he borrowed 22 from Dominico, nephew of Frances. We have most of the names which he promised and we expect to get from Friar Thomaso the writings of a formidable enemy. Will give a few gold pieces to Hebrews who have promised to write in proof of the following points. That the law in Deuteronomy relates only to inheritance .. that the marriage of Thamar with the sons of Judah was not consummated .. that the Levitical law is of the law of nature..".

While the Pope, Clement VII and Emperor were at Bologna March 1530 to settle their affairs after the Peace of Cambray, Henry VIII sent ambassadors thither to watch over his interests, including John.

Meanwhile Croke & Ghinucci were hard at work in northern Italy proceeding by stealth at first & pretending to be moved by a merely academic interest in the problems of Leviticus & Deuteronomy. But Croke was a whining, tiresome man who seems to have been able to quarrel with anybody. The Venetian authorities took fright at anything which might annoy Charles V, the Emperor, and King of Spain, and bade the English desist. Perugina and Bologna, both papal cities, were warned by the Vatican in Rome not to meddle in the affair. Queen Catherine's friends hindered the King's agents at every turn.

C. "John de la Fossa has been for six days without six ducats and unless G(hinucci) sends fresh orders to the merchants, Croke cannot secure the theologians in Milan and elsewhere and will be obliged to leave this place without a single ducat. De la Fossa will not pay without new letters from the Bishop, although Croke wants the money of own messenger arrived from Bologna".

D. 7 April 1530 "From what happened at the trial to which Croke was obliged to summon De la Fossa before he could get his money, thought Ghinucci distrusted him and ordered De La Fossa to pay no more money without giving him warning. Ghinucci had written to Croke that he must be contented with 25 gold pieces a week and De La Fossa had shown a letter from Ghinucci's brother give the same order".

E. Bernardino Mostye wrote to John de la Fossa "to John de la Fossa for the remaining 70 crowns which he refused to pay in consequence of orders from Ghinucci's brother that he should pay the remainder to the Prothonotary. Was very anxious at this as the estimation in which he was held seemed likely to be in danger, and also because he would be suspected of neglect in the Kings business and left to perish of hunger".

Finally Gallia Christiana notes that in 1531 between the two missions for King Henry VIII 'Johannem de Fosse' factus coadjutor Abbot Valassiae'.

F. 8 Aug 1535 Simon Heyes and Christopher Mont wrote to King Henry VIII "A kinsman of Langeus, M. de la Force to bring Melancthion to reason upon certain articles. If they can agree upon them perhaps M. will come to the French King".

G. 5 Sep 1535 Mont to the King "M(elancthion) and six other learned Lutherans with M. de la Force".

H. 7 Sep 1535 Chr. Mont wrote to Thos Cromwell, Earl of Essex (Mont was a code name for M. Ducroc, one of Cromwell's spy-masters). "Langius/William due Bellay, Sieur de Langeus, has accordingly sent on his kinsman (M. de la Fos was a cousin of De Langes) Monsieur de la Fos to Germany with money to bring (Phillip) Melancthion (Luther's disciple) to France with 5 other learned men. Francis has sent him a safe conduct, a gold chain and money. (Francis I was King of France). All the Lutheran doctors and rabbis have written to Langey that they will accept any terms of agreement not absolutely unjust and impious."

Mont to Cromwell 1535 "Hinc factum est ut langius cognatum suum Monsieur De La Fos ad Germaniam premiserit una cum pecunia, ut Melanthonem una cum aliis quinque doctos in Galliam perducat, omnibusuqe necessariis instruat. Litteras quoque fidet publice a Gallorum rege super salvo adventu in Galliam ad Melanthonem pertulit et cathenam quoque auream et aliquam pecunie summan, rex Gallus per hunc de la Fos misisse Melanthoni dicitur, qui Melanthon jam ternis litteris se adventuram in Galliam langio promisit."

I. In the same year a Voré de la Fosse went to Wittenburg on a private mission to see Phillip Melancthion from Paris. Vore is a misprint but it is still difficult to place the name — certainly not Jean or Jehan.

J. In 1535 Phillip Melancthion dedicated his 'Loci Communes' to King Henry VIII and received 200 crowns in reward. Almost certainly Melancthion converted John de la Force to the new form of Protestantism, Lutheranism (or Calvinism later on).

However later Melancthion changed his mind about Henry VIII

and wrote 'let us cease to sing praises of the English Nero' after Catherine of Aragon's divorce was granted.

John died in 1537 and left a family include a son John who was a prosperous lawyer in Amiens. His grandson was the famous Jean de la Fosse 'Curé Ligeur de Paris' who wrote a political diary.

Chapter 17

"St. John " Companion in tribulation"

Sir Anthony de La Force and Perkin Warbeck, the Pretender

Anthony, the younger son of Sir Bernard, and brother to Peter/ Pierre the goldsmith who lived in Canterbury, was born in the Auvergne in 1475.

At an early stage in his life he met and became friendly with Perkin Warbeck, soi-disant younger son of Edward V; Richard of York or Richard of England, as he signed himself.

Most historians regard Warbeck as a complete imposter, born in Tournai in 1472 or 1474. A recent book however sets out to disprove this theory — to prove in fact that Warbeck *was* the Duke of York and that Sir James Tyrell, Captain of the Bodyguard to Richard III smuggled one or both Prisoners in the Tower out of England in 1483. It was also possible that Warbeck was the illigitimate son of Margaret of York, Duchess of Burgundy.

One theory is that Anthony was linked to Perkin Warbeck at a very early age so that the latter's knowledge of English and of Court life should be improved. Anthony's father had first hand knowledge of four English and two Spanish sovereigns, and courts in London and Madrid. Much of this must have affected Anthony so that by the age of 9 or 10 he would have been a courtier himself with basic skills of diplomacy. This may sound incredible now, but men matured very early in life during the Middle Ages!

The records show clearly that Anthony was with Warbeck in Flanders, France and Scotland. It is perfectly possible that he accompanied Warbeck to Portugal, Austria and Ireland as well.

Warbeck went to Lisbon for the signing of "Richard's Treaty" in June 1484. Anthony's father, Sir Barnard, was still English Ambassador, to the Spanish Court and may possibly have advised the two young men on their diplomatic mission to Portugal.

In 1491 Warbeck made his first visit to Cork. In 1492 he went with Anthony to see Charles VIII, King of France, in Paris regarding his quarrel with Henry VII of England. The Treaty of Etaples forced Warbeck to leave France.

After many adventures they then returned to the court of Marguerite, Duchess of Burgundy, in the Low Counties. Anthony's grandfather Bernard, Lord De La Force, who was killed at the battle of Barnet in 1471, almost certainly started his fatal last venture from the Burgundian court in Flanders.

Anthony was certainly there at Deldermond in 1493 when both young men were being looked after by the Governor, Hugh de Melun, a Knight of the Golden Fleece. Margaret, the Dowager Duchess of Burgundy, accepted Warbeck as her nephew, and set about educating him as a Royal Yorkist.

Anthony might have gone with Warbeck to Innsbruck in 1494 to see Emperor Maximilian who recognised him as Richard IV.

Warbeck's second visit to Cork took place in July 1495, and Anthony may have fought in the various small battles and skirmishes in the Warbeck uprising.

In 1496 they both visited Paris, where King Charles VIII received Warbeck as Richard, Duke of York, with all appropriate honours due to that rank.

Anthony was now 21. Almost certainly he married in Paris and his sons were born there. Certainly Jaques and John and probably an Anthony and Bernard. Jaques was probably named after James IV King of Scotland who received Warbeck and Anthony kindly.

Late in 1496 Anthony was with Warbeck, as Richard of England, and Sir George Neville, at the Scottish Court in Edinburgh, and on 18th October went to Fuenterrabia in N.W. Spain to see his father, Sir Barnard, bearing with him the following testimonial. In the Egerton Manuscript MS616 folio 6 in the British Museum library Richard of York (Perkin Warbeck) wrote from Edinburgh 18th Oct 1496 to Sir Bernard in Spain, recorded also in the Calender of State Papers Henry IV 1485-1509: "Richard has been creditably informed that he (Bernard) had shown great love, favour and kindness to King Edward IV, his father, and rendered him signal services. King Edward on the other hand held him in high esteem. Begs him to use his influence with his friends in Spain. Grateful to his son, Anthony de la Forse who has accompanied him into different countries and goes now with this letter to Spain". "To our Trusty and right beloved Bernard de la Forse, Knight at Fuentarrabia in Spain."

In 1497 Warbeck was captured and remained in London until 1499 when he and the Earl of Warwick were hanged. He had tried to escape in 1498 but was recaptured. The Duchess of Burgundy made strenuous efforts to save Warbeck — but in vain. Sir George Neville fled to her court in the Low Cousntries in exile.

On 17th Aug 1498 the Bishop Elect of Astorga wrote to King Ferdinand and Queen Isabella "The King of France (Charles VIII) has presented to the Flemish Commissioners the following sums of money. The Count of Nassau 300 Marcs, to the president of Flanders 60 Marcs and to (Anthony) M De Fores 50 Marcs and the Secretary 40 Marcs. They are very well satisfied with the King of France". Spanish State Papers.

Anthony's father Sir Bernard had retired to the family town and home of Fources in Gascony in 1492 for a variety of reasons... he might have been ashamed of Anthony's escapades. He was wealthy from his trading, loaded with honours and wanted to reestablish roots in Gascony, having purchased a third of the family town!

For a time after Warbeck's death Anthony may have lived in Gascony or the Gironde. During 1498-1501 Anthony Delafont, of Realmont (Montreal near Fources) was trading with many cargoes from Bordeaux to London, this sounds like Anthony, backed by his father living in Fources, shipping cargoes, probably of wines to England.

In 1502 Gallia Christiana records "Antonius I de Feurs deu de Fours conciliarius (councillor) in Parlamento Parisiensi & Archideacanus Matisconensis, competitorem habuit & summovit Jacobum (James) de La Font quem modo ominavimus. Praerat adhuc anno 1502. Ecclesiae Carnotentsis".

In 1505, 6 and 7 Antoine de Feurs or Fours was shown in GC Book 12 p.655 as father of "Johannis de Feurs in Matisconsensis territorro, filius Antonius protonotarius (first chief notary) apostolicus prior d'Iregny, abbas Sancti Leonardi Ferrarensis, praefes (magistrate) concile inquisitionem in parlemento Parisiensi, major archidiacnos Nannetenois & Lugdunensis decanus, (deacon) episcopus Nivernonsis Mai 1505 in regestis Vaticani. Regi fidem juravit Blefis 8 Feb. 1505/6/7. (Vatican Records).

Anthony, aged 27, was now a responsible member of the French government in the Paris parliament with his sons James and John about to follow him. He had also been awarded church titles. He was elected to the Paris parliament of Charles VIII in 1495. In 1503 he was re-elected "des six conseilleurs elus, les deux plus favorisee Anthoine de Feurs seu Fours par 49 voix..." He was a Clerc or Magistrate, "docteur in utroque" archdeacon of Macon (in Burgundy) in 1504, made Bishop of Paris and later became the 85th Bishop of Nevers in 1507. (Source Maugis Hist. de Parlement de Paris, book 3).

About 1504 Anthony, now knighted and presumably totally forgiven by King Henry VII for his activities with Warbeck — which originally could certainly have been construed as treachery — was involved in a legal case in London.

Early Chancery proceedings vol. 3 p.173 (CI132/55), 1485-1500. "Sir Anthony Delaforce petitions the Archbishop of Canterbury, Chancellor of England". "Sir Anthony and Laurence Walgrave of Conventry were jointly and severally bound by simple obligation to John Unfrey for £6 owed to him by Laurence, which obligation was delivered to John Woodward of Coventry to be safely kept, to the intent that if Laurence allowed Unfrey to occupy a house belonging to L. of the annual value of 40s, for 3 years without paying rent the obligation should be regarded as void at the end of the 3 years. This time has passed but Unfrey is demanding the £6 against Anthony before the Sheriff of London. As the bond is 'simple' (not made under seal) he has no remedy unless the Chancellor directs the Sherrif to transfer the case to Chancery there to be ruled as right and conscience shall require".

Sir Anthony was presumably living in London at the time because the case was before the Sherrif of London.

Before we leave the saga of Anthony and Perkin Warbeck there is a fascinating but garbled story from one of the contemporary French historians. The Memoires de Comines vol.V p.172

recounts (translated) "Le Comte de Dammartin had acquired the titles of Comte d'Aumale and York from the French King Phillipe-Auguste (way back in the 13th century when William de Force was Earl of Albermarle). His ancestor fell into disgrace at the Court and with 'le cabinet du Roy Louis XI'. He followed the Court to Bordeaux, but in vain. The King sent him back to Germany without any friends except a Yeoman Farmer of Dammartin in Normandy named Anthoine le Fort with whom he returned where he was nurtured well for a long time with his son, god-child of the Duke de Bourbon (Armagnac)."

Louis XI reigned from 1461. Comines had got the salient features right. A "Duke of York" supported by his close friend Anthony de la Force solicited the King of France for favours. They did both leave France for Austria in 1492 (not Germany). Obviously the story of Warbeck (Duke of York) and Anthony was now enshrined in French folk-lore as an example of friendship.

Chapter 18

Sir Henry Wooton 1568
'An Ambassador is an honest man sent to lie abroad for the good of his country.'

Sir Bernard — Ambassador for Four English Kings

In some ways Bernard was the most famous of the Delaforce family. (His life was well documented in Thomas Rymer's Feodora and the Harleian Manuscripts). He was English Ambassador to Spain for the English Kings, Edward IV, V, Richard III and Henry VI.

Bernard was born in the Auvergne at one of the two La Force chateaux in 1446. Seven years later the Hundred Years War came to an end with a complete French victory.

Possibly Bernard had a brother called Anthony. Certainly he called one of his own sons Anthony. The two names continue for another 300 years. He certainly had a brother John, Seigneur de la Fource, a merchant trader and probably another — Pierre/Peter. On 18th June 1463 Bertrando Fortete 'etiam dicte ville mercatoribus Aurillae' and Bernardus del Forn 'sutor) (probably sutler, army supplier) — father and son were shown in the records of Aurillac in the Auvergne.

The British government's exchequer "Warrants for Issue" (i.e. payments) p.104 showed a Treasury payment to Peter Tastario, dean of St.Severin, Bordeaux, English Ambassador from Guìenne/Acquitaine in 1463 "for money given to Lewis de Brettaillis and Bernard de La Forsse for certaine secrete matiers". Aged 17 Bernard was now an English secret agent!

From August 1464, aged only 18, Bernard became envoy for

King Edward IV, then English Ambassador and eventually Knight at the court of the King of Castile in Spain. His family had connections with Navarre. The merchant traders of Bordeaux and London had business with Spain. His missions and travels are well documented. He negotiated with two Spanish Kings, Henry and then with Ferdinand.

His main task was to negotiate the marriage of King Edward IV of England's daughter Katherine to John, son of King Ferdinand of Castile. He was given various titles, of Armiger or squire, Magistrate, Ambassador and Knight. His briefings by the English Kings are long and specific and can be seen in the published State Papers. His missions were difficult and not particularly successful. The young Spanish Prince John died aged 19, having made another political marriage.

A. 9 Oct 1464 Bernard sent as Ambassador to King of Castile. His father being a Gascon Lord with extensive trading links with north west Spain, must have influenced this appointment.

B. 6 Aug 1466 Power for John Gunthorp, the Kings Chaplain and Bernard to deliver the Kings patent of the Treaty of Alliance with Henry King of Castile and to receive his patent in return.

C. 14 Mar 1470 Power for John Gunthorp, Chief Almoner, John Aliot and Bernard to treat with Henry, King of Castile. Bernard's title was Armiger or squire.

D. 1473 Bernard as Magistrate went with William Packenham to Castile.

E. 15 May 1474 Commission to Barnard de la Force & John Wyndesore Herald to exchange ratifictions of the treaty with Ferdinand as with Henry King of Castile.

F. 1475 Again with John Wyndsore Herald to Spain.

G. 28 Aug 1479 Power for John Coke and Bernard to negotiate a marriage between the Kings daughter Katherine and John son of Ferdinand King of Castile. John Coke was secondary in Office of Privy Seal.

H. 2 Mar 1481 Bernard went with Henry Ainsworth and Arnold Trussell to Spain.

I. 6 June 1481 Bernard went with Arnold Truffell to Goypuscoare N.W. Spain to negotiate trading agreements.

J. 2 Mar 1482 Commission to Henry Aynesworth, Bernard and

Arnold Trussell to conclude a marriage of Katherine with John.
K. 12 July & 30 Aug 1483 Power for Bernard to treat with King & Queen for redress of injuries (not known whether these are personal or commercial injuries or State problems).

In his book "Richard the Third", Paul Murray Kendall has this to say about Bernard in 1483. "Richard III appointed Bernard de la Forssa (re Isabella's wish to renew the league of Edward IV and Henry of Castile) who had performed many such missions for Edward IV, to go to Spain on this very business. Since Forssa had apparently not yet sailed, Richard despatched him further instructions in which he outlined his reasons for desiring a renewal of the previous league but made clear that he was willing to agree a new Treaty if Queen Isabella so wished. He wrote a very friendly letter to the Queen herself announcing the arrival of the Spanish Ambassador and telling her that Bernard de la Forssa was on his way to complete negotitions. Spain was far from weak but Ferdinand and Isabella's chief interest in England seems to have been centred in the hope that by making war on France, she would leave them (Spain) free to complete their conquest of the Moors".

Henry Tudor seized the English throne after the battle of Bosworth Field in August 1485, Bernard was in Spain and stayed there for some time. At this time he was probably involved with negotiations to renew the Treaty of Alliance (the oldest alliance of all, that of 1386) with Portugal. In 1489 as Henry VIIs ambassador, Sir Bernard was welcomed at Medina del Campo with much ceremony in connection with the poposed marriage of the English Prince Arthur to Catalina, age 4, Isabel and Ferdinands young daughter.

In the Egerton MS 616 folio 6 in the British Museum Richard of York (Perkin Warbeck) writes from Edinburgh 18th October 1496 to Sir Barnard. The Calender of State Papers Henry IV 1485-1509 record the same letter. "Richard has been creditably informed that he (Bernard) had shown great love, favour and kindness to King Edward IV, his father, and rendered him signal services. King Edward on the other hand held him in high esteem. Begs him to use his influence with his friends in Spain. "To our Trusty and right entirely beloved Bernard de la Forse, Knight at Feuentarrabia in Spain".

Bernard must have been a very able man. Not only did he maintain a position in London as a politician and trader, and make frequent visits to Spain, but in 1479 as Bertrand de Fers, Seigneur de Lapayrie (2km. from Fources in Gascony) he was counted amongst the "noblesse d'Armagnac". In 1484 he and brother Johanne de Forcesio were witnesses at Auch to Charles d'Armagnac being made Comte de Fezensac. They greeted the French King Charles VIII at Auch in 1491. Bernard's younger son Anthony was already well-known to the French King and court through his visits with Richard of York (Perkin Warbeck) to Paris.

In the Chancery Early Proceedings of 1467-85 Vol. 2 p.166; 1485-1500 Vol.3 p.28 there are two references to Sir Barnard. Both were civil actions in front of the Mayor and Alderman of London. "John Dort (The same man who asked King Edward IV in 1471 for a grant for prayers for Lord De la Forse, Bernard's father) and William Horton, sureties for Bernard de la Forca in action Colyns against the said Forca. F. is in Spain in the Kings business and suits against him are postponed by letter missive of the King". "Various merchants of Spain are sureties for Bernard de la Force".

Petitions by Thomas Randyll of London, tailor, Diego de Castro and Peter de Salamanca, merchants of Spain, to the Bishop of Ely, Chancellor "Bernard Delaforce was bound by his obligation to John a Wode, Treasurer of England to Richard III for £280. The debt being now due, a John barker of London, Goldsmith, pretends that £200 of it was assigned to him by John a Wode for a debt made by the King Richard III and has affirmed a plaint before the sheriff of London against Bernard Delaforce. The case was removed to Chancery but in the absence of Bernard and the petitioners the case was granted to London where John Barker, having great favour and being brother-in-law to the mayor, intended to condemn Bernard. As now Bernard, "for certain matters concerning the league between the King and the King of Spain, is beyond the sea in Spain and will be here in this land soon by mid-summer and that he should be in time charged for the said £200, if the said John Barker should recover against him," the petitioners ask the Chancellor to issue a writ of "certiorari" to the mayor and sheriff of London "to have before the King in his Chancery at a certain day the plaint or action there to be examined and directed according to right and conscience and this for the love of God".

Bernard was honoured with titles and grants by Edward IV, Richard III and Henry VII.

(a) On 3rd March 1479 Buckden in the Calender of Patent Rolls records a Grant was made to Bernard de la Force by the government of "40L (pounds) yearly from Michaelmas last at the receipt of the Exchequer until he shall be provided for life with lands to the same value".

(b) In the Harleian MSS 433, the record of writs and letters of authority issued by John Kendall, Richard III's secretary from the Signet office over the royal sign manual, there is authority for annual payment of fees of £20 to Sir Bernard. Also recorded were his detailed instructions as to his embassy at Fuenterrabia to the Kings of Castile and Spain.

(c) In 1490 Bernard de la Fers 'by way of reward' was granted C(100) Marks (Pounds) by King Henry VII.

(d) on 6 June 1490 King Henry VII wrote 'Licence to Barnard de La Forse of Spain to ship goods in Spanish ships to England and that the same ships having discharged their cargoes may return to safety". Permission to use foreign ships was most unusual. Bernard probably earned a fortune in Spain.

There are many source references to Bernard. T. Rymer Feodora Xii p.193/8/200 and 228. Harleian MSS 433 f.235. Original letters 2nd series 1 pp. 152/4. Letters and papers 1 pp.21-23, f.241 pp.23-25, f.244bl pp.48-51.

To round off Bernard's unusual history, after receiving King Henry VII's trading permit in 1490 and a reward of C Marcs, he returned from N.W. Spain (Fuenterabbia) to the town of his ancestors — Fources in Gascony. There in 1491 as Bertrand de Fources 'restitution' was made of 'un tiers de Fources et de la Rocque-Fources, et creation de foires à Fources pour Bertrand de Fources seigneur de lieu". Two government Arrets were published to this effec; Registers JJ222, 34 folio 11 and 292 folio 134, signed by King Louis XI from Montils-Lez-Tours.

In 1492 "Les heritiers universels de Pierre Fores, sartre (tailor) de Concots (halfway between Cahors and Montauban) devront far las nossas e la festa — le festin (feast) — apres la premiere messe

(Mass) de leur frère Bernard, Clerc/Magistrate". This might imply a form of Will by Peter Force, tailor and Sir Bernard's brother, that his successors will have a feast for Sir Bernard.

On 14th January 1498 Bertrand de Forcez rendered homage to Louis XIV King of France and Navarre as "Seigneur,était acquitté des mêmes devoirs feodaux (feudal duties) en 1494". "The King is dead, long live, the King". Sir Bernard was correctly making sure that the new King knew where Bernard's loyalties lay. His son Sir Anthony was a member of the Paris parliament at the time.

Benard's family consisted of three sons: Peter (de) Force baptised 1472 who became a Goldsmith of Canterbury and Faversham, Kent, and died in 1523. A long line of goldsmiths, 'bankers', silversmiths, pawnbrokers and stockbrokers followed throughout the 16th, 17th and 18th centuries.

Anthony, the younger son, born 1475, has a chapter to himself.

The eldest son Bernard, was born about 1470, and there are several mentions of him. 1509 Bertran de Forc(e) paroisse de Len (Lelin) near Gotz/Auch, Castelgelons, was given permission to return to his lands 'chargé de femme & plusieurs petits enfants'.

1512 Bernard de Forsans was in Montpouillon in Gascony, and in 1519-22 Bertrand Du Fousse/Defosse shipped cargoes from Bordeaux to Bilbao in Spain. Bernards continued until at least 1725, appearing in London and Paris either as goldsmiths, traders or politicians or a combination.

2073/24/1 British Museum Library

Edward IV brief to Bernard
"Relations with Spain"
(MS.Harl.433,f.241.)

Instrucctions geven by the king to Barnard de la Forssa to be shewed and opened to the kinges cousyns, the king and quene of Castelle.

FIRST, after the presentacion of the kinges lettres to his said cousyns with recomendacions in suche case accustumed, he shall shewė and remembre the said king of the trendre love, trust, and effeccion that the

A.D. 1483. July.

king oure brother now decessed (whome God pardon) had and bare towards his said cousyns, latting them wit that his highnes is and evere entendeth to be of like disposcion towardes them in alle thinges that he may conveniently doo to their honnor and pleasure. And in likewise by alle meanes convenient the said Barnard shalle shewe that the king trusteth that his said cousyns wolbe of like benevolence and disposicion towards him.

Diet agreed to by Edward IV., and Ferdinand and Isabella.

And where in the yere last passed the kinges said brother sent his ambassiate to his said cousyns for diverse maters then not fully concluded, and amonges other for thentreteignyng of the peas, ligue, and amyte passed and concluded betweixt his hignes and Henry late king of Castelle, against which many attemptates have be and daily be committed; whereof, if due reformacion were not had, the said peax, ligue, and amite cowd not long contynue: it was therfore appoynted and concluded with his said cousyns to have had a diette in Spayn at Midsomer then next following, or afor, to the which the kinges said brother was fully agreed.

But for asmoche as it pleased Almighti God to call him out of this miserable worlde unto his mercy afore the tyme appoyned for the said diette; after whose decesse no gret maters might conveniently be appointed afore the king coronacion and ordering of his realme:

A new day to be named.

The said Barnard shall, for that and other causes suche as shalle best serve after his descrecion, excuse the tarying of comyssioners that shuld have come to that diette, and, by the auctorite and power to the said Barnard comitted by the kinges comission, agree and appoynte[1] with the kinges said cousyns or their commissioners to a new day of meting for reformacion of the said attemptates, suche as shall pleas the kinges cousyns aforesaid.

A.D. 1483. July.

And that the said barnard after thappoyntmentes of a day of meeting soo agreed, in alle goodly hast acertain the king and his counsell of the same, to thentent that commissioners may be sent thider sufficiently instructe and auctorized for due reformacion of the said attemptates to be had and made of their partie.

[1] appointed, MS.

"Answer to the Message of Isabella of Castile".
(MS.Harl.433.f.244b.)

Intruccions ʒeven by the king to Barnard de la Forssa, whome his highnes at this tyme sendeth to his derrest cousyns the king and the quene of Spaigne.

First, after the presenting of the kinges lettres to theim of credence, with suceh recommendacions and good wordes as shalbe thought most convenient and acceptable to theim, he shall shewe his credence in manner and forme folowing:—

That the king our soverayn lord hath recived a lettre of credence from his derrest cousine the quene of Spaigne by hir orator the bachiler de Sasiola, and by the same hath clerly understande the gret luff and singuler benevolence that hir highnes beres towardes his grace, and therfore thankes her in his hertiest maner, latting her wit that his highnes is of noo lesse good will towardes hir husband and hir, but woll in all convenient wises be as glad to do that, that my be to the honour and wele of theim and their realmes as any prince lyving.

A.D. 1483. August.

And forsomoche as by vertue of credence commited to hir said orator, and by him shewed to the king by mouth and also writing, his grace hath understande his said cousins to be utterly disposed to have with him good and ferme peace, lieges, alliaunces, and confideractions, to thentent that they shuld be joigned, alyed, and confederate in perfite liege and confideracion as good and feithfulle cousins and cofiderates:

The said Barnard shall in that behalve say that the king therfore thankes his said cousins in his hertiest maner and is thereof as desirus as they be, and wolle to be perfeccion thereof intende by alle weyes and meanes convenient and resonable. And how that incontinent upon the said credence so opened the king, seing that the said orator whiche had no specialle commission in writing, nor instructions so large as shuld be requisite to the making of so gretea ligue, made to be serched up the lique that was last taken betwene the late king Edward, his brother, and king Henry of Castille, late brother of the said quene, whome God pardone. Wherby it was thought unto him and his counsaille that the beginnyng of the best intelligence betwene both

England proposes a renewal of the league made between Edward IV. and Henry IV. of Castile.

parties shuld be grounded upon the articles of the said ligue, considering that by long and ripe advise and deliberacion the articles of the said ligue were practized and concluded.

And over this the said Barnard shalle shewe that the king our soverayn lord, not willing anny long tracte of tyme or other impediment of so goodly and behovefull entent shuld be on his partie, and specially when he is so instanced by the said orator to send thider in all goodly hast for full expedicion of the same, his highnes hath at this tyme sent thider the said Bernard to common of the best and spediest wayes.

A.D. 1483. August.

In which communicacion the said Barnard shalle by alle meanes of policie dryve theim to conforme [1] the olde ligue without making of a newe; to the whiche if they can be founde by his wisdome agreable, than he shall now desire to have suche forme of commission made by the kinges cousins ther to suche as shalle please them to deliver to him their part of the ligue sealed as he hath to deliver the kynges parte also sealed, keping him close alwey from knowledging that he hath suche commission or ligue sealed unto suche tyme as he utterly understande their myndes of suche commission and delivere to be made by theim.

And in case they wolle in no wise agree to make any suche confirmacion of the ligue now made, but utterly insiste to make a new, either like or more large with some new articles, then he shall labor by his wisdome the wayes that suche orators may be sent with him into England, as may have of the kinges cousins their fulle auctorite and power to common, appoincte and conclude, as by theim the said mater may take good affecte [2] and conclusion.

Morover the king is content that whethir the ligue shalbe desired to be alle new made, or any addicions to be had to the olde, the said Barnard speke frely with theim of suche new articles as they desire, and that he common and debate upon theim in suche wise as by his discrecion shalbe thought best for the king and his land, avoiding as moche as he can any gret and certaine charges that the king might be put unto; provided alwey that by any thing so to be spoken, commoned, or treated the king be not bounden above the olde articles, but be at his hole libertie in alle suche new maters unto the commyng of thenbassate of Castille into England, and till they and the kinges commissaries have throughly passed in all poyntes.

Item, where the said Bernard hathe an other commission to treate and appointe upon attemptates aswele with the governors of the provinces as with the counsaille of the king and quene, and to appoincte a diete for the same; the king wolle that he doo and procede in thoos maters according to the said commission, and to suche instruccions as he had delivered unto him therupon afore.

A.D. 1483. August.

[1] sic in MS. [2] and conclude,—effecte) repe ated in MS.

Chapter 19

"He was a verray parfit gentil Knight"
Chaucer 1340-1400.

The Gascon Lord and the Battle of Barnett

Bernard de la Force was born about 1425-30 probably in the Auvergne at one of the three chateaux near Aurillac.

His father was Bertrand de la Forsa, Prior then Abbot of Meymac abbey north west of Mauriac in the fief of Ventadour. He was the 21st Abbot, and "Gallia Christiana" mentions him in 1384/6/7, 1396, 1412, 1423 and 1443 (Book 2 p.600). His grandfather was Bernard de Forcia, Prior, then Abbot of St. Leonards of Montreal, near Fources in 1374, who had a distinguished career from 1354 to 1386.

Bernard married about 1445 and his son Bernard was born in 1446. In the period 1446-1453, when the English were being driven out of France, Betrand De Fas/Du Fos was a 'capitoul' or consul in the Toulouse area (which would have included Aurillac) with 'Armes de Gueules, a une épée antique d'or or posée en bande, la pointe en bas, l'ecu bordé d'azur'.

In the Calender of French Rolls (Membrane 5) King Henry VI granted on 15th march 1459/60 'a safe conduct for Bernard de la Force of Aquitaine for the ship 'Marie' of Ypusco, Spain trading from San Sebastien, Fuenterrabia, via Rouen and Calais for England'. His brother John de la Fource was also given a licence by Henry VI (Membrane 3) "to trade between France and England to compensate him for losses sustained by his loyalty".

In 1463 Bernard and his son Bernard were shown on the Aurillac city charts, one as a 'sutor' or merchant supplying the army and the other as a merchant. Both father and son had friends in London including John Dort, a Gascon trader.

On 30th June 1471 in the 2nd year of Edward IV's reign, the Privy Seals Rolls of the Tower of London record (file 2) "John Dort, Gascoyn, supplicates the King in order to sustain two priests for two years in the Church of St. Martin in the Vintry, London, to say masses and prayers for the soules of the Lord de La Forse and Isarn de la Bernia, Lord de Gensac, slain at the battle of Barnet (14 April 1471) in the Kings service, whose bodies are buried in the said church, for leave to trade for a yere with a ship or ships of 200 'tunnes'.

The battle of Barnet was fought on a cold grey Easter Sunday morning between the Yorkists and the Lancastrians, but including many professional mercenaries from Gascony. The Duke of Burgundy had fitted out and financed an expeditionary force for King Edward, who landed in March 1471 on the River Humber. As Warwick, the Kingmaker, was killed on the battlefield, the result was a Yorkist victory.

History does not relate whether John Dort's request was granted. Possibly it was, because the dead Lord's son Bernard had become Ambassador to Spain for King Edward IV seven years earlier and he was obviously a valuable servant of the Crown.

The history of the family continues in a second book. They were descended from the old Kings of Navarre in N.W. Spain. Charlemagne hanged three generations of this family in the period 781-812 AD, when they were Dukes of Gascony. From 920-1100 they were Feudal Princes of Verdun and Saves (near Montauban). A Knight fought at the battle of Hastings for the Conqueror, owned lands in Domesday Book. Others went on the First and Third Crusades, and became Earls of Albermarle by marrying into the Conqueror's family. One was a close friend of King Richard, Coeur de Lion, and his son was one of King John's few friends, but relucantly signed with the other barons at Runnymede.

Chapter 20

John Donne 1571-1631
"No man is an island entire of itself,
Every man is a piece of the continent, a part of the main."

The Delaforces and Delforces in Australia

The "discovery" of the Australian and American Delaforce families was fortuitous. A Delaforce cousin visiting Australia looked in a telephone directory and discovered a Keith Delaforce. They met and became friends. Keith was recently retired and besides growing Chrysanthemums almost professionally, is also a very keen genealogist. He had already researched the family history in Australia, had produced an excellent tree, had copies of William and Frances Janes marriage certificate and had secured photographs of the first two generations in Australia. At a Delaforce family reunion in November 1979 held at Caboolture, north of Brisbane, Queensland about 130 Delaforces attended. Another reunion is planned for 1984.

One of Keith's relations had been visited in Australia by Warren Delaforce from USA. Warren and his cousin Dorothy were also keen genealogists and had prepared the American family tree descending from James Moses.

Keith has now produced a family tree for the Delforce family in Australia. From a London library collection of Australian telephone directories a letter was sent to ten different Delforces in Australia. Three answered with helpful details and so their family tree is shown in the appendix. They descended from George Delforce who was born in England between 1830-1840 emigrated

William Delaforce,
ex-convict Second Fleet,
founder of Australian family

about 1860 and from his two sons George and John are descended the current family living around Brisbane, Newcastle and Sydney.

At the end of this chapter are some of the main sources of genealogy for Australia, although, as it happened, Keith had little need to consult them since he had followed instinctively the basic rules. Visit all known relatives and ask them for every possible detail of their parents and grandparents, backed up by photographs and certificates.

The first convicts were transported to Australia — to Sydney Cove near Botany Bay — in 1788. Captain Cook's first voyage to the East Coast of Australia was in 1770. The English expedition led by Captain Cook landed at Botany Bay (several hundred miles north of Van Diemens Land) in that year. It was recommended as 'suitable for the establishment of a Colony of convicted felons.' The arrivals of the First Fleet and their uniformed overseers were the founders of the Colony of New South Wales, as an English territory under the rule of King George III.

Every possible detail of the First Fleet, composed by Bryan Thomas, in Sydney 1976, is available from Midlands Ancestor, the excellent quarterly magazine published by the Birmingham & Midland Society for Genealogy and Heraldry. The names are shown of the ships, officers, crew, their wives, and of course, the convicts. All the details of the cargoes (110 firkins of butter, 1 piano, 1 printing press, and hundreds of other items) are recorded faithfully in the two page spread. All historians interested in Australia should obtain a copy.

In 1818 Governor Macquarie sent out an expedition under John Oxley, surveyor-general, which included twelve convicts. After finding and naming the Hastings river, they found a suitable well-watered site and named it Port Macquarie (200 miles North of Botany Bay and Sydney) "The port abounds with fish, the sharks were larger and more numerous. The first hills and rising grounds were covered with large kangaroos and the marshes afford shelter and support to innumerable wild fowl." The more important reasons for the new settlement were the isolation of the convicts, the cultivation of 'new' plants, shrubs and tropical fruits and the opening up of the road to New England from the Coast.

To this Paradise came — on 19th April 1821 — three ships from

Sydney with the pioneer party of 60 selected convicts, 41 soldiers, 12 specialists and 50 strong healthy labourers under Captain Francis Allman of the 48th Regiment.

Thanks to the "History of Port Macquarie" published by the Hastings District Historical Society, a wealth of detail is available about this settlement.

Many experiments were made with vegetable and fruit crops. Sugar cane was successfully grown, and rum appeared shortly afterwards! Pineapples, cotton, coffee, pigs, cows, poultry — all were encouraged, although coffee was not successful.

The first white settlers met with a hostile reception from the aborigines and several settlers and convicts were killed in a massacre in 1843.

William Delaforce, born 28th May 1817, elder son of William and Mary, lived in Shoreditch, stood trial in London on 3rd July 1834 for house-breaking (family rumour says that he stole a loaf of bread, or a waistcoat, but not both!) and was given a 7 year sentence. Along with 260 other convicts, he sailed on 28th July 1834 on the S.S. Hooghly on its 4th voyage with convicts to Australia. The Master was George Bayly and the voyage took 120 days.

William's convict number was 34.2554. He was aged 17 — could read and write — was a single man, Protestant, and was a carter's boy from London. he had no previous convictions. He was 5'3" tall — ruddy and freckled complexion, with brown hair and blue eyes. he had anchor tattoos under both arms. A comprehensive log! William's first assignment was to Mr Sam Terry at Mt. Pleasant near Windsor, west of Sydney. Then he contracted sandy blight and after 10 months in Windsor Hospital, he was transferred to Parramutta, west of Sydney. Back to Sydney barracks. Then to the Phoenix hulk — prison ship. Finally he was sent to Port Macquarie by the steamer 'Little Billie'. William's adventures were 'ghosted' in a booklet by 'Woomera', first published in 1900 entitled "The life and experiences of an ex-convict". The 32 pages show the hard brutal life the convicts led. William had many beatings, by 'mis-conduct' earned another year's imprisonment, but became a Freeman in 1843, aged 26.

William married Frances Jane Shane (Sheharn) daughter of a shoemaker, on 10th October 1851. She came from Cork in

Ireland. His name was shown on the register as Deleforce. The marriage was performed by William McKee, Minister of the Presbyterian church of St. Andrews, in Port Macquarie.

William became a dairy farmer at Rawdon Island near Port Macquarie. Six children were born and survived to rear families. Liscillier b.1852, d.1934, married a Mr McCormack, then a Mr Blossom, then a Mr Charles Wilson. Jeseph b.1854, d.1934, married Sarah Marriott. (Joseph was named after his uncle, William's younger brother). Isobella b.1856, d.1938, married Tom Mansfield. William b.1858, d.1939, married Agnes Barnes. William the father died of cirrhosis of kidney, or dropsy on 7th June 1900, at Fernbank Creek, aged 83 and was buried at Port Macquarie Church of England Cemetery. William's grand and great-grandchildren are shown in the family tree at the end of this book.

Sources

In England — there is an excellent reference library in Australia House, Aldwych, London WC1. The Public Records Office, Chancery Lane, London should be consulted: "NSW Original Correspondence (CO 201) 1784-1821. Entry Books relating to Convicts (CO 207, 202, 360 and 369). Convicts NSW & Tasmania (HO 10, 64 volumes, HO-11 21 volumes). Census of 1828 (HO 10/21-27). The Genealogical Society in London also has extensive records including Directories. See also articles in the "Genealogist" March & June 1981 by Dr Joseph. Printed books available in England include:–

"Census of New South Wales, Nov. 1828" by M.R. Sainty/K.A. Johnson.

"The Convict Settlers of Australia" by L.L. Robson.

"Crimes of the First Fleet settlers" by John Cobley.

The British Museum library and Guildhall library also have other printed sources available.

Montrose Genealogical Services, 83 Riley St., Tuart Hill, W.Australia 6060, publish a genealogical computer index, including sources such as Shipping Lists, Voters Rolls, Probate Registers, Telephone Directories and Newspaper Archives.

British Emigrants to the Antipodes (pre 1900) is a joint index by Dr M. Watts, 77 Church Lane, Lowton, Warrington; Mrs M. Russell, Ulpha, 32 Granada Rd. Denton, Manchester, and the Western Australian Genealogical Society.

The James McClelland Research organisation, dedicated to Australian History, have published 12 books including — Returned Soldiers Associatiion — Convict, Pioneer & Immigrant History of Australia — A Guide to locating & searching Family, Convict, Pioneer & Immigrant Records of Australia.

The Australian Biographical & Genealogical Record, details from Dr. A.P. Joseph, 25 Westbourne Rd. Edgebaston, Birmingham B15 3TX.

In Australia — the Mormon Church, Church of Latter Day Saints have genealogical libraries in New South Wales (Emu Plains, Greenwich Sydney, Mortdale, New Lambton), in Victoria (Northcote, and Moorabbin), in Queensland (Brisbane), in Southern Australia (Firle and Marion), in Western Australia (Yokin) and in Canberra.

The UK Federtaion of Family History Societies in Plymouth lists all the major Australian societies including three national ones:

(a) Australian Inst. of Genealogical Studies, PO Box 68, Oakleigh, Victoria 3166, publish "The Genealogist".

(b) Society of Australian Genealogists, Richmond Villa, 120 Kent St., Observatory Hill, Sydney NSW 2000.

(c) Heraldry & Genealogy Society of Canberra, PO Box E185, Canberra ACT 2600.

(d) Gen. Soc. of Northern Territory, PO Box 37212, Winnellie, NT 5789.

(e) Queensland FHS, PO Box 171, Indooroopillay, Brisbane 4068.

(f) Gen. Soc. of Queensland, 1st Floor, 329 Logan Road, Stones Corner, Queensland 4120.

(g) Gen. Soc. of Victoria, Room 1, 1st Floor, Block Arcade, 98 Elizabeth St., Melbourne, Vic. 3000.

(h) S. Australian Geneal. & Her. Society, PO Box 13, Marden, S.Australia 5070.

(i) W. Australia Geneal. Society, PO Box 7, West Perth, W. Australia 6005.

(**j**) Gen. Soc. of Tasmania, PO Box 640G, Hobart, Tasmania, 7001.
(**k**) Nepean District FH Soc., 125 Maxwell St, South Penrith, NSW 2750.

The main Australian Archives are in Canberra: the National Library of Australia is at NSM 136/69, Canberra ACT 2600: The Mitchell Library in Sydney is a major repository of records and historical documents: so too are the State Library of Victoria, Swanston St., Melbourne and the Public library of NSW, Macquarie St., Sydney NSW 2000. Library of Australian History, PO Box 795, North Sydney, NSW 2060.

Chapter 21

Ralph Waldo Emerson 1803-1882
"America is a country of young men."

The American Families

The Delaforce family at various times emigrated to America, occasionally in handcuffs, more often not. They just failed to qualify as the original Pilgrim Fathers who settled in New England in 1620, but one of them, Peter Force, helped sail the "Mayflower" to America in that year as a member of the crew. (Source Smithsonian Institute). Peter was probably a great-grandson of Peter Force (1475-1530) born in the Auvergne (son of Sir Bernard de La Force and brother of Sir Anthony). Peter Force was a goldsmith of Faversham and Canterbury in Kent. Peter Foytz of Norton Folgate, London, of 1559 was perhaps related. There are several other members of the family in America early in the 17th century but there is no proof that they were related to Peter.

One of the earliest families was that of Matthew de La Force (source Virkus Compendium of American Genealogy) who was born about 1645 and married Elizabeth Palmer in 1667 in Albany, New York (Source Mormon IGI Index). Matthew came from England. His father was Matthew LaFors, born about 1620, who married in about 1640 at St. Olaves Benet, London. A sister, Martha, was born in February 1648.

The first Matthew recorded in the family history was in 1239, Matthew de Forte "Antipolitan" and in 1284 as "Matthaei de Forti, judicis Avenionsis, domino Phillipo" (a Judge in the Auvergne). His son Mathieu de Fortibus was a "juge de Quercy" in 1309. In 1552 Mathys de Fossez was a drapier or cloth manufacturer as a Huguenot refugee living in Ghansesstrate, Bruges, near John, James and Nicholas. In 1569 Mathurin Fort was a "huissier" or court usher in Bordeaux. In 1631 Mathewe Fursse died in Silferton, Devon, possibly the father of Mathew LaFors.

Matthew and his wife Elizabeth Palmer settled at Gravesend on Long Island, NY and later moved to New York City, which had been taken by the English in 1664. Their son Matthew Force initially married Joan Prior in 1691 at St. Marylebone's in London, and then as Matheas De Foss landed in Delaware in 1693. (Source Reindeers Settlers in Delaware).

The Puritans suffered and were persecuted at this time in England and some emigrated to America when the monarchy was restored in 1660. Matthew married again in 1697 to Sarah Morris and they lived in Woodbridge, Middlesex. (Source IGI Index). Their children included John born in 1697, Elizabeth in 1699, and Mary in 1701.

Matthew and Elizabeth Palmer also produced Thomas, born 1668-72 (source Virkus), who lived in Westchester NY, and Woodbridge New Jersey. He was a sergeant in Captain George Bradshaw's Queen's Company of New York. Matthew and Elizabeth's daughter Damaris married John Ogilsbie in 1684 (IGI Index). Their daughter Elizabeth married Samuel Smith in 1692. Thomas was 'deeded' 25 acres of land at Woodbridge by his brother Matthew.

Matthew's family continue after Thomas, with his son Obadiah, born 1691, who lived in New York and Essex County, married a Miss Manning and died in 1789. The Boston massacre and famous tea party occurred in 1770. Their son Manning, overseer of the poor, was a member of the Newark Troop 1769-1788. He married Lucretia Winchell in 1751. Their son William Force 1752-1827 was a corporal in the American Reserve and married Sarah Ferguson in 1788. One son, Manning Force, born in 1789 married Nancy Monro and went into the Church. They had two children, William Monro and Jemima Baxter. William, b.1817 married Mary Elizabeth Cooke in 1840 and became Clerk of the Supreme Court. Their daughter Mary Frances Force appeared to be the only child. her oldest son was called William Force Marvin and her youngest daughter Mignonette de la Force Marvin.

William and Sarah's other son was called Peter, 1790-1868 born 26 Nov. at Passaic Falls, New Jersey. He married Hannah Evans and had two sons Manning Ferguson b. 17 Dec. 1824 in Washington DC and died in 1899, and William Quereau 1820-1880.

The Dictionary of American Biography, vol. 6 by Johnson & Malone lists both Peter and his son Manning Ferguson.

Peter was an archivist and historian. He worked initially in the printing trade, became a lieutenant in the war of 1812, later Mayor of Washington. He established the newspaper "National Journal". Politically he was a Whig. He was an editor of much historical material and published the "American Archives" which he later sold to the Library of Congress for $100,000. He published 6 books altogether. His younger son Manning Ferguson was a soldier, jurist and author. He became a Major in the 20th Ohio Regiment, a Colonel in the Civil War, in camp with General Grant, commanded the 2nd Brigade under General Sherman. He received the Gold medal of honour, became a Brigadier-General and eventually Major-General. He married Frances Horton on 13 May 1874. As an author he wrote, like his father, 6 books.

The second early family probably descended from Thomas Fouch, age 16, and Hugh Fouche, his brother, age 17, who were transported to Virginia from Gravesend in 1635. In 1656 "the Report of the Commissioners of the Admiralty in London upon a proposal by Thomas Fossann to make Saltpetre upon the islands in America belonging to the Commonwealth. Letters should be written to the Governors of Barbadoes, St.Christophers & Antigua desiring them to permit Fossan & his agents to dig for saltpetre in those islands." The Committee set up consisted of Lord Lisle, General Montagu, Lord Strickland, Earl of Malgrave, Colonel Jones and Sir Charles Wolseley. Saltpetre was an important element in the manufacture of explosives and the influential committee followed Thomas' recommendations. Unfortunately in 1658 Thomas Fossan 'deceased' an an officer of the American military expedition. In 1685 Thomas and John Forcey, or Facey or Faucey, who were rebels amongst the Duke of Monmouth's supporters, were transported to Barbadoes via

America on the ship "Betty". Possibly they were sons of the saltpetre enthusiast. In 1716 Thomas' wife Susanna Delaforce age 46 (i.e. married about 1686) was living with 5 children in St.Michaels Parish, Barbadoes.

The third early 17th century family was that of Benjamin Force, born about 1670, who married Elizabeth in 1689 and lived at Wrentham near Boston. Since their three sons were christened Benjamin (1690), Thomas (1693) and Matthew (1695) it is likely that Benjamin was a son of Thomas and perhaps a nephew of Matthew (i.e. Thomas and Matthew were brothers).

The fourth 17th century family was that of Mark FForce, born about 1670, and who was married initially to Deborah Maccane in 1698 and later to Sarah Hills in 1709. (Source New England Historical & Genealogical Registers). Mark was probably Benjamin's brother.

There are several other Force families living in New York, Brooklyn, Chicago, etc. Some are descended from Matthew, some from Peter and others from the gentlemen in chains — Joseph, James, William and Stephen/Etienne.

There was a large family of Forces descended from James b.1790 in the USA, married to Hepza and living at Lacolle, close to the New York Border. James almost certainly descended from James Foss who sailed for Boston in 1768.

The William and Joseph Force family now of Brooklyn and Illinois probably descend from Joseph, a convict, who sailed in 1770 from England. The New York Census of 1790 shows a Solomon, a Sylvester, a Timothy and a Zebulon Force.

The shipping records (passenger and immigration lists index) chronicle Delaforces sailing the Atlantic who may have been part of Matthew's or Thomas' families.

Anne (age 18) and Barbara la Force (age 22) sailed in 1709.

Pet(er) la Fosse sailed for Georgia in 1735.

Elizabeth Forsee sailed for Maryland in 1744.

Claude La Fosse sailed for Louisiana in 1756.

James Foss, who sailed for Boston in 1768, was possibly a brother of William.

Mrs Defossee age 50 who sailed to Mississipi in 1820, was possibly Sarah Ferguson, William's wife.

M. Delfosse aged 48 who sailed to New Orleans in 1823 was possiby a Manning, also a M. Delfosset age 36 who sailed to Baltimore in the same year.

Charles Forss sailed for Philadelphia in 1829,.

William Force sailed for New York in 1830 aged 17. He may have been a convict.

Now the records show various convicts (Coldham, 'English Convicts in Colonial America') Two Stephen (or Etienne) Delfoss sailed for Philadelphia in 1718, presumably father and son, and Etienne la Forte, aged 35 sailed for Louisiana in 1719, but he was not necessarily a convict.

James Force, who sailed for America in 1767, was also a convict and so was Joseph Delaforce in 1770 on board the "Scarsdale".

The main Delaforce family now living in the USA (apart from the author's sister in California), derived from Edward Delaforce who lived in Hare Alley in London, where he was born 19th Feb. 1779. He married in 1802 Mary Lambert at Christ Church, Newgate Street in Battersea, a London suburb south of the river Thames. He died aged 65 and was the foreman of a silk weaving factory.

In September 1846 James Moses Delaforce, Edward's third son emigrated to America with his two sons James Edward and Edward William Joseph. They settled in Milan, Michigan as farmers, and sold timber and firewood. James Edward was also a farmer, and owned a machinery repair shop.

The family continued with James Moses' grandsons, Arthur James, George Henry and Willis.

The twentieth century Delaforces include Richard Gordon, George Robert and Warren Arthur, and the family continue to live in Michigan at Milan, Ann Arbour, Marine City and Detroit.

The sources for USA shown in this chapter are but a small fraction of those available within that country. Their purpose is directed at the family historian in the UK who may have a family or relatives in the USA, and wishes to establish genealogical links with them.

Most of the printed sources now mentioned are available in the UK at major libraries (certainly the British Museum library) and probably the Society of Genealogists.

The next step is to consult the various Indexes of Emigration to the USA to try and identify names, dates and some idea of destination.

Telephone directories of major American cities are held in a few major libraries in the UK. The response rate to possible, even probable, relatives shown in these directories will be about 1 in 10, perhaps 2 in 10, but rarely more. But those answers may help immmensely, depending how far back the links are in the chain.

The last stages apart from a working holiday visit to the States are as follows:

(a) Join an American Family History Society if you are now sure of a 'settlement area'. Some are listed in the sources that follow.

(b) Consult (by post) the efficient Mormon Society archives (which lists 210 Force baptisms & marriages 1667-1887).

(c) Consult the US National Archives, complete their investigation forms and send their modest search fees to them.

Sources: In the UK

(a) Public Records Office, Chancery Lane, London — see Calenders of State, Colonial, American and West Indies Papers — 44 volumes 1574-1738. Also at the British Museum library and Guildhall library open shelves.

(b) PRO Lists and Indexes No. XXXVI and XLVI (American Loyalists). See PRO leaflet No.56.

(c) Journals of the Commissioners for Trade & Plantations, 14 volumes.

(d) Huguenot Society publication XXIV "Lists of naturalisation of Foreign protestants in the American colonies under Stat.13 GEO II".

(e) City of London Record Office, Guildhall, London has useful material on emigration and transportation.

(f) Society of Genealogists, London has collection of American Family Histories, periodicals.

Published Information

(g) "Compendium of American Genealogy" by Virkus.
(h) "Abridged Compendium of American Genealogy".
(i) "Enc. of American Quaker Genealogy" by Hinshaw.
(j) "Top. Dict. of 2885 English Emigrants 1620-1650" C.E. Banks/E.E. Brownell.
(k) "Emigrants in Bondage" M. & J. Kaminkow, Baltimore.
(l) "New World Immigrants".
(m) "Transcript of three registers of passengers from Gt. Yarmouth to New England" C.B. Jewson.
(n) "American & British Genealogy & Heraldry", Chicago, P.W. Filby.
(o)"Bibliography of ship passengers lists 1538-1825 to N. America" A.H. Lancour.
(p) All books by Peter Wilson Coldham "English Convicts in Colonial America 1617-1775" etc.
(q) "Immigrants to the Middle Colonies" by Tepper.
(r) "Port Arrivals of Boston" Whitmore.
(s) "Emigration to New York" by Edwards.
(t) "Settlers in Delaware 1693" by Reindeers.
(u) "Original Lists of Persons of Quality" by J.C. Hotten.

In the USA

"New York Genealogical & Biographical Records" NY 1909/10. Consult US National Archives & Records Service, General Services & Administration, Eighth St. and Pennsylvania Avenue, NW, Washington 25, DC 20408, who will send appropriate forms requesting specific information in various categories.

"NY Census 1790" is in printed form.

General Society of Church of Jesus Christ Latter-Day Saints, 50 East North Temple, Salt Lake City, Utah 84150. They will send application forms for information from CFI.

Library of Congress, Washington DC — major repository of records and historical papers.

Association of Professional Genealogists P.O. Box 11601, Salt Lake City, Utah 84147.

Family History Societies in USA

Some of them are members of the UK Federation of FH Societies in Plymouth.

(**a**) International Soc. for British Gen. and Fam. History, PO Box 20425, Cleveland, Ohio 44120.

(**b**) National Genealogical Society, Mrs P. Johnson, 1921 Sunderland Pl., NW Washington DC 20036.

(**c**) Historical Soc. of Pennyslvania, 1300 Locust St., Philadelphia 7

(**d**) Florida Genealogical Society, L.D. Jordan 1508 Geoorgia Ave., Tampa, Florida 33609.

(**e**) Harris County Gen. Soc. Mrs E.L. Burke, PO Box 391, Pasadena, Texas 77501.

(**f**) Houston Gen. Forum Mrs L.M. Leighton, 7130 Evans, Houston, Texas 77061.

(**g**) English Interest Group, Minnesota Gen. Soc., 9009 Northwood Circle, New Hope, Minn. 55427.

(**h**) Santa Barbara Co. Gen. Soc., PO Box 1174, Goleta, California, 93116.

(**i**) Seattle Gen. Soc., PO Box 549, Seattle, Washington, 98111.

(**j**) Utah Gen. Assoc., Mr R.C. Flick, PO Box 1144 Salt Lake City, Utah 84110.

(**k**) New England Hist. Gen. Soc. 101 Newberry St, Boston, Mass 02116.

The Society of Genealogists in London receive practically all American Family History Society magazines and should be consulted for the regions not covered in this list.

Huguenot Societies in USA

1. Hug. Soc. of America, New York Genealogical & Biographical Society Building, 122 East 58th St. New York City 10022.
2. Hug. Soc. Founders of Manakin, Colony of Virginia, c/o Librarian, Mrs P. Tulane Atkinson, Hampden Sydney, Virginia.
3. Hug. Soc. of Pennsylvania, Hall of the Historical Society of Pennsylvania, 1300 Locust St. Philadelphia, Pa.
4. Hug. Soc. of South Carolina, 25 Chalmers St., Charleston, S. Carolina 29401.

The Emigrant Check by the Surname Archive, Mr Francis Leeson FSG, 108 Sea Lane, Ferring, Sussex BN12 5HB, has index of nearly 100 published and unpublished sources of UK emigrants to America, Canada and BWI between 1600-1850.

The Currer-Briggs Colonial Records Index contains names of 50,000 persons from unpublished sources in England and Virginia for the period 1560-1690.

Ship Passenger Lists to USA 1538-1825 published by Carl Boyer, PO Box 333, Newhall, Cal. 91322. USA.

Passenger & Immigrant Lists Index by P.W. Filby & Mary Meyer, Gale Research Co. of Detroit. USA.

"Searching for your ancestors" Gilbert Doane, Univ. Minnesota Press.

"Colonists in Bondage, USA" by Abbot Emerson Smith.

Chapter 22

The Canadian Family

There was no reason to suppose that there was, and is, a Delaforce family in Canada. But there is one — alive and well and flourishing. This is a classic tale for the family historian. It all started because in the Huguenot Society records of the London hospital for Huguenots, called La Providence, there are the following paragraphs.

"August Force entered hospital 1886, died there in 1894. he had been a teacher of the French language in London but was borne in Quebec, Canada on 19 June 1810. He was the son of Pierre Michel Force and Catherine Brandon of 21 Tottenham Street/Road of London (so Pierre would have been born about 1785). Auguste's grandfather Francoys Force left France early in the last century and settled in London in partnership with M. de L'Arbre in the silk trade (presumably a weaver). He afterwards went to Canada where your petitioners (Auguste) father was born and lived there until the year 1816 when he returned to France with his wife and only child, the petitioner. Your petitioner has now lived in England for 30 years, formerly a teacher of French in various schools. Petitioners' great-grandfather left France immediately after the Revocation of Nantes in 1685". Now these dates do not add up convincingly. Assume the great-grandfather was a very young boy in 1685 and was married about 1700 in England, his son Francois would have been born in the period 1700-1720. But as Auguste was born in 1810 his parents Pierre and Catherine were married in the period 1795-1810 and born about 1760-1770.

The Federation of Family History Societies publish a most informative booklet twice a year. No less than eight Canadian Family History Societies are members and their addresses given.

A concise version of the Francois/Pierre/Auguste saga was sent to the Ontario Genealogical Society, asking if any of their members were interested in Delaforce, Delforce or Forces. Back came a most helpful and courteous letter which gave the current addresses (from a telephone directory) of a small number of Delaforce/Laforces.

A quite detailed letter was posted to each address from France giving some information on the various famlies and asking for help in identifying not only the Forces but the new discoveries. A month later back came a detailed letter from Barry and Carol Delaforce from Unionville, Ontario. Barry works for IBM and his father Ralph worked for the Toronto Transit Commission. Ralph's parents, Sydney Ralph Leopold Delaforce and his wife Ellen née Little emigrated from Islington, London in 1910.

A few months later with the help of a few marriage certificates purchased from St. Catherine's House the Canadian family roots were clearly proved. Sydney Ralph Leopold's brother was George Frederick Fleurriette. Their father was George Frederick married to Eliza née Lake. Their Grandfather was George Frederick Delaforce the wine merchant, who was married three times. So the Canadian family and the Port Wine Shippers are directly related. The family name of Fleurriette was of course an immmediate clue and link back to the marriage of Samuel and Elizabeth Fleurriet married in Southwark in 1770. Three generations of George Fredericks were railwaymen, corporal on a military train, railway clerk, railway accountant, etc. Barry and Carol turned out to be enthusiastic and skilled researchers.

The Laforce families emigrated from France at the time of the Edict of Nantes and sailed direct to Canada; Guillaume was possibly the earliest, who was born in 1607 at Saint laurent de la Barriere in Saintonge, not in Poitou, France, but near the Mississippi river in the USA. He moved to Trois-Rivieres, Quebec about 1646. They acquired a nickname, Pepin, from lake Pepin and the "Genealogie des Familles Canadiens-Francaises" lists five generations of this family. In the 15th century the Poitou de Forces were Seigneurs de la Barriere, near Fors in Poitou.

There do not appear to be any more clues (as yet) to the original silk weaving partnership of the first Forces to visit and perhaps settle in Canada. there were two Francois de la Fosse/Force silkweaver families in London. Francis Noah married to Ann Van Den Holder of Brussels had a very large family of at last 12 children all baptised at the French Threadneedle Street church in London in the period 1688-1707. Also Francis who married Susanne Bouyu (Bowyer) in 1699 at St. Martins in the Fields, London. Either of these two families could have been "Francoys Force's" parents. But Carol and Barry searched the efficient Canadian census records for 1825/31/51/61 and 71 and came up with Force families in Lacolle, Quebec area. James and Hepza Force and a large family lived on a 56 acre farm. James was born in 1790 in the USA. Solomon and Anna Force lived nearby with their family and so did Margaret, a spinster. The next generation was John A. Force married to Jane who lived on a 48 acre farm in St. Jean County, Quebec; Alonzo married to Caroline, and Timothy married to Elizabeth (they had 14 children).

James Force's father or probably grandfather was transported from London as a convict in 1767 to New York on the SS "Thornton". He was born in Stepney to James Delaforce and Elizabeth Harris — the eldest son — of a weaving family — in Dec. 1753.

One last mystery — who was Guy de la Force who commanded the Army Post at York Fort, Hudsons Bay in 1696?

Some of the sources available for tracing ancestors and relatives in Canada are now shown. The initial advice is to join one of the efficient Family History Societies in the appropriate State:

Alberta Gen. Soc. PO Box 12015, Edmonton, Alberta T5J 3L2.

British Columbia Gen. Soc. PO Box 94371, Richmond, BC V6Y 2A8

Manitoba Gen. Soc. Mrs E. Briggs, PO Box 2066, Winnipeg, Manitoba R3C 3R4.

Ontario Gen. Soc. Mr J.E. O'Meara, PO Box 66, Station Q, Toronto, Ont. M4T 2L7.

Ontario Gen. Soc. (Toronto branch), Mrs D. Martin, PO Box 74, Station U, Toronto M8Z 5M4

Prince Edward Island Gen. Soc. PO Box 2744, Charlottetown, Pr. Ed. Island, C1A 8C4.

Quebec FHS, PO Box 1026, Station Pointe, Claire, Point Claire, Quebec H9S 4H9.

Saskatchewan Gen. Soc. PO Box 1894, Regina, Saskatchewan S4P 3E1

For those who can visit Canadian sources on the spot, the Public Archives 395 Wellington St., in Ottawa are a major repository for records and historical papers. Canadian census records are available at most major public libraries in Canada — certainly in Toronto and Quebec. (But of course one needs to know of a time and a place before looking at census records).

The Mormon Church of Latter Day Saints have genealogical libraries with microfiche baptismal data. There are eight in Alberta (Calgary, Cardston, Edmonton, Lethbridge, Raymond, Red Deer, Grande Prarie and Taber), four in British Columbia (Cranbrook, Burnaby, Kelowna and Victoria), four in Ontario (Hamilton, London, Ottawa and Etobicoke) and one in Saskatchewan (Saskatoon).

The Institute Genealogique Drouin of Montreal have microfiches with 61 million names of French Canadians. But additionally many excellent printed books are available:

"The Dictionary of Canadian Biography": Dictionnaire Genealogique des Familles Canadiens by Cyprian Tomqlay: "List of Parish Registers held in the Public Archives of Canada" by Coderre & Lavoie: "Dict. National des Canadiens Francois 1608-1860" Instit. Drouin: "A History of the Canadian West" by A.S. Morton.

Abbé Daniel "Histoires des grande familles Francaises du Canada": Abbé Le Jeune "Dict. Gen. Histoire du Canada" Books by Archange Godboue.

Canadian telephone directories are available in the UK at certain major libraries, Canadian Embassy (trade section). Trade directories and other records at the Society of Genealogists.

Chapter 23

Oliver Goldsmith 1728-1774
"A man he was to all the country dear,
and passing rich with forty pounds a year;"

Francis Bacon 1561-1626
"Riches are for spending"

Last Wills and Testaments from 1625

Many of the Delaforces in the last five hundred years left wills, not because they were necessarily rich, but mainly because it was a custom. From 1858 all wills are kept at Somerset House in London and searches are comparatively easy. Before 1858 wills or a grant of administration are to be found among the records of the court where probate was granted i.e. where the will was given an official stamp of approval empowering the executor to act. The proving of wills and the granting of administrations lay with the ecclesiastical courts and some manorial courts. The Prerogative Court of Canterbury (PCC) was the most important from 1383 to 1858 and their wills are deposited at the Public Record Office. The London Commissary Court and Archdeaconry Courts of London for roughly the same period are kept at the Guildhall library in the manuscripts section. The Public Records Office in County Hall also has some London wills. Copies of the most important old wills are held by the Author of this book.

The long summary that follows is a vital part of this genealogical story. Some wills gave information about two or even three generations. Incidentally the phrase 'cut off with a shilling' meant that the person concerned then had little or no right to sue the estate for more money. No mention at all in a will could be a cause for litigation.

The Fishmongers of London

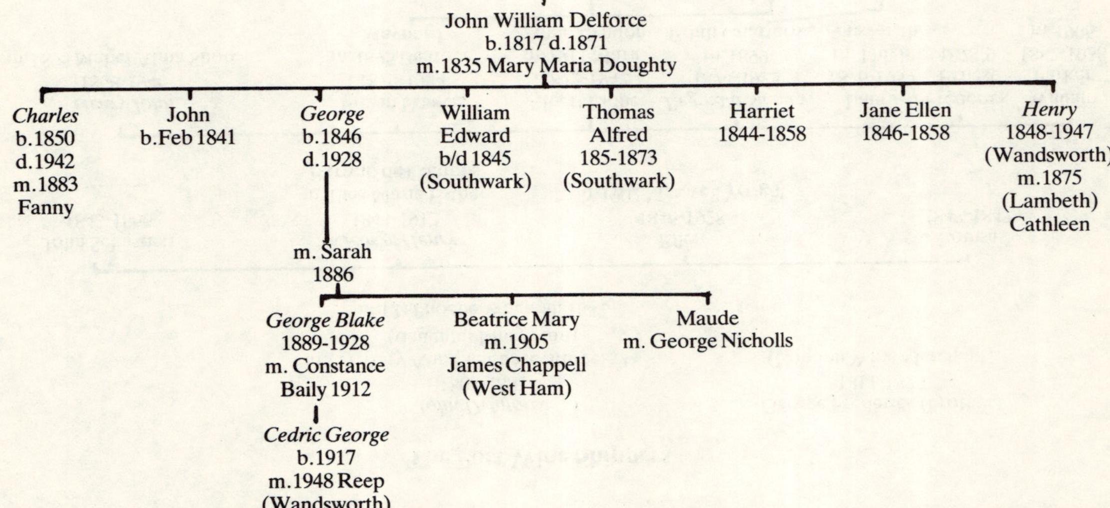

NOTES: The original family lived at 36 Henry Street, Kent Road, Southwark – at No. 46 Crispin Street, Christchurch, Spitalfields–and at 31 Warner Street, Dover Road, Surrey. The churches for baptisms and marriages were Christchurch, Greyfriars, Newgate , St. Saviours and St. George the Martyr in Southwark. Partners in family firm in italic type.

The Port Wine Shippers

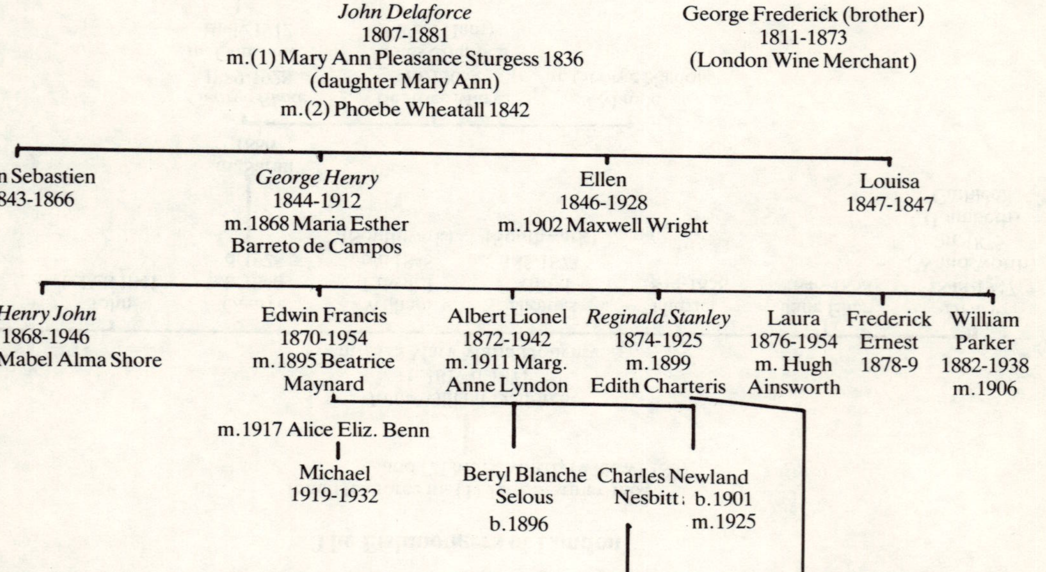

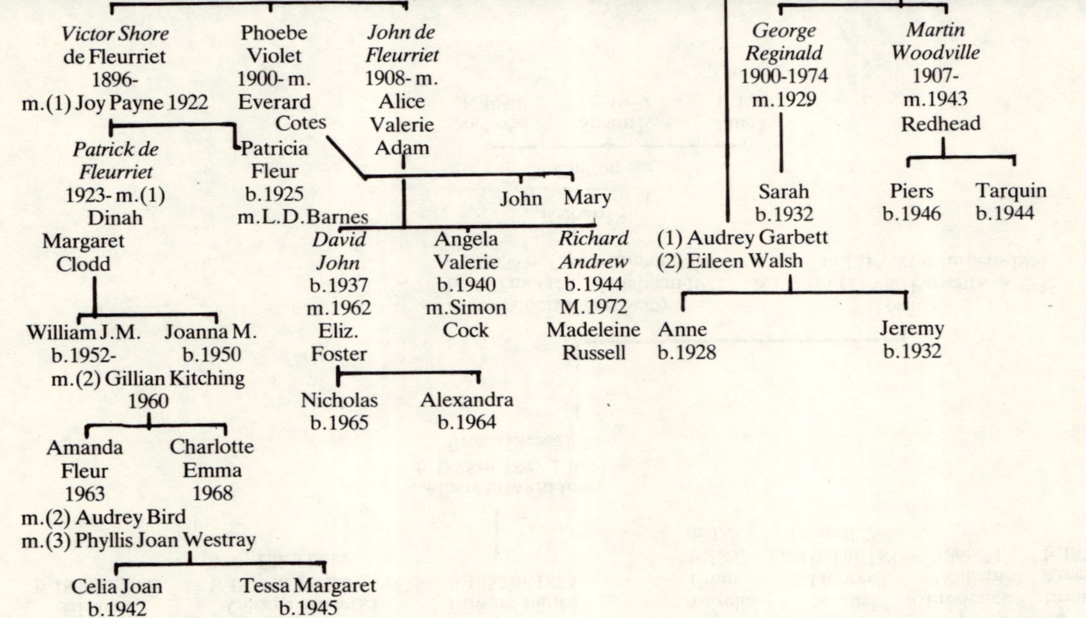

Port Wine Shippers in italic type

George Frederick and the *Canadian Family*

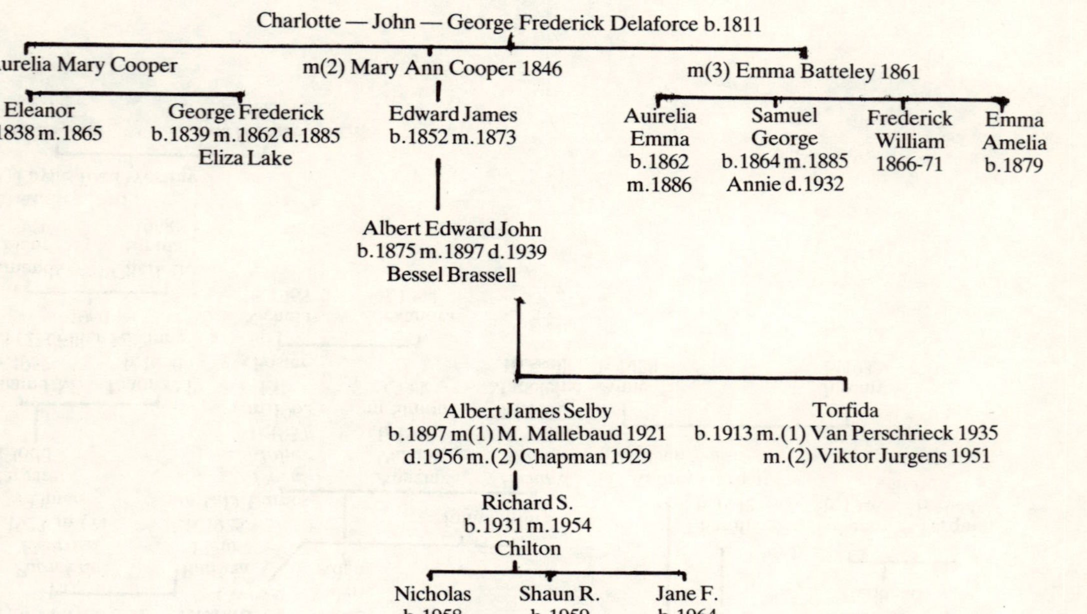

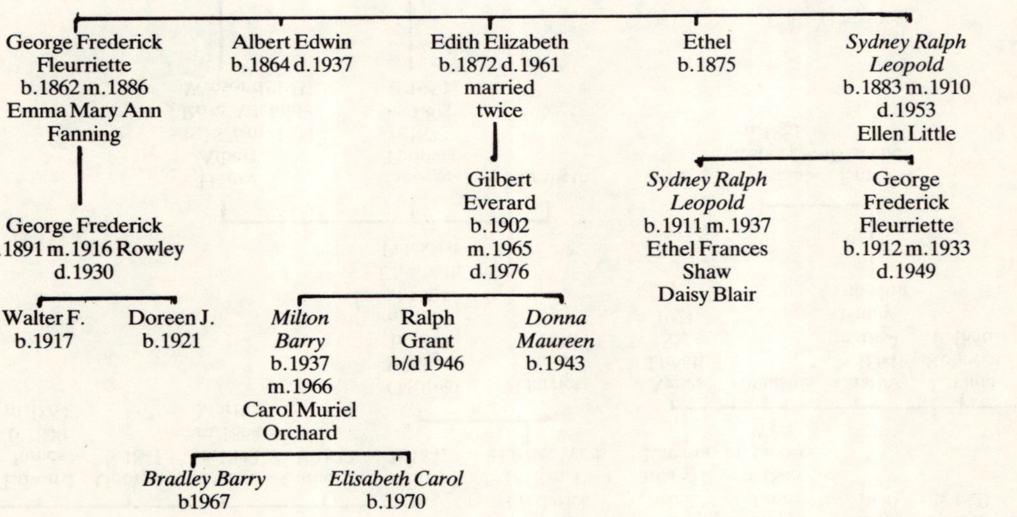

Canadian Family in italic type

The Silk Weavers of London

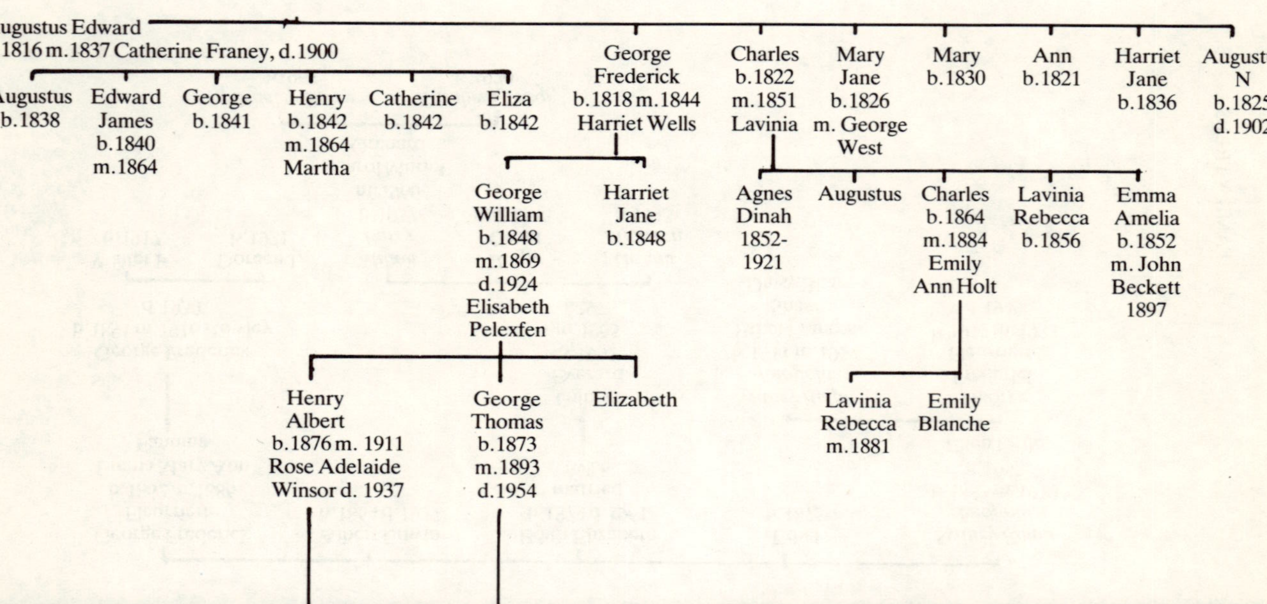

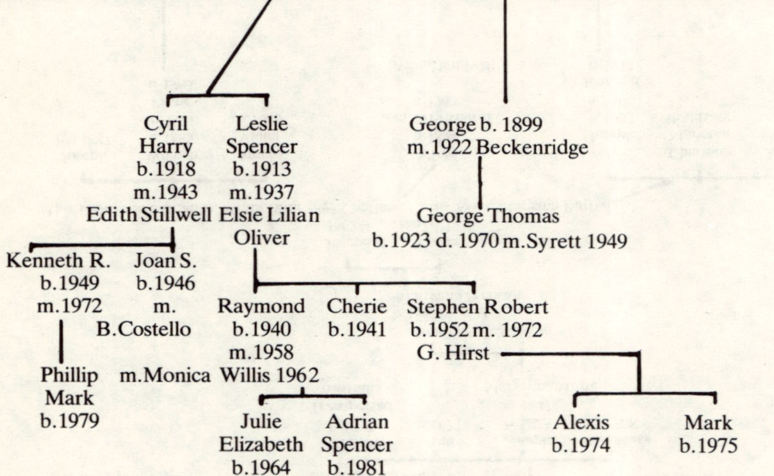

NOTES: Augustus Edward was a silkweaver and also his sons, of Bethnal Green. Augustus Edward and his brother Edward (see American family) were sons Edward & Elizabeth Windmill (1753-1826) of Red Lion Street, Spitalfields, Stepney. Edward a widower remarried 1791 to Ann Newth.

Silkweaver Families

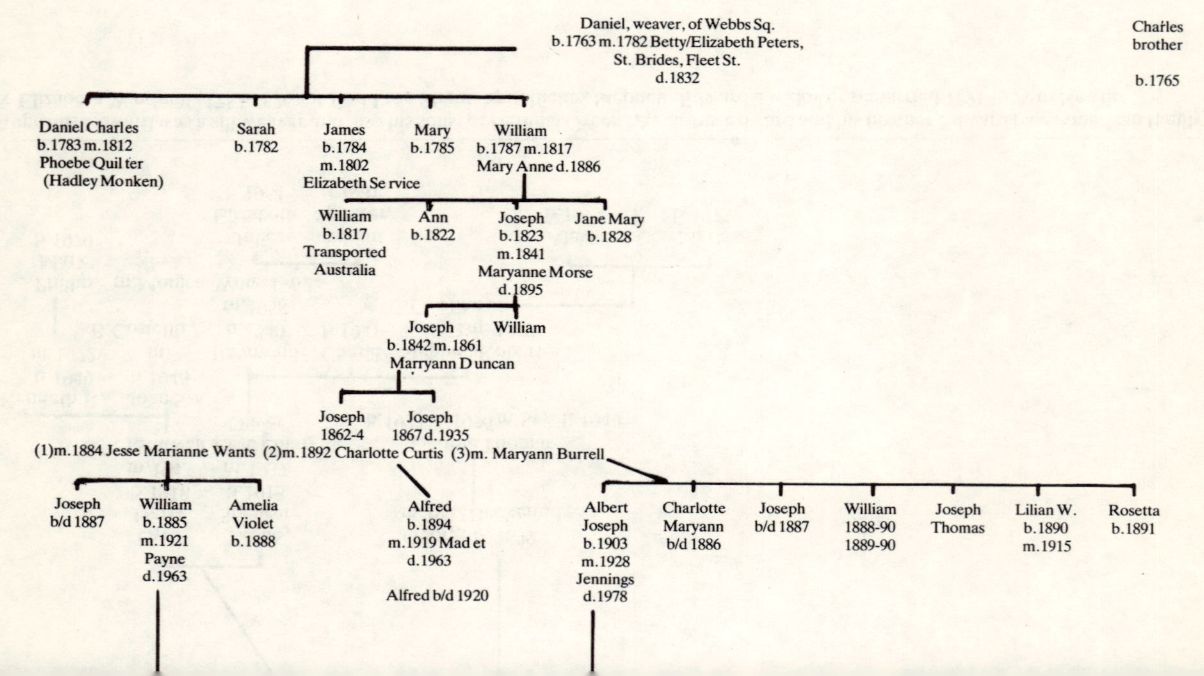

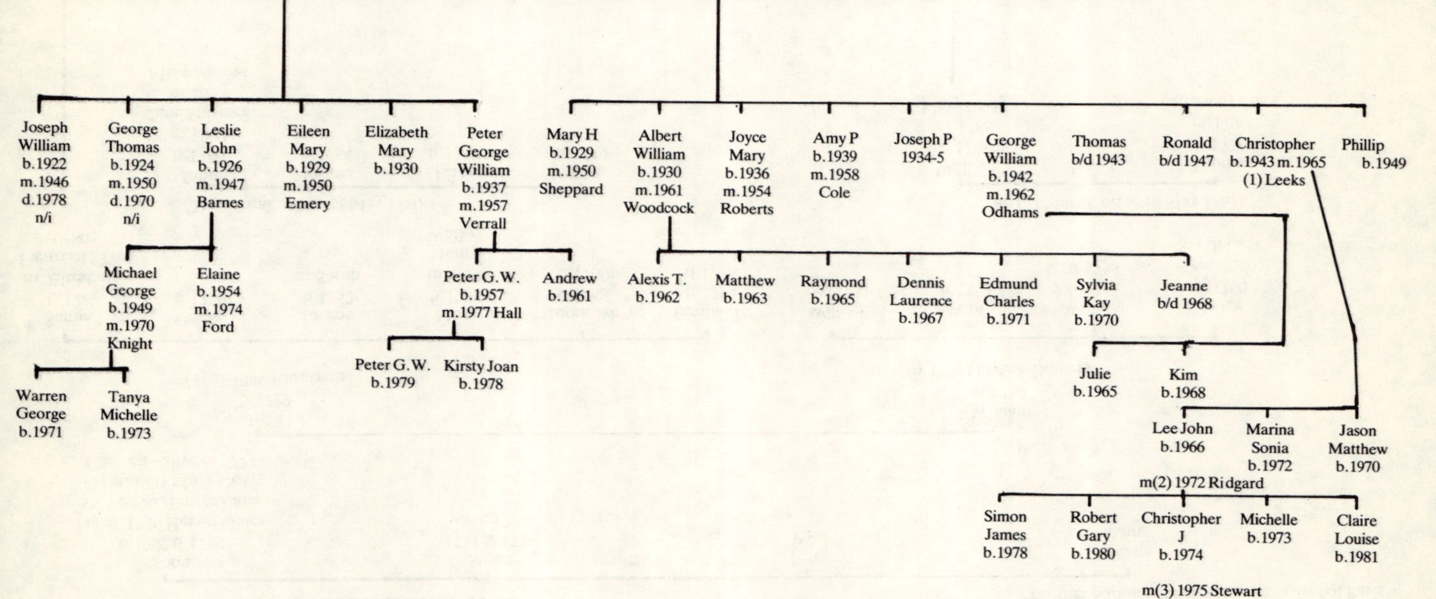
Joseph William b.1922 m.1946 d.1978 n/i
George Thomas b.1924 m.1950 d.1970 n/i
Leslie John b.1926 m.1947 Barnes
Eileen Mary b.1929 m.1950 Emery
Elizabeth Mary b.1930
Peter George William b.1937 m.1957 Verrall
Mary H b.1929 m.1950 Sheppard
Albert William b.1930 m.1961 Woodcock
Joyce Mary b.1936 m.1954 Roberts
Amy P b.1939 m.1958 Cole
Joseph P 1934-5
George William b.1942 m.1962 Odhams
Thomas b/d 1943
Ronald b/d 1947
Christopher b.1943 m.1965 (1) Leeks
Phillip b.1949
Michael George b.1949 m.1970 Knight
Elaine b.1954 m.1974 Ford
Peter G.W. b.1957 m.1977 Hall
Andrew b.1961
Alexis T. b.1962
Matthew b.1963
Raymond b.1965
Dennis Laurence b.1967
Edmund Charles b.1971
Sylvia Kay b.1970
Jeanne b/d 1968
Warren George b.1971
Tanya Michelle b.1973
Peter G.W. b.1979
Kirsty Joan b.1978
Julie b.1965
Kim b.1968
Lee John b.1966
Marina Sonia b.1972
Jason Matthew b.1970
m(2) 1972 Ridgard
Simon James b.1978
Robert Gary b.1980
Christopher J b.1974
Michelle b.1973
Claire Louise b.1981
m(3) 1975 Stewart

The French Connection

Sieur Jean Delafous/Delafours/Delafons, jeweller, ex-Guisne, Chatellrault etc.

b.1671 m.1702 Susanne Massienne of Paris

? brother Samuel Delafosse clockmaker of Paris

Children:

- John, b.1702 d.1779, (1) m. 1726 Hester Gales St. Vedast, Foster Lane, (2) m. 1731 Mary Dory Chelsea – alive in 1779
- Susan, 1711 & 1716, alive 1779
- Peter Paul
- Mary Anne

Children of John:

- John, b.1729, (1) m.1749 Elizabeth
- William, b.1730, m.1750 (1) Ann Bowers

Children of John (b.1729) and Elizabeth:

- Samuel, b.1749, m. Elizabeth Fleurriet 1770, d.1805
- Daniel, b.1759
- Joseph, b.1752, m.Sarah
- Mary, b.1756, m.1774 Henry Walker
- Jeremiah, b.1758, d.1760
- Benjamin, b.1754, d.1756

John (b.1729) (2) m. Sarah Willmor May 1780:

- John, b.1780, m.1802 Jane Starmer, m.1807 Mary Morris
- Joshua, b.1784
- Isaac, b.1787
- William, b.1789

Children of William (b.1730) and Ann Bowers:

- William, b/d 1751
- Ann, b.1753
- William, b.1756, d.1758
- Peter, b.1760, m.1786 Sarah Lane

William (b.1730) m. (2) Mary Coffee 18 May 1761:

- William, b.1768, m.1786 Mary Perry
- James
- Thomas, b.1770, m.1790 Elizabeth Elliot

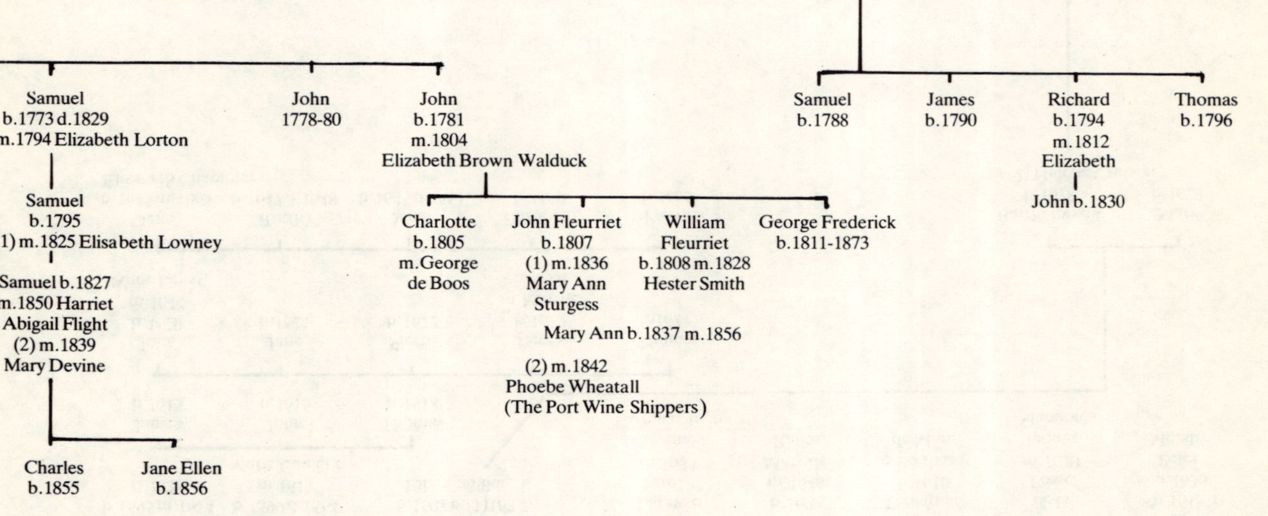
Samuel
b.1773 d.1829
m.1794 Elizabeth Lorton
John
1778-80
John
b.1781
m.1804
Elizabeth Brown Walduck
Samuel
b.1788
James
b.1790
Richard
b.1794
m.1812
Elizabeth
Thomas
b.1796
John b.1830
Samuel
b.1795
(1) m.1825 Elisabeth Lowney
Samuel b.1827
m.1850 Harriet
Abigail Flight
(2) m.1839
Mary Devine
Charles
b.1855
Jane Ellen
b.1856
Charlotte
b.1805
m.George
de Boos
John Fleurriet
b.1807
(1) m.1836
Mary Ann
Sturgess
Mary Ann b.1837 m.1856
(2) m.1842
Phoebe Wheatall
(The Port Wine Shippers)
William
Fleurriet
b.1808 m.1828
Hester Smith
George Frederick
b.1811-1873

The 17th Century Silkweavers

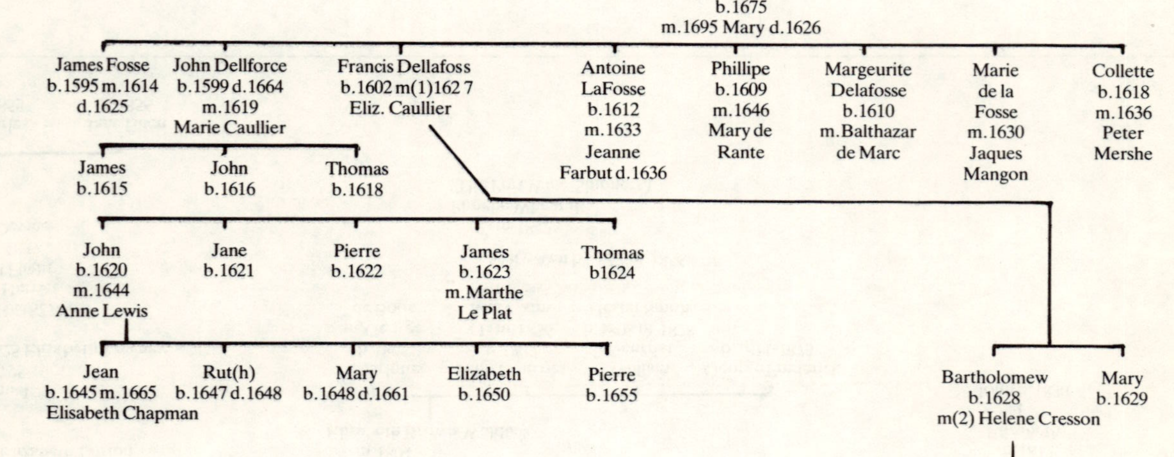

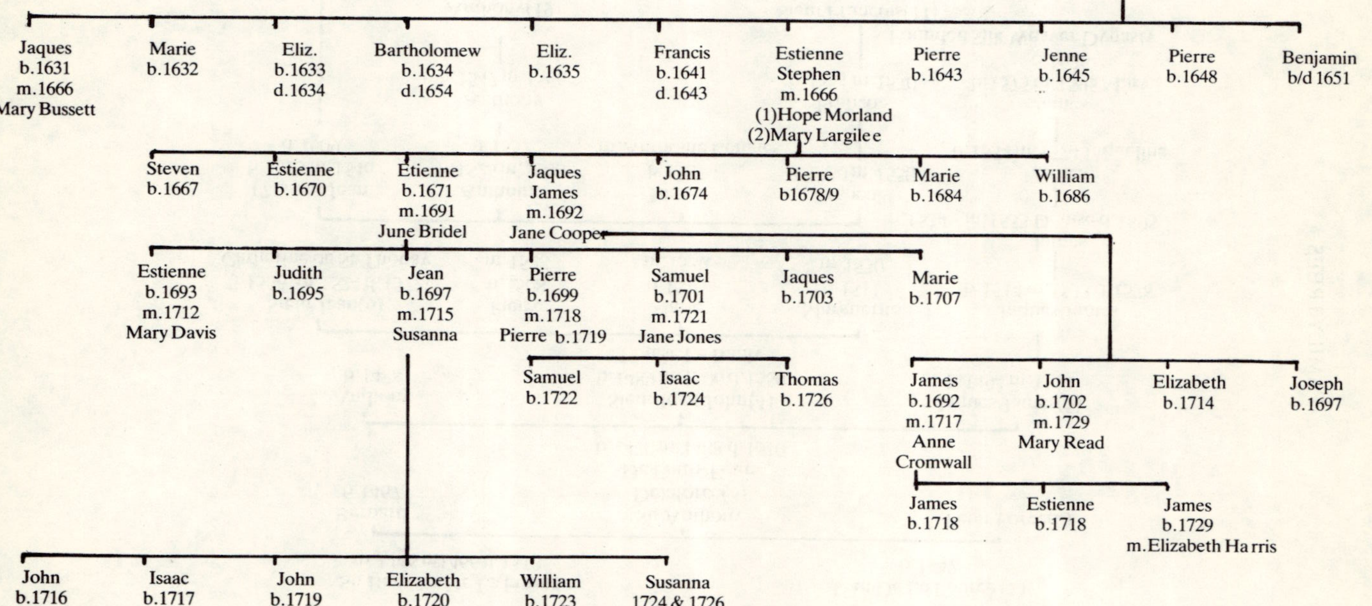

NOTES: Main churches were Threadneedle Street, St. Botolphs Bishopsgate, St. Leonards Shoreditch, St. Mary Bethnal Green, Christchurch Spitalfields. Every variation of the name Delaforce was used – about 12 spellings.

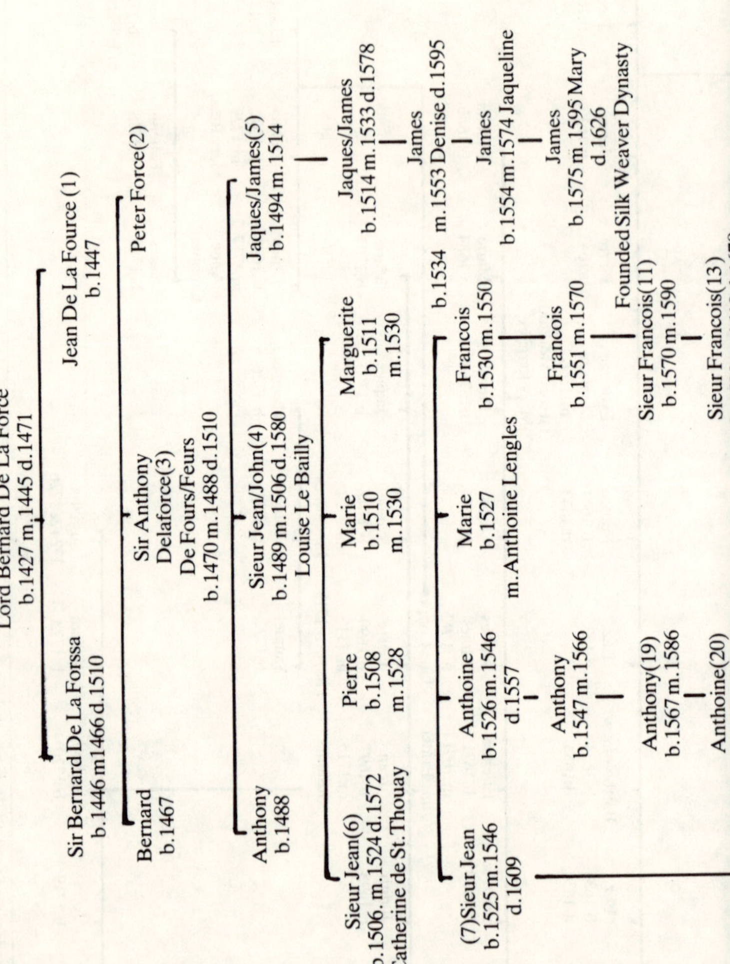
The Knights Genealogy
Lord Bernard De La Force
b.1427 m.1445 d.1471
Sir Bernard De La Forssa
b.1446 m1466 d.1510
Jean De La Fource (1)
b.1447
Bernard
b.1467
Sir Anthony
Delaforce(3)
De Fours/Feurs
b.1470 m.1488 d.1510
Peter Force(2)
Anthony
b.1488
Sieur Jean/John(4)
b.1489 m.1506 d.1580
Louise Le Bailly
Jaques/James(5)
b.1494 m.1514
Sieur Jean(6)
b.1506. m.1524 d.1572
Catherine de St. Thouay
Pierre
b.1508
m.1528
Marie
b.1510
m.1530
Marguerite
b.1511
m.1530
Jaques/James
b.1514 m.1533 d.1578
(7)Sieur Jean
b.1525 m.1546
d.1609
Anthoine
b.1526 m.1546
d.1557
Marie
b.1527
m.Anthoine Lengles
Francois
b.1530 m.1550
James
b.1534 m.1553 Denise d.1595
Anthony
b.1547 m.1566
Francois
b.1551 m.1570
James
b.1554 m.1574 Jaqueline
Anthony(19)
b.1567 m.1586
Sieur Francois(11)
b.1570 m.1590
Founded Silk Weaver Dynasty
James
b.1575 m.1595 Mary
d.1626
Anthoine(20)
Sieur Francois(13)

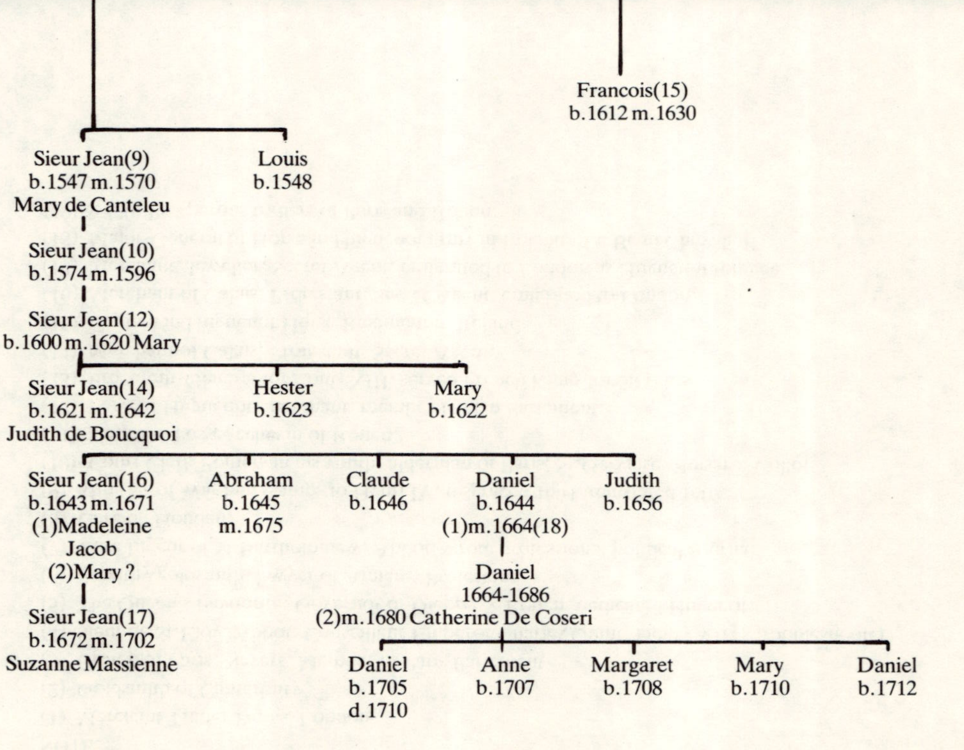
Francois(15)
b.1612 m.1630
Sieur Jean(9)
b.1547 m.1570
Mary de Canteleu
Louis
b.1548
Sieur Jean(10)
b.1574 m.1596
Sieur Jean(12)
b.1600 m.1620 Mary
Sieur Jean(14)
b.1621 m.1642
Judith de Boucquoi
Hester
b.1623
Mary
b.1622
Sieur Jean(16)
b.1643 m.1671
(1)Madeleine
Jacob
(2)Mary ?
Abraham
b.1645
m.1675
Claude
b.1646
Daniel
b.1644
(1)m.1664(18)
Judith
b.1656
Daniel
1664-1686
Sieur Jean(17)
b.1672 m.1702
Suzanne Massienne
(2)m.1680 Catherine De Coseri
Daniel
b.1705
d.1710
Anne
b.1707
Margaret
b.1708
Mary
b.1710
Daniel
b.1712

NOTES:

(1) Merchant Trader Paris – London
(2) Goldsmith of Canterbury
(3) Bishop of Paris, Nevers, Member of Paris Parlement
(4) Sieur de St.Eloy, Abbot, Conseilleur Emperor Charles Quint. Henry VIII's troubleshooter.
(5) The Queen's Favourite, Governor of Dieppe & Rouen, dedicated Hugenot.
(6) Wealthy goldsmith, lawyer of Amiens, Protestant.
(7) Curé Ligeur of St.Bartholomew, Abbot, wrote professional political Journal.
(8) Curé de Houdan.
(9) Minister of War and Camps to Henri IV, disgraced 1604, reinstated 1607.
(10) Court Clerk Poitiers in his youth, alderman of Paris, St.Gervaise, Boisard, Collot.
(11) Sieur Du Fosse, echevin of Rouen.
(12) Fervent Huguenot, merchant, member Rouen Parlement.
(13) Procureur-General for Louis XIII, served French Kings for 50 years.
(14) Merchant of Calais, Protestant, Secret Agent.
(15) Captain in Huguenot Horse Regiment in Ireland.
(16) Merchant of Calais, Protestant, Secret Agent, emigrated to London.
(17) Merchant, Jeweller, Secret Agent, emigrated to London as Huguenot refugee.
(18) Major-General of Horse in Huguenot army in Ireland. 'Le Beau Chevalier'.
(19) & (20) Prosperous traders of Paris and Rouen.

The Delforce family in Australia

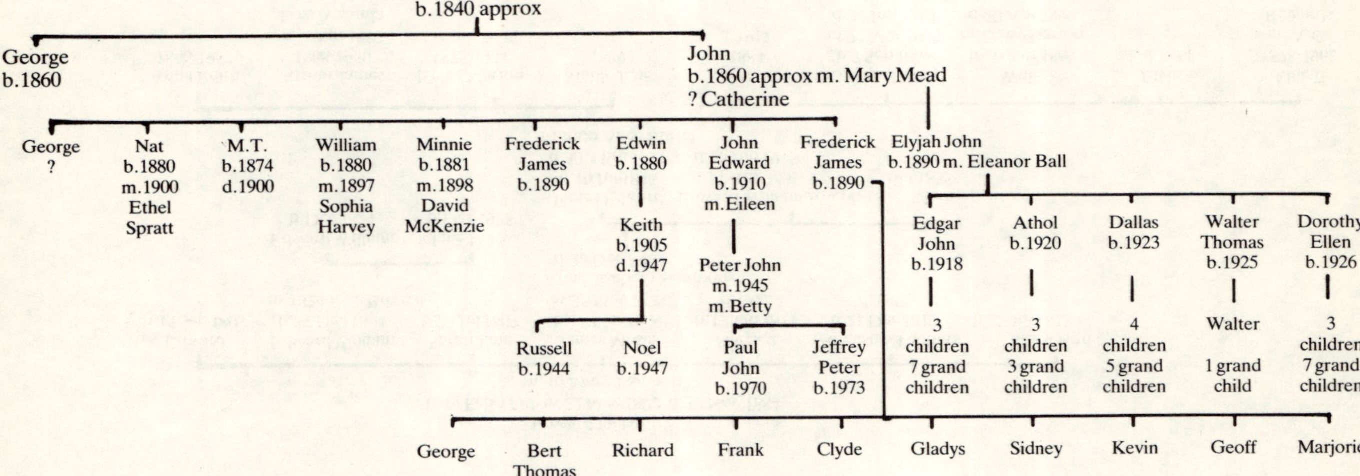

NOTES: Dates are approximate.
It is possible that George was the third son baptised 1841 in Bethnal Green, to Augustus Edward Delaforce and Catherine Franey, the silkweaving family, but more likely was George Delforce, the fishmonger.

The American Family

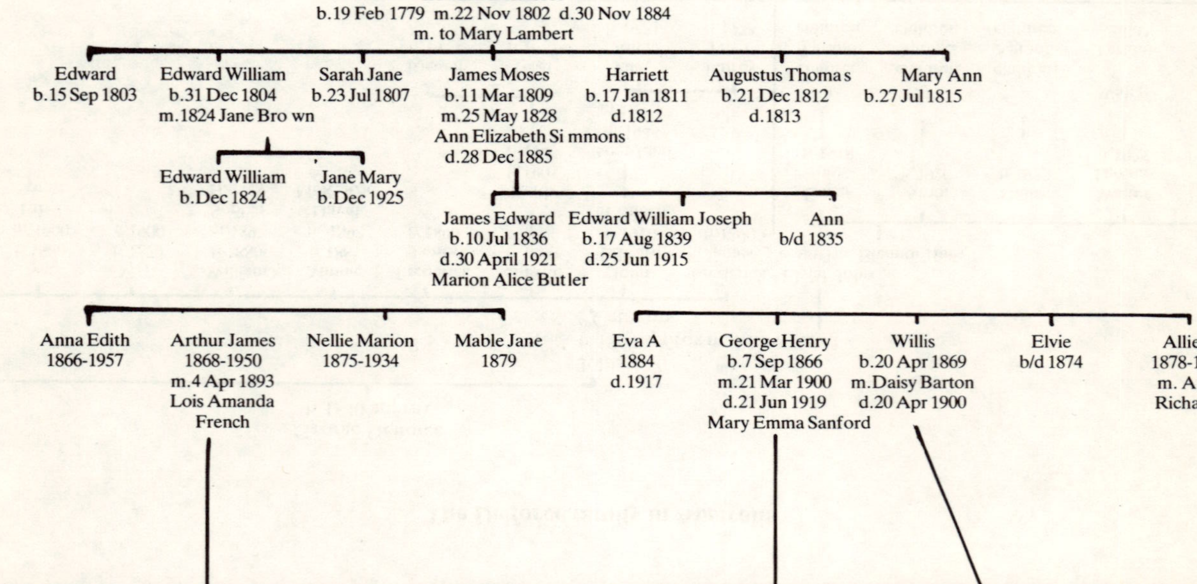

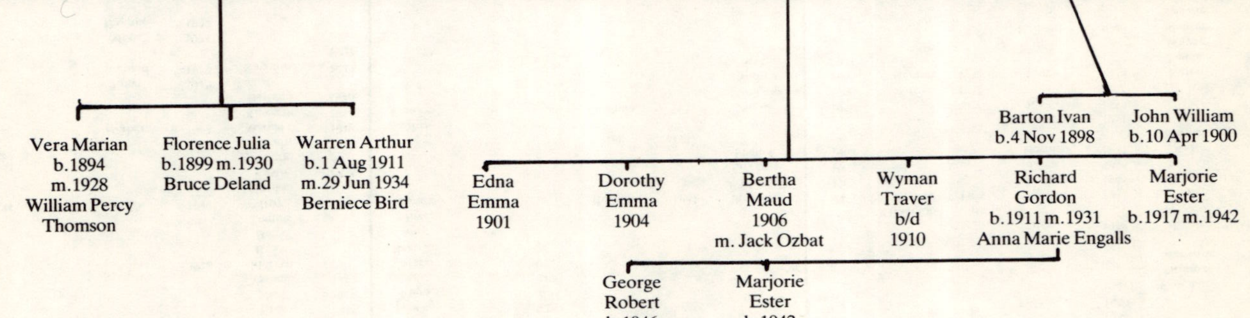

NOTES: Edward 1779-1844 was Foreman, Silk Factory, Battersea, London. Lived in Hare Street; married Mary Lambert, Christhcurch, Greyfriars, Newgate St. All their children were baptised at St. Leonards, Shoreditch. Edward was brother to Augustus Edward who produced large London family of silkweavers.

James Moses was married at St. Mary's Church, Battersea. He and his family emigrated to USA in Sept. 1846, lived York Township, Milan, Michigan.

The Australian Family

William Delaforce – born 28th May, 1817 Shoreditch or Bethnell Green – died 7th June, 1900 Port Macquarie NSW Aust.
married 10 October 1851
Frances Jane Shane – born 1832 Cork Ireland – died 1915 Sydney NSW Aust.

hildren:		Born 1852 Died	
	Liscillier	Born 1852 Died	1934
	Joseph	1854	1934
	Isobella	1856	1938
	William	1858	1939
	Clara	1860	?
	Frederick	1862	1952

Joseph married Sarah Marriott

Children	*Born*	*Died*	*Children*	*Born*	*Children*	*Born*
Clara	1876	1959	1			
Edith	1880	1920	2			
Ernest	1882	1939	Harold	1911	Alan	1935
					Judith	
					Barbara	
					John	
					Robert	
			Myrtle	1913	7	
			Gordon	1915	Henry	1941
					Douglas	1943
					Raymond	1945
					Elsa	1947
					Noel	1948
					Yvonne	1949
			Adin	1918	Mervyn	
					Bruce	
					Betty	
					Dennis	
Herbert	1884	1957	Neville	1911	Roy	
					Gordon	
					Kevin	1938
					Jeffery	
					Dorothy	
			Herbert	1913	Margaret	1942
					Kenneth	1944
					Barbara	1946
			Lona	1915	6	
			Richard	1919	Raymond	1947
					Lorrell	1902
			Mona	1921	4	
			Daphne	1927	4	

William married Mary Barnes							Frederick married Agnes Barnes					
Children	*Born*	*Died*	*Children*	*Born*	*Children*	*Born*	*Children*	*Born*	*Children*	*Born*	*Children*	*Born*
Frederick	1885	1937	Lindsay	1914	John	1951	Maud	1892	5			
					Wayne	1959	William	1895	Fay			
			Frederick	1916	Janice	1942			Josie			
					Lynnette	1945			Billie			
			Eileen	1919	2				Janet			
			Roy	1922			Joseph		Thora			
			George	1924	Barbara				Patsey			
					Michele		Leslie	1901	Agnes	1928		
					Rowan				Betty	1929		
					Nigel				Peggy	1931		
			William	1935					Joy	1934		
Stanley		1972							Frederick	1939		
Clara									Joseph	1941	Rosemary	1961
Ethel		1947									Norman	1963
Mary		1974									Marianne	1965
Beatrice		?							Ethel	1946		
Alice	1900								Eric	1948	Jason	1970
Olive												
							Raymond	1903				
James	1905		Rodney	1934	Anthony	1961	Harold	1908	Graham	1943		
					Maria	1963			Heather	1945		
					Gregory	1964			Ellen	1946		
					Michele	1968			Harold	1947	Avis	1971
			Rex	1937							Michael	1973
Edna									Irene	1951		
Gordon	1910		Graham	1935	Alexis	1958			Junita	1953		
					Cameron	1960	Austen	1912				
					Andrea	1965	Kenrick	1915	Barry	1938	Karen	1965
					Scott	1971					Janelle	1967
			Neil								Wayne	1969
									Kenneth	1940	Sharon	1967
											Dianne	1969
									Judith	1942		
									Gregory	1949		

Children	Born	Died	Children	Born	Children	Born	Children	Born	Died	Children	Born	Children	Born	Children	Born	Children	Born	Children	Born
Ethel	1886	1964	4																
Lillias	1888	1965	4																
Henry	1890	1964	Kathleen	1923	2														
			Keith	1924	Allan	1948													
					Terry	1952													
			Joyce	1926	3														
Violet	1892	1941	5																
William	1895	1962	Pearl																
			Clifford		Barry														
					Ronald														
					Marlene														
					Betty														
					Annette														
			Allen		Joyce														
					William	1946													
					Robert														
					John														
					Neville														
					David														
					Darryl														
					Bradley														
					Cecil														
					Margaret														
					Beverley														
			Eric		Joy														
					Anne														
					James														
					Glen														
					Ellie														
					Gail														
					Thomas														
					Terry														
			Cecil																
			Alice																
			Clyde																
			Ella	Mark															
Isobel	1897	1964	9																
Leslie	1900	1973	Winston	1929	Rodney	1955													
					Terry	1958													
			Ruth	1934	2														
			Naomi	1945	3														

Appendix

The 17th, 18th century Silkweavers of London

Name	*Born*	*App.*	*Master/Freed*	*Father*	*Name*
Danyell	1603	1617	F1623 10 Jul		De Fowce
Francis	1602	1616	F1627 28 Nov	Jaques	Delaforce
John	1599	1624	F1635 25 May	Jaques	del Forto
Peeter	1605	1624	F1635 25 May	Jaques	de Fallso
Jaques	1617?	1631	F1638	?	de Fos?
James	1641	1656 Dec	F1664 5 Sept	Anthony	Delafosse
John	1645	1659	F1666 17 Dec	John	Delafe…
Stephen	1641?3	1657	F1663	Francis	Delafosse
Phillip	1609	1623	F?	Jaques	Delafoss
Antony	1612	1626	F?	Jaques	Delafosse
Francis	1653?	1667	1674/5	Phillip	Defore/Deforce
John	1649	1663	1670 13 Jun		Desfosses/Delafosse
James	1652	1668			Delafosse
Charles	1645	1660	F1669 18 Jun		Delfoss refused 1669
James	1662	1676 Feb	1683	Stephen	Delafosse
Isaac	1663	1677 May	1684 9 Jun		Delafosse
Phillip	1633	1650	F1684 30 Jun		Delfosse (Valenciennes)
Charles	1664	1678	1685 8 Sept	Charles	Delfoss (same as above)
John	1653	1668 Nov	1675		Delfoss/Delaplaus
Stephen	1667	1681	1709 5 Sept	Stephen	Delafosse
Francis Noah	1671	1685 Jun	1692	Phillip	Delfosse/Delfoss
Charles	1674	1688	1695		Defose (Royal Lustring Co)
Isaac	1674	1688	1695		Delfosse (Royal Lustring Co)
John	1672	1686	1693 3 Apr	Stephen	Delavoer/Delforce
Isaac	1685	1699	1706 Dec	Isaac	Deford?
James	1671	1685	1692	Stephen	Delaforce
Peter	1685	1699Jun	1707	James	Delford/Dolforce (Stepney)
Charles	1687	1701	1709		Delforce (Bethnal Green)
John	1690	1704 Jan	1712 Apr	John	Delfosse/Delaforce
John	1692/3	1707 Jan	1718 5 Dec	Isaac	Delaforce/Delfort
John	1702	1718 May	1722 4 Jun	James	Defforce/Lefause/ Dollifou

Name	*Born*	*App.*	*Master/Freed*	*Father*	*Name*
James	1694	1708	1715	James	Delaforce
Stephen	1693	1709	1716		Delafosse
Phillip	1709	1723	1730	? Phillip	Dufour/Delforse
John	1710	1724 Sep	1731	John	Delforce
Jacob	1717	1731 May	1750 Mar(!)	James	Delforce
Charles	1719	1733	1744	Charles	Delafosse
Susan	1716	1733	1740	James	Delaforce
John	1723	1737 June	1744 July	James	Delaforce
James	1729	1743	1758	John	Delfosse
James	1730	1744 Aug	1769 Jun(!)	James	Delfors
James	1731	1745 Aug	1753 Apr	Peter (Tailor)	Delaforce
Jacob	1750	1764	1771	Jacob	Delforce
William	1734	1748 Oct	1752	John (Weaver	Delaforce
Daniel	1755	1769	1776		Delaforce
Thomas	1755	1769 July	1776	William	Delaforce
Judith	1755	1770	1780		Delaforce
Thomas	1756	1770 July	1777		Delaforce
Jacob	1758	1772 June	1779	Jacob	Delaforce
Charles	1766	1780 June	1787	Charles	Delaforce/Delfors
James	1779	1793 Aug	1801 Feb	Thomas (Weaver)	Delaforce
Mary	1785	1800	1810		Delaforce
Aug.Edward	1793/87	1807	1814		Delaforce
Thomas	1785	1800	1807	Delaforce	
Aug.Edward	1816	1830	1837	Aug.Edward	Delaforce

F = Foreign weaver